A Zapotec Natural History

A Zapotec Natural History
Trees, Herbs, and Flowers,
Birds, Beasts, and Bugs in
the Life of San Juan Gbëë

EUGENE S. HUNN

The University of Arizona Press   Tucson

The University of Arizona Press
www.uapress.arizona.edu

© 2008 The Arizona Board of Regents
All rights reserved. Published 2008
First paperback edition 2016

Printed in the United States of America
21 20 19 18 17 16   7 6 5 4 3 2

ISBN-13: 978-0-8165-2617-8 (cloth)
ISBN-13: 978-0-8165-3433-3 (paper)

Cover design by Lori Lieber
Front cover: Marielena Cruz Hernández holding pinecones, May 1997. *All cover photographs by Eugene S. Hunn.*

Publication of this book is made possible in part by the proceeds of a permanent endowment created with the assistance of a Challenge Grant from the National Endowment for the Humanities, a federal agency.

Library of Congress Cataloging-in-Publication Data
Hunn, Eugene S.
  A Zapotec natural history : trees, herbs, and flowers, birds, beasts, and bugs in the life of San Juan Gbëë / Eugene S. Hunn.
    p. cm.
  Includes bibliographical references.
  ISBN 978-0-8165-2617-8 (hardcover : alk. paper)
  1. Zapotec Indians—Ethnobotany—Mexico—San Juan Gbëë. 2. Zapotec Indians—Ethnozoology—Mexico—San Juan Gbëë. 3. Zapotec Indians—Ethnobiology—Mexico—San Juan Gbëë. 4. Ethnobotany—Mexico—San Juan Gbëë. 5. Names, Zapotec—Mexico—San Juan Gbëë. 6. Plant names, Popular—Mexico—San Juan Gbëë. 7. San Juan Gbëë (Mexico)—Social life and customs. I. Title.
  F1221.Z3H86 2008
  615'.321089976807274—dc22
                         2008003986

♾ This paper meets the requirements of ANSI/NISO Z39.48-1992 (Permanence of Paper).

This work is dedicated to the memory of
Biol. Donato Acuca Vásquez.
He made much of this work possible.
He died doing what he loved,
an inspiration to us all.

Contents

Part 1

List of Illustrations   ix

Preface   xi

Acknowledgments   xv

1 Introduction   3

2 *Guièdz* / The Town   19

3 *Ló Liù Sànfwân* / The Land   55

4 *Lḛ̀* / Names for Plants and Animals   78

5 *Dòoz* / The Milpa   118

6 *Ncuàan* / Medicines from Plants   151

7 *Guièe* / Flowers   198

8 *Xpḛ̈ëd* / The Children   224

Literature Cited   239

Index   253

Part 2

Online at www.uapress.arizona.edu/Books/bid1957.htm.

Illustrations

Figures

Marielena and Cándido Cruz with ethnobotanist   4
Pedro Miguel with maize seed for planting   5
Driving animals to the milpa   73
Mother and son plowing   126
Martina Romero planting corn and bean seeds   127
León Hernández working with his oxen   128
Emiliano Miguel loading maize   130
A sample of local maize landraces   133
Verónica Santiago with edible mushroom   147
Memorial floral cross   200
Pedro Miguel inspecting a decorative "star"   216

Tables

2.1 "Economically active population" employment sector   38
2.2 Population trends   39
2.3 School attendance by age   41
2.4 Literacy rates   42
2.5 Level of education, 15 years of age and older   43
2.6 Commodities in private households   44
2.7 Amenities in private households   44

Figures, tables, maps, text, and sound clips referred to in part 1 can be accessed in part 2 online at www.uapress.arizona.edu/Books/bid1957.htm.

Preface

A *Zapotec Natural History* provides a comprehensive summary and analysis of the cultural roles of plants in the daily lives of the people of San Juan Gbëë, a Zapotec-speaking community in Oaxaca, Mexico, documenting in detail the traditional environmental knowledge widely shared within San Juan, with particular emphasis on local knowledge of plants. It is published in two parts, the first in standard print format, the second in electronic format online together with over 1,000 images. Part 1 details how this fund of environmental knowledge is integrated within the everyday lives of the people of San Juan. I introduce the community and the local natural environment and then consider in turn the application of this knowledge for subsistence agricultural production, in medicine, and in ritual. Part 2 includes tabular summaries that elaborate upon the material in part 1 and presents a comprehensive annotated list of the plants, animals, and fungi recognized and named in the Zapotec language of San Juan Gbëë. The local Zapotec biological vocabulary is applied to over 700 locally recognized kinds of plants, nearly 400 kinds of animals, and some twenty types of fungi.

This natural history is based on twelve years of field research by the author. Part 1 includes the following chapters:

Chapter 1, Introduction. I argue that the traditional environmental knowledge (TEK) of communities such as San Juan may be an essential tool for the conservation of biodiversity in the future. I define here my position with regard to the contentious issue of bioprospecting, describe my perspective as an ethnobiologist, and provide a brief account of the field of ethnobiology.

Chapter 2, *Guièdz* / The Town. I describe San Juan Gbëë: its geographical position, history, the subsistence economy, social and political organization, and religious practices, and offer a linguistic prognosis. I argue that the town is not "poor," as many outside experts might assume, but "rich" in its own terms. I analyze census materials to evaluate the impact of out-migration. Finally, I describe how my fieldwork in San Juan began and the community's reaction to my presence.

Chapter 3, *Ló Liù Sànfwân* / The Land. The ecological stage is set by narrating a series of explorations, first from Oaxaca City to San Juan, then round about San Juan to the upper and lower limits of the communal territory. I describe major plant communities and types of dominant vegetation.

Chapter 4, *Lè* / Names for Plants and Animals. How people in San Juan use their native language to describe their environment. The focus is on the more than 1,000 Zapotec names in common use and on the conceptual world those names entail. The San Juan system of biological classification is systematically compared with that of modern biological systematics, applying the analytical framework developed by Brent Berlin.

Chapter 5, *Dòoz* / The Milpa. I describe the local subsistence system, beginning with an account of milpa agriculture in the context of debates about the nutritional adequacy of the traditional Mesoamerican diet. I provide an inventory of edible plants (plus fungi, insects, and game animals), including cultivars (in particular, local landraces of maize and beans) and wild edible plants. I describe the annual agricultural work cycle, the complementary roles of orchards and gardens, practices to conserve soil fertility and control crop pests, and animal husbandry as a critical adjunct to the agricultural enterprise. I describe the selection of plants used to make plows, in home building, and for other technical activities.

Chapter 6, *Ncuàan* / Medicines from Plants. I describe the role of traditional medicine in San Juan today, the limited role of traditional specialists, and local perspectives on varieties of "modern" medicine. I analyze the local vocabulary for illnesses and symptoms, particularly the nature of the "hot-cold" distinction. I describe the primary modes of preparation and application of herbal remedies, then review the roles of some 270 plant species used locally to treat some 100 categories of illness. I offer limited comparative ethnopharmacological commentary.

Chapter 7, *Guièe* / Flowers. I take up the debate in ethnobiology with regard to whether traditional environmental knowledge is primarily motivated by utilitarian concerns or by a disinterested intellectual curiosity. I stress the importance of aesthetic and symbolic values of plants, particularly in light of the poetic fascination with flowers characteristic of

Mesoamerican civilizations. I describe the major Zapotec categories of flowers, wild and domesticated.

Chapter 8, *Xpëëd* / The Children. I summarize evidence that very young children in San Juan master a vocabulary of several hundred plant names by the age of twelve, if not by age seven. They learn in the fields and gardens while helping their families, rather than in the classroom, and do so seemingly without effort or formal instruction. This "precocious acquisition" contrasts sharply with the ignorance of the natural environment that is the heritage of so many urban children in the United States today. In conclusion I reflect on the future of this traditional heritage of environmental knowledge as rural subsistence-based communities such as San Juan increasingly engage the global market.

A Phonological Sketch

A note on the Zapotec orthography is in order here. Gbëë Zapotec phonemes include labial, alveolar, velar, and labiovelar occlusives, in fortis and lenis series, plus alveolar and palatal affricates and fricatives, also fortis and lenis (table P1). The three semivowels do not contrast on the fortis-lenis dimension. Labial and alveolar semivowels following velar occlusives are analyzed as unitary labiovelar phonemes. The sound written *"ngu-"* is analyzed as a unitary consonant phoneme (a nazalized labiovelar sonorant). These analytic decisions and orthographic conventions are justified in more detail in Reeck (1991:262–70). Labial (*"f"*) and velar (*"j," "x"*) fricatives and the palatal nasal (*ñ*) are found only in Spanish loans, as is the silent *"h"* (which is not pronounced but written to conform to Spanish orthographic conventions in loan words).

As a naïve native English speaker, I have experienced particular difficulty hearing the fortis-lenis contrast, as this is similar to but not quite the same as the unvoiced-voiced contrast characteristic of English and Spanish occlusives, affricates, and fricatives. The contrast is particularly subtle for nasal and lateral sonorants. In word-final position, lenis sonorants are scarcely audible. One strategy useful for learning this distinction is to note how vowels are shortened when followed by a fortis as opposed to a lenis nasal or lateral sonorant. If still in doubt, one may elicit the word in a construction where the sonorant in question is followed by a vowel, e.g., *"mèl-á"* 'it is a star' versus *"mèl̲-á"* 'it is a fish'.

The vowel system (table P2) is perhaps easier for a native English speaker than for a native Spanish speaker, as the "sixth vowel" is the familiar "*æ*" (written in the print text as "*ë*") of English "hat" or "cat." The simple, for example, "*a*," versus glottalized vowel, for example, "*aa*," contrast is also not entirely foreign to English speakers, as we are accustomed to the glottalized vowel of the admonitions "uh-uh" and "oh-oh." Gbëë Zapotec glottalized vowels sound much like these admonitive interjections when word final or when followed by a lenis consonant but are reduced before fortis consonants to a preglottalization of the following consonant. One should be aware also that glottalization may be transferred to the preceding word in compounds or phrases, e.g., **gâz** + ***lùu*** → **gâazlù** 'you will bathe' (Reeck 1991:265).

Acknowledgments

Many people have provided generous support and encouragement along the way. If I have neglected to give them due recognition here, my apologies. First of all, this work builds upon a twelve-year collaboration by the people of San Juan Gbëë and me, a joint effort that I trust will continue.

Colleagues

I am indebted to the following for generous advice and support:

In Oaxaca: Alejandro de Ávila, director, Jardín Etnobotánico, Centro Cultural de Santo Domingo, Oaxaca, who jump-started my Oaxaca research and introduced me to the Sierra Sur.

At the Centro Interdisciplinario de Investigación para el Desarrollo Integral Regional (CIIDIR), Oaxaca: M. en C. Remedios Aguilar Santelises, director of the herbarium; M. en C. Gladys Isabel Manzanero Medina, specialist in Cactaceae; M. en C. Alejandro Flores Martínez, ecologist; M. en C. Emma Cisneros, herpetologist.

At the Sociedad para el Estudio de los Recursos Bióticos de Oaxaca, A. C. (SERBO), Oaxaca: M. en C. Sylvia Salas, president, SERBO, Oaxaca; Leo Schibli (deceased); Biol. Donato Acuca Vásquez, ornithologist and full partner in this research (deceased); Biol. Alfredo Saynes, botanist, now at the UNAM; Biol. Elizabeth Torres Bayena, botanist, now at the Instituto Estatal de Ecología de Oaxaca.

At the Instituto Tecnológico de Valle de Oaxaca (ITVO), Xoxocotlán, Oaxaca: M. en C. Marco Antonio Vásquez Dávila, ethnobiologist; Biol. Hugo León Avendaño and Biol. Alfonso Aurelio, mycologists.

At large in Oaxaca: M. en C. Salvador Acosta Castellanos, botanist; M. en C. Graciela Alcántara, ethno-ornithologist; M. en C. Jaime Ernesto Rivera Hernández, botanist; M. en C. Luís Cervantes Servin, botanist; Dr. Marcus Winter, archaeologist, INAH, Oaxaca; Dra. María de los Ángeles Romero Frizzi, historian, INAH, Oaxaca; Dr. Martha Reese, anthropolgist, Oaxaca and the University of Cincinnati; Drs. Ronald Waterbury and Carol Turkenik, Oaxaca; Dr. Michael Chibnik, Oaxaca and Iowa State University; Dr. Arthur D. Murphy, then president of the Instituto Welty de Estudios Oaxaqueños.

In the Sierra Sur: Meinardo Hernández Pérez, linguist and native of San Juan; Roger Reeck, SIL linguist; Dr. Miguel Ángel Espinosa S., doctor, San Pedro Mixtepec clinic.

In Mexico City, at the Botanical Garden, Universidad Nacional Autónoma de México (UNAM): Dr. Javier Caballero, director; Dr. Robert Bye and M. en C. Edelmira Linares, ethnobiologists and good friends of many years; Dr. Abisaí García Mendoza, Agavaceae specialist.

At the National Herbarium (MEXU) at UNAM: Dr. Gerardo A. Salazar, director, orchid specialist; M. en C. Mario Sousa; M. en C. Oswaldo Tellez; Dra. Rosalinda Medina López, *Bursera* specialist; Jerónimo Reyes Santiago, expert in Cactaceae; Dr. David Gernandt, pine specialist; and Francisco Ramos Marchena, who provided initial determinations for the bulk of my collections.

At the Institute of Biology, UNAM: Dr. José L. Villaseñor, specialist in Asteraceae; Dr. Jerzy Rzedowski, *Bursera* specialist; Dra. Susana Valencia Avalos, specialist in *Quercus*; Dra. Patricia Escalante, curator of the bird collection.

At the Centro de Estudios Lingüísticos y Literarios, El Colegio de México, Dr. Thomas C. Smith-Stark.

Thanks also to Dr. William W. Dressler, University of Alabama, and Dr. Dan Moerman, University of Michigan, for reviewing the medicinal plant chapter; to Dr. George F. Estabrook, University of Michigan, for many stimulating discussions, particularly with regard to goats; to Mark Egger, Seattle, for helping locate rare endemic species of *Castilleja*; and to Stacy Waters, Evan Perry, and Cody Logan, DXARTS, University of Washington, for absolutely essential technical support in the preparation of the online content.

Students

Dr. Jennifer Sepez, Dr. Thomas Murphy, Dr. Akesha Baron, Biol. Miriam Aldasoro Maya, Dr. Oscar Barrera-Núñez, Brian Van Hoy, Lisa Schneider.

Townspeople

Hermilo Silva Cruz, municipal president, 1996–1999; Florentino Hernández Hernández, municipal president, 1999–2002; Felipe Martínez García, municipal president, 2002–2005; Higinio Hernández Hernández, municipal president 2005–2008; Feliciano "Chano" Martínez López, *síndico*, 1996–1999; Valentín Martínez Miguel, blind man, writes in Braille (died 2005); Pánfilo Santiago Cruz and Verónica Santiago Cruz, consultants; Antolín Hernández Hernández, brother of Florentino; Pedro Miguel Zurita and Bernardina Hernández Hernández, consultants; Silvino Miguel Zurita and Vírgen Martínez Hernández, shopkeepers, neighbors; Solomón Miguel Zurita, Pedro and Silvino's brother, municipal vice-president, 1999–2002; Javier Miguel Martínez, Silvino's eldest son; Raúl Miguel Martínez, another of Silvino's sons; Eucario Hernández Miguel, old-timer (died 2006); medicinal plant panel: Agripina Martínez Cruz, Pedro Hernández Miguel, Elia Jarquín Hernández, Ranulfo Cruz López; Israel Zurita Jarquín (son of Elia, librarian); Cándido Cruz Hernández, consultant; Roselía Hernández Cruz, Cándido's wife, consultant; Inez Vírgen Cruz Hernández, consultant; Justina Cruz Hernández, consultant; Marielena Cruz Hernández, consultant; Lilia Sánchez Cruz, Inez's older daughter, consultant; Maximiliano Sánchez Hernández, nephew of Roselía, consultant and guide; Lorenzo Mendoza, consultant and guide; Dario Mardonio Cruz Pérez, municipal vice-president, 1996–1999; Floriana Cruz Zurita, consultant; Victoriano Fabian Mendoza, patriarch at Rancho Conejo; Felipe Fabian Mendoza, son of Victoriano, Rancho Conejo, consultant; Sofía Fabian Cruz, midwife, San Pedro; Lucila Martínez Martínez, our landlady, lawyer in Oaxaca; Rufina Martínez, our landlady's mother, shopkeeper in Miahuatlán; Rosa Cervantes, from Veracruz; the children of San Juan, my teachers.

Funding

National Science Foundation; University of Washington, Graduate School Research Fund; Jacobs Research Fund.

Special Mention

Carlos Córdova Camacho and Rocio Gómez, friends, neighbors, Oaxaca; the staff of Casa Arnel, home away from home in Oaxaca; last, but by no means least, my wife, Nancy, constructive critic and companion through it all.

A Zapotec Natural History

CHAPTER 1

Introduction

THIS IS A story about *science, of, by, and for the people* of one Mexican town, San Juan Gbëë in the state of Oaxaca. The science in question is natural history, with a particular emphasis on botany. I describe in detail the knowledge of the local flora and fauna, derived from systematic observation and centuries of accumulated experience, that is the patrimony of San Juan, an indigenous Zapotec community. The people of San Juan live with and by means of this biota.

It is the story of Marielena, ten years old as I began my project, of her fascination with the plants in her garden, the weeds in her family's milpa, the wildflowers and medicines she finds along the trails that radiate from town (fig. 1.1). It is the story of Lilia, her five-year-old niece, who has followed in her footsteps (fig. 1.2). Marielena's parents, Cándido and Roselía, invited me into their home on my first visit (fig. 1.3). Marielena's mother, her five daughters and two granddaughters, and Cándido's mother, who lives next door, constitute a strong four-generation matrilineal family line.

This book is the story of Eucario, age sixty-eight, who as a young man, before the construction of the Pan American Highway, drove mules over well-beaten paths loaded with *petates* from neighboring San Cristóbal to the Isthmus of Tehuántepec, returning with salted fish. In his later days he loved to sit in the shade of his *palapa* at the edge of town admiring his fields and the expansive view down the valley to the north (fig. 1.4). It is the story of Valentín, also sixty-eight years old, struck blind by disease at the age of eighteen, who until nearly the end of his life worked his own fields with the help of a grandchild. Don, or Zhey, Eucario died in 2006; Zhey Valentín, the previous year. He wrote vivid descriptions of birds and flowers in Zapotec with his braille-writing machine (fig. 1.5). It is the story of Pedro, age forty, acolyte in the Catholic church, who experiments constantly with his crops to improve on tradition (fig. 1.6).

It is the story of a town at a turning point, a town deeply rooted, its people conscious of their 1,000-year history, proud of their native

Marielena and her father, Cándido Cruz, instructing the ethnobiologist on wild plants near their milpa, July 25, 1996.

language, jealous of their forests, serious about their duty to communal service, yet eager for education and well aware of the world down the road. It is the story of Pánfilo, a man of twenty-eight, who, like many young people, left San Juan to learn a trade (masonry in his case) and make some money (fig. 1.7). He met Verónica, a young woman also from San Juan, while working in a coastal city. They came home, married, and are now raising their three children. Pánfilo works with his father in their milpa and hires out his services as a mason. He knows his town well, once recounting the fates of over 1,000 townspeople recorded twenty years previously in a household census. It is the story of Raúl also, fifteen when I first arrived in San Juan (fig. 1.8), curious to learn about my country, eager to learn English, now a pioneer in California. It is the story of Hermilo, age forty-eight, past president of San Juan (fig. 1.9). He is a dedicated subsistence farmer and a brilliant linguist, in the estimation of Roger Reeck, SIL linguist, who lived here in the 1970s. Though a Protestant, Hermilo champions the community and is guardedly optimistic about its future.

Pedro Miguel with maize seed for planting, June 17, 1998.

Why San Juan?

What is so special about San Juan Gbëë that books should be written about it? San Juan, like every town, is a mirror in which to see ourselves. It is a very human place. But more to the specifics of the case, San Juan is of particular interest for being on the front lines of a global confrontation in which those who value and would preserve diversity—whether biological or cultural—are on the defensive before the seemingly overwhelming force of the ever-expanding human consumption of resources, land, and energy. The "human footprint" continues its relentless march (cf. Wackernagel and Rees 1996). We are consuming our planet. At the same time, rural villages and towns that retain a measure of self-sufficiency in producing much of the food they eat, building their own houses, and weaving their own clothing, while collecting and preparing the medicines they use to cure themselves, are presumed to be poor and backward, rare anachronisms not long for this world. San Juan is one such community. Is it doomed to be swept aside by the advancing tide of capitalist expansion?

This cannibalism of the earth is driven by the twin engines of human population increase and an insatiable global consumer economy. Yet thousands of local and indigenous communities such as San Juan, scattered across the rural tropics, hold traditional lands that shelter critical habitat, rich in biodiversity. Is it mere coincidence that regions which harbor these rural communities, rich in cultural diversity, are very often at the same time regions of exceptional floral and faunal diversity (Maffi 2001)? Is this an accident of history? Have these overlapping islands of cultural and biological diversity been spared the ravages of "development" only by virtue of their common isolation, now rapidly disappearing? Or, perhaps these communities have actively husbanded those biodiverse lands, forests, and waters with an eye to the interests of their posterity? If so, might we trust them to guard these riches in the future as they have guarded them in the past? This latter view is not popular with the most vocal proponents of biodiversity conservation (Diamond 1988; Redford and Stearman 1993; Kay 1994; Caro 1998). The evidence that indigenous communities have the knowledge and the will to conserve the biological heritage of their lands is sparse, scattered, and subject to varied interpretations (Smith and Wishnie 2000; Hunn et al. 2003). More often it is assumed that to preserve biodiversity it is necessary to keep people out. My goal here is not to resolve this complex and pressing question, but rather to tell the story of one indigenous community that for centuries has occupied a biologically rich corner of one of the most biologically diverse countries in the world, Mexico, balancing their human desires and needs against the requirements of sustainable diversity.

I will emphasize one aspect of the complex relationship between the people of this community and the environment they occupy, that is, their knowledge of that environment, their traditional environmental or ecological knowledge, sometimes labeled TEK, for short. Some critics object to this shorthand, TEK, on the grounds that "traditional" implies a rigid and unchanging outlook or that "knowledge" implies a Western dichotomy of thought and feeling, that it decontextualizes the "knowledge and wisdom" of indigenous worldviews (Nadasdy 1999). Alternatives offered include IK, "indigenous knowledge"; LEK, "local ecological knowledge"; or TKW, "traditional knowledge and wisdom." This last option emphasizes that for many indigenous communities, what we set in opposition—science and religion—for them constitute a seamless whole (Berkes 1999). Personally, I prefer TEK. It has a slight historic priority, and I understand "tradition" to be a dynamic, collective intellectual response to the challenges and opportunities of a constantly evolving natural and social environment (Hunn 1993). Traditional environmental knowledge emerges necessarily from a deeply rooted communal relationship to the local landscape. It is thus also both "indigenous" and "local." Knowledge in such communities is, as a general rule, in no way set off from worldview or *cosmovisión*, to use the felicitous Spanish term, the encompassing understandings of the moral order that should govern the human place in nature. That is the "wisdom" of TKW (Berkes 1999).

A Brief Essay on the Nature of Science

Many bitter academic debates reduce to semantic misunderstandings. The rhetorical flourishes of proponents of one point of view wield words in ways that needlessly antagonize proponents of alternative perspectives. An informative and substantive debate might have been possible had key words been employed with an appreciation of their complex and subtle nuances of meaning. *Science* is a case in point. Proponents of "hard" science demand that certain procedures be followed and that "scientific" investigations be designed to test hypotheses deduced from explicit, formal, ideally mathematical theoretical models, and that such tests involve experiments that "control" for extraneous variation. For many of us, such an approach is *prototypically* scientific. However, it does not follow that investigations that deviate in one or more respects from this prototype are therefore *not* scientific or that they represent an inferior mode of science less worthy of our interest (and financial support).

Many undeniably scientific advances of great importance fail to match this prototype of superior science. For example, modern linguistic theory within the Chomskyan paradigm involves neither mathematical theory nor controlled experimentation, yet it is fiercely rigorous and has produced powerful advances in our understanding of the cognitive psychological and evolutionary bases of human language (Pinker 1994).

Contemporary biology recognizes Charles Darwin's contribution as its ultimate foundation, yet Darwin's approach was in the tradition of natural history, neither formally theoretical nor experimental. Darwin amassed a lifetime of observations of patterns in nature and puzzled long and hard to find some convincing mechanism to account for the intricate connections he perceived among these observations. Of course, contemporary biology is fast becoming a formal laboratory science dedicated to mapping the genome and demonstrating how specific genetic changes produce effects in the form, function, and behavior of living organisms, to the point of aggressive interventions designed to control the natural processes Darwin could only guess at. This bias in favor of "hard" science spawned in anthropology and cultural studies a "critical science studies" program that is at times virulently antiscience, seeking to undermine the authority of modern science by exposing its cultural, social, and political entanglements, its historic roots in a patriarchal, colonialist, and capitalist "West" (Marcus and Fisher 1986; Tyler 1991; Haraway 1994). However, in attacking particular excesses of scientific zeal, this program suffers from the same semantic oversimplification of those it attacks; that is, its proponents equate "science" with some few stereotypical expressions of that vast and entirely human endeavor properly so-called.

What, Then, Is *Science*?

Is it a unique expression of the European Renaissance rooted in Greek philosophy, or might we expect to find an indigenous science in a Zapotec village such as San Juan Gbëë? If, following González (2001:22), science may be defined quite simply as a "quest for truths about the world," or, after Malinowski (1974 [1925]), as "knowledge, based on experience and fashioned by reason" (i.e., knowledge that is both empirical and rational), then I believe we may expect to find science most everywhere, and in TEK in particular.

Granted, science has taken rather dramatic turns in the history of Western Europe and its intellectual colonies since the Renaissance. However, if we wish to set apart this particular historic manifestation of science, we may refer to it as "modern science" (Anderson 1996:143) or "cosmopolitan science" (González 2001), or better yet, "modern sciences," to avoid essentializing a diverse endeavor. These modern sciences may then be contrasted with "folk sciences" and other expressions of the scientific imagination that might not fall comfortably under either term.

I would argue that the outstanding differences between modern and folk sciences are first of all a consequence of transformations in the scale of scientific enterprise, rather than attributable to any fundamental advance in the quality of human thought, as many presume. Modern science is a multitrillion-dollar global enterprise, carried out by certified professional "scientists," in the employ of universities and governmental or corporate research institutes. Modern science is a juggernaut urged ahead by a million helping hands. By contrast, folk science is carried forward by a *campesino* observing how his corn crop responds to vagaries of soil and weather, chatting over dinner with a neighbor, comparing notes, or a *curandera* evaluating the recovery of a village child sick with fever. Does the fact that folk scientists say nothing of viruses, DNA, and quasars expose some fault in their thinking? Certainly not. Not that such "things" are of no consequence for them. Just that they have not the means to experience them directly.

Will Modern Science Absorb Folk Science?

Agrawal (1995) argues that in the contemporary world no body of traditional knowledge remains beyond the influence of global scientific perspectives and that it is therefore misleading to speak of local knowledge as "indigenous." I disagree. In the case of San Juan Gbëë, granted, the townspeople are aware of modern medical options—of pills, injections, and surgery. However, suffering from "fright" or *chaneque,* a cold or a fever, diarrhea or *empacho,* they find relief in indigenous herbal remedies to adjust the dynamic internal balance of "heat" and "cold" on which they believe their health depends. Their knowledge of modern scientific medicine as an option has neither transformed nor displaced indigenous theory and practice in the diagnosis and treatment of illness (see chap. 6).

The same may be said of indigenous agriculture in San Juan. Medieval European plows drawn by teams of oxen open furrows for planting seeds of maize and beans domesticated here 7,000 years ago. A substantial fraction of the plants in San Juan orchards and gardens are post-conquest introductions, mostly from Europe, and new exotic species are continually brought home as curiosities. Exotic and native ornamental flowers alike are offered on graves and at village ceremonies dedicated to the spirits of the dead, as at Todos Santos, or in appeals to the god of thunder for rain, as at the Fiesta de la Santa Cruz. Such practices reveal a deeply rooted Mesoamerican aesthetic that values flowers as "poetry" and as "prayer" (see chap. 7). In short, despite continuing exchange of ideas and material, San Juan environmental knowledge remains "traditional" and "indigenous"; that is, it is understood, transmitted, and applied by local people, for their own ends. It is *their* knowledge, intimately connected to their daily life experiences.

Ethnoscience

A *Zapotec Natural History* is an account of a system of traditional environmental knowledge, TEK. The subject matter may also be construed as *ethnoscience*, a term that gained a special currency in the 1960s with the emergence of the field of cognitive anthropology (Sturtevant 1964). While TEK and *ethnoscience* name closely allied intellectual subjects, they are not synonymous. This lack of semantic equivalence is due largely to the different historical contexts in which each term was developed and deployed. For cultural anthropologists of the 1960s ethnoscience exemplified the "New Ethnography" (ironically, quite far removed from the postmodern "New Ethnography" of the 1980s). It advocated an ethnographic method designed to be scientific, replicable, and, above all, faithful to the *emic* cultural realities anthropology had set out to capture in print. Thus, ethnoscientists were careful to describe folk scientific knowledge in the language of the people who developed, distributed, and deployed that knowledge. Use of the term *ethnoscience* implied that "science" is a universal phenomenon, much as an earlier generation of anthropologists had expanded the scope of terms such as *family, religion, art, economics,* and *law,* asserting that there was no human society that lacked kinship (though they might fail to distinguish siblings from cousins), religion (though they believed in many gods or imagined deity in animate forces of nature), art (though their arts were expressed in the practices of daily life), economics (though they might lack money and markets), and law (though lacking lawyers and law codes). Rather, anthropologists showed how all peoples recognize kin, imbue their worlds with moral value, express refined aesthetic sensibilities, shrewdly calculate the exchange of valued goods, and resolve all manner of disputes by public appeals to evidence, testimony, precedent, and rational argument (Hutchins 1980). Likewise, "ethnoscience" implies that a form of scientific analysis is in play in all human societies.

TEK emerged as a concern in the early 1980s. An international committee to preserve TEK was authorized under UNESCO auspices in 1983, directed by Gregory Baines. Initially, the scientific status of TEK was not a primary concern. Rather, scholars and indigenous activists focused on giving TEK recognition and legal status as cultural patrimony and finding resources to help indigenous communities preserve this patrimony in the face of the global cultural homogenization of the postcolonial era. However, to recognize that TEK is scientific is to grant such bodies of knowledge a measure of the legitimacy widely accorded "science" in the contemporary world.

Science: Theoretical or Applied?

Ethnobiologists have long debated the "utilitarian" as opposed to "disinterested" motives that drive the accumulation and conservation of knowledge within a cultural tradition (Hays 1982; Hunn 1982; Berlin 1992). The issues are complex, but most would agree that traditional knowledge plays a key role in the successful adaptation of a people to their local environment. Taken as a whole, folk biological knowledge is undeniably useful. On the other hand, it is clear that if people were motivated to learn only that which is of proven utility, new knowledge could not be developed, as the recognition of the utility of an element of knowledge first requires that it be known, recognized. Thus, "disinterested" curiosity is itself of great utility. Comparative analyses of ethnobiological knowledge systems have demonstrated that the recognition of plants or animals as "things" to be known depends heavily upon their intrinsic distinctiveness as natural species, within the limitations of naked-eye natural history (Berlin 1992;

Hunn 1999a). Nevertheless, a utilitarian bias is noticeable in that more "useful" plants and animals are more finely resolved culturally than those less useful, other things being equal (see chap. 4).

This debate is reflected in the invidious distinction so often drawn between pure and applied sciences. It is undeniable that modern science is driven to a substantial degree by practical concerns, such as the availability of research funding, and such funding, whether from government or industry, is strongly constrained by market considerations. Pharmaceutical companies will invest in the development of a potential drug only if the corporate managers judge it likely that an adequate market exists for such a drug. Thus, drugs to treat diseases that affect only small numbers of people or that affect people too poor to pay full fare for the drugs are less likely to be developed by pharmaceutical companies than drugs, such as Viagra, that have clear profit potential. Government funding for science, also, is hardly immune from such considerations, given the political fallout from spending tax dollars on projects without clear public benefits, very often measured in terms of financial impacts.

In conclusion, I believe that both utility and "pure" curiosity about the working principles of our world drive both modern and folk sciences. Nevertheless, it is clear that certain modern sciences, particularly those with highly developed experimental protocols, such as physics, chemistry, and genetics, are abstractly theoretical in ways quite unlike the "theoretical" bent of folk scientists. For example, Blurton-Jones and Konner, in their classic essay on !Kung San ethnoethology (1976), that is, the folk science of animal behavior, argue convincingly that !Kung hunters, however carefully and critically they may observe animals, tend to explain their behavioral peculiarities with a shrug. For example, they respond to the question of why a lion might abandon meat soiled by the prey animal's feces, with "That's what lions do." If Isaac Newton had dismissed the fall of the apple as just what apples do, modern physics might have been stillborn. Yet, I hope to convince you that the people of San Juan Gbëë have developed a traditional body of knowledge of local plants and animals worthy of that distinguished title "science"; it is a natural history of impressive scope and detail that reliably informs their daily struggle for health and sustenance and that testifies to the fascination local people have for their natural surroundings.

A Personal Note

I am an ethnobiologist. This odd beast is part anthropologist, part linguist, part field biologist, part evolutionist, part conservationist and social activist. My fellow ethnobiologists are a motley crew, their peculiar perspectives emerging from their unique histories, academic, personal, and political. Those of us trained in anthropology are often strangers among our cultural anthropologist colleagues, who rarely know or care what sort of plant it is that a villager sends her child to find to make the tea to treat the child's bad dreams. Those of us trained in biology are estranged from our conservation biologist colleagues, who so readily assume that the problem is people, without regard for the economic and political systems that define the parameters of their action and inaction. We are all distressed by a groundswell of hostility from indigenous activists, who suspect that we are but agents of the continuing misappropriation of their cultural and natural heritage. Still, we persevere, hoping that by our appreciation and understanding of the humanity of these "people of the earth," these "indigenous people," the Inuit, Déné, *tanan-ma*, and *binni za*, as they know themselves, we might encourage support for all indigenous peoples in their struggles to keep their lands and lives intact.

I was amazed to discover the depth and breadth of San Juan children's knowledge of the plants around them, and their passion to learn more (see chap. 8). These children, by age seven, far outstrip my peers in their common knowledge. Perhaps this is evidence of E. O. Wilson's hopeful *Biophilia* (1986)—the notion that humans are innately attuned to the life around them—an affinity honored more often these days in the breach.

I intend to preserve a record of the knowledge of plants and animals of San Juan by the simple measure of writing down as much as I can of the environmental knowledge the people of San Juan share. However, it is not so simple. Their knowledge is embodied in their language, a form of Zapotec readily understood only within a radius of some twenty kilometers by some 10,000 people native to the zone. Zapotec languages are difficult for English native speakers to "hear," as they employ tonal contrasts and vowel quality distinctions and modes of consonantal articulation we long ago learned to ignore.

I have acquired a limited command of Zapotec phonology and can more or less faithfully transcribe Zapotec plant and animal names. However, that is of no help in my efforts here to communicate to an English-speaking audience what seems a wonder to me: quite independent of any outside expert intervention, a community of subsistence farmers has in their own words learned to describe in exquisite detail the rich biodiversity of their country. There seems no alternative but to use Latin, the language of global science, as a bridge between Zapotec and English (Hunn 2006). Latin provides a *metalanguage* by which we may show how Zapotec-speakers grasp the phenomenological reality of nature. However, the reader is at a distinct disadvantage, deprived of the experience of nature that informs San Juan traditional environmental knowledge. To compensate I have selected visual images—several hundred of which are accessible online. These images may convey something of the aesthetic power of an exotic flora as well.

The bare numbers are stark but nevertheless impressive. In part 2 I list the Ethnoflora: 452 folk generic taxa, 341 (75 percent) of which are monotypic and 111 (25 percent) polytypic. Polytypic generics include 371 specific taxa, of which 46 are covert prototypes; eight (1.7 percent) of the specific taxa are polytypic, including a total of 23 varietal taxa, one of which is a covert prototype. I thus recognize 717 terminal taxa and 843 total generic, specific, and varietal taxa. These taxa correspond to a minimum of 1,075 varieties of 1,065 species of 557 genera of 140 vascular plant families.

Why this obsession with names, with mere words? you might ask. Sapir and Whorf argued that words are the tools of thought (Carroll 1956). The Sapir-Whorf hypothesis of linguistic relativity states:

> Human beings do not live in the objective world alone, . . . but are very much at the mercy of the particular language which has become the medium of expression for their society . . . the "real world" is to a large extent unconsciously built upon the language habits of the group. . . . The worlds in which different societies live are distinct worlds, not merely the same world with different labels attached. (Sapir, *Selected Writings*, p. 162)

Thus, a large vocabulary for a domain deeply implicated in our lives provides indispensable leverage in dealing with those aspects of the world most important to us. However, with all due respect to Sapir and Whorf, we do not "invent" the worlds we live in. The worlds we describe in our native tongues are not purely conventional virtual realities, but actual, immanent realities we misconstrue at our peril. Thus, words for plants and animals made life possible for the people of San Juan now and throughout their long history.

I am deeply concerned about the consequences of the loss of indigenous languages such as San Juan Gbëë Zapotec, since the imperial tongues, that is, Spanish or English, that would replace them reserve an elaborated biological vocabulary for a small coterie of professionals and leave the great majority of speakers clueless. I believe it is worth the effort to understand how a modest peasant community such as San Juan Gbëë could have preserved such etymological riches despite 480 years of political, economic, religious, and cultural colonization by European-derived traditions and values. Yet they have done so, scarcely missing a beat (Hunn and Acuca Vásquez 2001), to the present youngest generation.

A Brief Intellectual History of Ethnobiology

I have found it useful to distinguish four phases in the history of ethnobiology, which correspond also to four emphases—complementary, not mutually exclusive—among ethnobiological researchers today.

Ethnobiology 1 might be termed "pre-theoretical ethnobiology." As an intellectual endeavor it dates to before recorded history, since the first curious human engaged some stranger in a conversation about useful plants in hopes of learning something that might be profitably applied in his or her own life. No doubt peoples have always exchanged useful information about foods, medicines, and materials derived from their local floras, to their mutual benefit. However, as a systematic, written exercise, such exchanges of ethnobotanical information date at least to the sixteenth century. The Franciscan friar Bernardino de Sahagún dedicated his long career to the conversion of the Aztec peoples to Christianity following Cortés's invasion of Mexico. To further that effort, Sahagún organized a systematic study of Aztec knowledge and practice, employing bilingual Aztec students of noble birth to interview respected elders about an expansive range of topics: the religious, social, political, and economic life of the Aztec Empire, so recently brought to ruin. Book 11 of the monumental *Florentine Codex*, written in Nahuatl and first published in 1577, treats of Aztec knowledge and use of plants and animals (Sahagún 1950–69). Of the same era is Francisco Hernández's three-volume *Historia de las Plantas de Nueva España* (1959, originally published 1577). Hernández was a court physician to King Philip II of Spain, sent to Mexico expressly to record Aztec medicinal knowledge, widely recognized then as superior to European medicine (Ortiz de Montellano 1990:25–29). Though biased by a belief in the ultimate superiority of Spanish culture and faith, these early efforts were extraordinary for their time in their meticulous attention to detail and—in Sahagún's case—tacit respect for the value of local lifeways and local knowledge.

Mark Plotkin's much-publicized ethnobotanical adventures among contemporary South American tribes (1994) in search of new medicines carry this first ethnobiological tradition forward, but without the lifelong immersion in the lives of the local people practiced by Sahagún. One might question the efficacy of such efforts to discover miracle cures today, in the age of multinational corporate pharmaceutical giants, exhaustive governmental oversight of new drugs, and the growing awareness by indigenous peoples that they are being asked to share their hard-won knowledge of plant cures to treat diseases of affluent people elsewhere. Which is not to say that Ethnobiology 1 is an effort that should be abandoned, rather, that ethnobiology must embrace a wider range of human concerns if it is to contribute to human understanding, welfare, and justice, broadly conceived.

Ethnobiology 2 emerged in the 1950s in tandem with the development of cognitive anthropology, the anthropological spoke in the cognitive science wheel (Gardner 1985). We might call it "cognitive ethnobiology." Harold Conklin's meticulous analysis of Hanunóo ethnobotanical systematics (1954) set a very high standard for ethnobiological ethnography. But Conklin was averse to broad generalization. Thus, we had to wait until Brent Berlin's Tzeltal Maya research (Berlin, Breedlove, and Raven 1974), with inspiration from Ralph Bulmer's reflections on Kalam ethnozoology (1974), motivated a "general [cognitive] theory" of ethnobiological classification. Though imperfect, Berlin's "general principles of folk biological classification and nomenclature" (Berlin, Breedlove, and Raven 1973) provide the analytical framework for the present analysis. Chapter 4 elaborates issues central to cognitive ethnobiology.

Ethnobiology 2 was judged narrowly formalist by both critics and proponents in the 1970s. This set the stage for the emergence of Ethnobiology 3. This "ecological ethnobiology" sought to characterize local knowledge of plants and animals in its rich context of practice, knowledge put to use in dealing with issues of day-to-day survival in difficult environments by hunter-gatherers, fishermen, and farmers. These critics argued that the study of ethnobiology should be subordinate to the study of *ethnoecology*, or TEK, and of traditional resource management (TRM). Ethnobiology should address pressing issues of human survival in the modern world, such as: "Does a detailed awareness of local biodiversity encourage conservation of that diversity?" Or, "Is that knowledge dedicated to maximizing personal profit?" Such questions are now central to the field and are addressed in chapters 5, 6, 7, and 8.

The most recent development, Ethnobiology 4, emerged in the 1980s. Ethnobiologists came to grips with the fact that the subjects of ethnobiological scrutiny, the "traditional" and "indigenous" peoples whose environmental knowledge the field had devoted its primary efforts to salvaging, must be involved as full partners in any legitimate ethnobiological inquiry. Were such efforts legitimate intellectual pursuits or, rather, a morally questionable intrusion into and exploitation of the lives of peoples victimized by the scholars' own societies? Ethnobiology 4 could be the final ethnobiological chapter if the study of ethnobiological knowledge becomes so fraught with questions of power and violation as to preclude the delicate collaboration such ethnographic research requires. If Ethnobiology 4 is ethnobiology of, by, and for "indigenous" or subject peoples, does this preclude collaboration between indigenous scholars and those of us who happen to have been born elsewise? I hope not, for I believe there are valuable lessons to be learned on both sides of the indigenous divide. Perhaps the very survival of indigenous peoples requires that their opposite number, the immigrant peoples, who now far outnumber them, appreciate that all will benefit from their continued presence among us. Though these volumes are written in English, and are thus not readily accessible to the people of San Juan, I have published a summary of local knowledge of medicinal herbs in Spanish with an extensive Zapotec technical vocabulary. I have distributed this booklet free of charge to the families of San Juan. I plan additional volumes as requested by community leaders, which will summarize much of the content of *A Zapotec Natural History*.

Ethnobiology 1, 2, 3, and 4 do not represent an evolutionary progression through which superior forms of analysis displace the inferior forms that preceded them. Rather, the historical development of ethnobiology through these four phases is cumulative, each new perspective enhancing the older emphases. I believe strongly that for ethnobiology to reach its full potential we must weave all four strands together.

CHAPTER 2

Guièdz / The Town

Cultural Overview

The People

THE ZAPOTECS TODAY live in the Mexican state of Oaxaca (map 2.1) in nearly 300 rural villages and towns, as well as in the state capital and tourist mecca, Oaxaca City. You might also run into Zapotecs in California or elsewhere in the United States helping harvest crops in fields and orchards or serving tables in the ubiquitous Mexican restaurants. What do all these Zapotecs have in common, wherever they may live and work? There is no simple answer, but they all have roots in their Zapotec homeland in the mountains and arid valleys of the southern Mexican plateau. Many speak a Zapotec language as their first language, though most now also speak Spanish, the language of schools, markets, and government throughout Mexico since the Spanish conquest in the early sixteenth century.

The Zapotec people today make their homes in a wide range of habitats and speak many different Zapotec languages. Experts disagree on how many Zapotec languages there are, because these languages often change gradually as one travels from village to village across Oaxaca. Linguists have in the past recognized five to nine Zapotec languages (Whitecotton 1977:15; Smith Stark 2001), but it is clear that each of these "languages" encompasses great variation, preventing mutual intelligibility. A recent estimate by *Ethnologue*, a summary of world language diversity, recognizes no fewer than fifty-eight Zapotec languages (SIL 2004).

Most Zapotecs are direct descendants of the people who built Monte Albán, a magnificent city constructed 2,500 years ago on a mountaintop that commands a view of the densely settled, fertile valley of the Atoyac River and of the contemporary city of Oaxaca (Blanton et al. 1999). The founders of Monte Albán are thought to have helped invent the writing and calendar systems that were later elaborated by the Classic Mayan civilization (Marcus 1976, 2003).

San Juan Gbëë is one of 571 independent local communities (*municipios*) in the Mexican state of Oaxaca (maps 2.2, 2.3). It is an indigenous community (fig. 2.1); that is, virtually every resident speaks the local Zapotec as their first language, though many also speak Spanish. The community is self-governing according to local *"usos y costumbres,"* traditional customary practices, rather than by national party politics. The town was established at its present location in 1690 (Rojas 1992), after moving one kilometer southeast from its previous location. Local tradition affirms that sometime before the arrival of the Spanish, San Juan and its neighbor, San Pedro Gbëë, were a single pueblo where the Río Grande joins the Río Calabazar two kilometers north of contemporary San Juan (maps 2.4, 2.5). On a ridge above this ancient village site are unexcavated ruins of the Classic period, thus more than 1,350 years old (Winter 1997) (fig. 2.2). The community is endogamous and to this day there are no more than a handful of spouses not native to the town. The term *indigenous* is often considered to be so difficult to define as to be meaningless. Such is not the case with San Juan. However, the people of San Juan today do not think of themselves first of all as "Zapotecs" or even as "indigenous people," but rather as citizens of their town, San Juan Gbëë, and of their country, Mexico.

San Juan today is home to 932 permanent residents (according to the most recent national census, conducted in 2000), which is, of course, but a tiny fraction of the population of Mexico and less still of the world. However, it is essential to recognize that there are perhaps as many more San Juaneros living in nearby cities. These citizens retain their family ties and their emotional attachment to the land. They come back for community celebrations and to memorialize their deceased relatives. They will return if called to serve a *cargo*—that is, a "civic burden" or duty such as *presidente municipal, síndico*, or *regidor*, interrupting careers in the wider world. Their town encompasses 54 km^2, the upper half a nearly pristine pine forest, lightly harvested but subject to periodic forest fires. If they need land to farm, it is there for them, although the best fields, those closest to the town, are *terrenos privados*, purchased by citizens from their town, inherited by their children, farmed by the family together, or farmed *a medias* by those with less land. However, the bulk of the community's lands are *terrenos comunales,* and may be used by any citizen to hunt, graze animals, gather firewood, or collect flowers and herbs. Citizens may cut trees or stone to build a house or clear a new milpa on these communal lands, but only with the express permission of the Comisariado de Bienes Comunales, a committee of twelve citizens, serving in rotation, who review and affirm such petitions. This is communal land, not the "tragic commons" of Garrett Hardin's classic essay (1968).

San Juan's claim to its communal territory derives from the community's occupation of the land since before the Spanish conquest and is affirmed by colonial title deeds. This has not prevented disputes with neighboring towns over the precise boundaries. For example, San Juan is embroiled in a bitter conflict with its southern neighbor over rights to an additional 14 km^2 of high-elevation forest land. There have been fatal confrontations, one as recently as 1990. But San Juan kept its communal lands throughout the Porfiriato—the prerevolutionary period of Mexican history dominated by the dictator, and Oaxaca native son, Porfirio Díaz, when communal lands were confiscated for sale to foreign capitalist interests in pursuit of national economic growth. (This in part explains why there are relatively few *ejidos*—post-revolutionary communal land grants —in Oaxaca.) Still, the community's firm control of its lands and natural resources is a legacy of Emiliano Zapata's revolutionary credo, "The land belongs to those who work it," which inspired Mexico's constitutional guarantee of a measure of local sovereignty for indigenous municipal governments.

> Article 27, Provision VII: The centers of population which, by law or in fact, possess a communal status shall have legal capacity to enjoy common possession of the lands, forests, and waters belonging to them or which have been or may be restored to them. (1917 Constitution of Mexico)

Many indigenous communities elsewhere lack this security of tenure. It is San Juan's best hope for the future.

Spanish Catholic missionaries of the Dominican order were granted Oaxaca as their domain and were charged by the pope and the king of Spain to convert to Christianity the Zapotecs and their neighbors: Mixtecs, Chinantecs, Mazatecs, Cuicatecs, Mixes, Chontales, etc. (The Oaxaca state government recognizes sixteen indigenous ethnic groups, of which the Zapotecs are just one.) The Dominicans were remarkably successful. Today nearly every Zapotec village and town clusters around a Catholic church, which the priest visits from time to time as he makes the rounds of his parish circuit. Yet in accepting Christianity, the Zapotecs held on to many of their traditional religious beliefs and practices, finding Christianity and their traditional beliefs in many ways complementary rather than contradictory.

The people of San Juan Gbëë name their town "Cliff of the Moon" in Zapotec. They say their town was founded by a wandering people who settled beneath a cliff near the present town. High on this cliff was a white moon-shaped rock, subsequently stolen by mysterious "priests." The Moon, the Sun, and Thunder are still worshipped as deities that give heat and moisture to sustain their crops of corn, beans, and squashes on which their lives depend. Their Zapotec is closely allied with that spoken in several dozen villages scattered across the headwaters of the Río Tehuántepec and south of the Sierra Sur divide. These villages in turn share language patterns with Sierra Sur Zapotec villages to the west. The Zapotec towns of the central valleys are at some further remove (Smith Stark 2001).

The Isthmus Zapotecs settled in the tropical lowlands of the Isthmus of Tehuántepec a few hundred years before the Spaniards invaded. These Zapotecs are renowned throughout Mexico for the power and independence of their women—who dominate the local markets, dressed in rainbow patterns of their traditional *traje*, or costume (Chiñas 1991, 1993)—and for their political independence (Campbell 1994).

Other Zapotecs live in the rugged Sierra Norte north of the city of Oaxaca. Benito Juárez, Mexico's Abraham Lincoln, was a Zapotec Indian born in Gueletao, a Sierra Norte town. Ironically, Profirio Díaz, widely reviled as the dictator who sold Mexico to outside interests, claims Mixtec ancestry and is still a hero for many Oaxaqueños.

The Setting

San Juan Gbëë is a tight cluster of some 200 houses (map 2.6)—many built in a distinctive local style, the roofs supported by heavy hand-hewn beams of pine cut from the community's forests that stretch from just above the town at 6,800 feet (2,050 m) elevation up to the 12,000-foot

(3,700 m) summits of the Sierra Sur. San Juan is on the north slope of the Sierra Sur and thus in the "rain shadow" of that range (fig. 2.3). (Rainfall and temperature statistics are not available for San Juan but can be interpolated from data collected at three regional sites, San Jose del Pacifico at 2,500 m, Santa María Zoquitlán at ca. 1000 m, and San Carlos Yautepec at 1,800 m, as shown in charts 2.1 and 2.2.) A few miles south over the crest toward the Pacific are lush cloud forests where much of Oaxaca's famous coffee is grown. However, the rain shadow is too dry for coffee, so the people of San Juan grow mostly food crops they will eat themselves. Close below the town to the north, San Juan's cultivated fields merge with a low, open forest of spiny, thorny, or poisonous desert plants such as columnar cacti (many with edible fruits) and agaves or century plants (some of which provide *aguamiel* for *pulque*, a traditional alcoholic beverage). The land is precipitous. Farms cling to the upper slopes of spur-ridges that ultimately drop off nearly vertically into deep canyons where clear streams tumble, eventually to join the Tehuántepec River on its looping course to the Pacific Ocean.

If you take a walk below town out past the crosses that guard the souls of the townspeople, you are certain to fall in with a boy or girl herding the family's goats. Men and women plowing, planting, weeding, or harvesting their corn and beans will stop what they're doing to check out the stranger, as few outsiders stray so far from the paved highways (fig. 2.4). If you call out "*Dyuzh*," the local all-purpose Zapotec greeting, they'll reply in kind. But then they'll ask, "*Pa tsie luu?*" or "*Pe run to?*" which means, "Where are you going?" or "What are you doing?" Now you know you're in real Indian Mexico, where even Spanish is of limited use.

The people of San Juan are poor by our standards. Most earn but a few hundred dollars a year, if that. They need money to buy clothes, to pay for medical care (since many people distrust the free medical services of the government clinic in the next town and are not yet convinced their new clinic is to be trusted), or for advanced education. However, they are rich in land. The *municipio* owns more than twenty square miles (54 km^2), land that their ancestors have farmed for 2,000 years, judging by the ancient ruins of a ball court, temple, and palace just below town. Thus, there are nearly fifteen acres (6 ha) for each of the 932 men, women, and children now living in town.

Traditional Subsistence Strategies

Even the poorest family can plant sufficient land to feed themselves (see chap. 5), though the crop is subject to many uncertainties: drought, hail, insect pests, or perhaps illness that could incapacitate a family member just when the work is most pressing and exhausting. One may also build a house of local adobe, stone, and timber, needing only to notify the town authorities to obtain permission. If one of the family gets sick, there are dozens of plants growing in the family garden or in the fields and forests near town that have proved effective for many ailments (see chap. 6). Knowledge of how to use these plants to cure is widely shared and among the earliest lessons children learn as they work beside their parents and grandparents in their fields (see chap. 8).

This ancient subsistence way of life is hard and may not satisfy young people's ambitions: to dress in style, to earn enough money to buy a car or truck, to go to the university, or to become a teacher, businessman, lawyer, doctor, or famous musician. Some San Juaneros have been very successful, and their examples are both an inspiration and a temptation to escape the limits of the traditional peasant life.

Social and Political Organization

San Juan is the *cabecera*, or head town, of the *municipio* of the same name. It is one of 571 such *municipios* in Oaxaca. *Municipios* are like counties in the United States except that, in the case of predominantly Indian towns, they are largely self-governing. Their internal politics follow customary rules authorized by the whole town assembly. They may reject the efforts of national political parties or state government agencies to meddle in their affairs, though they welcome government schools, clinics, and roads.

Half the people who lived in San Juan in 1980 had left by 1998. The vast majority of these emigrants work as petty traders or laborers in nearby towns in the valley of Oaxaca, on the Pacific coast, or in the Isthmus of Tehuántepec. They return regularly to San Juan to enjoy fiestas or to help in the fields. Thus, the exodus is still local and often temporary. During the 1980s and 1990s some of these emigrant townspeople returned to San Juan. Nevertheless, between 1970 and 1990 the town's population declined 20 percent, though it has stabilized since. In 2000 a few young men joined the flood of illegal immigrants to the United States. One young man works as a ranch hand in California's Central Valley; two others have found work in textile factories in Georgia. If out-migration gains momentum again, the town could die.

What keeps the people of San Juan from joining the flood of Mexican migrant labor that has swamped Mexico City's fringes (now one of the largest cities in the world) and washed across the United States border? I believe it is pride in their town and love of the land filled with flowers with the rains. A number of San Juaneros with successful business and professional careers in the state capital or beyond have returned to accept a *cargo*, voluntary service in the town administration, which requires their constant attention and no small expense, for up to three years. Perhaps they realize that life in San Juan is a life among relatives and lifelong friends, a life of relative tranquility and beauty in comparison to what they have seen in the cities.

Linguistic Acculturation

The eminent biologist E. O. Wilson fears that as a consequence of an inexorably expanding human population plus our extravagant energy consumption in pursuit of an ever "higher standard of living," species are being driven to extinction faster than we can discover them (Wilson 2002). This loss of biodiversity may be compared to burning libraries. Less widely recognized is a parallel historic trend, the mass extinction of human languages. Of 6,000 languages known to have been spoken around the world in recent times, over 90 percent are seriously threatened with extinction this century (Maffi 2001).

There is an intimate connection between the language that people speak and their culture, that is, their ideas about virtually everything, about the way the world is and how it should be, about how to make a living, how to live in peace, and the meaning of life. So when a language dies—most often because the younger generation prefers to learn a more prestigious language instead—much of the wisdom inherited by the elder generation is also lost. The old stories no longer get told, because there is no one to listen to and understand them, and TV is so much more engrossing.

One or another Zapotec language is still spoken by some 350,000 people in Oaxaca; the number of Zapotec speakers is not at this point declining. However, this does not mean its future is secure as a medium of cultural transmission. The number of speakers of Zapotec and other Indian languages in Oaxaca and throughout Mexico is a constantly shrinking percentage of the total population (Aubague 1986). The total population of Mexico is increasing more rapidly than the populations of Native speakers. Four hundred years ago nearly everyone in Oaxaca spoke an Indian language. In 1990, just 39 percent did. Of those who do speak an Indian language, a growing majority are bilingual, having learned Spanish in school or through interactions with monolingual Spanish-speaking teachers, doctors, and administrators who control access to governmental services. In 1990, 87 percent of Zapotec speakers were bilingual. These two factors combine to marginalize the Zapotec linguistic presence in Oaxaca. Contemporary Zapotec speakers must live now and in the future in a world dominated by Spanish.

San Juan Gbëë has so far been fortunate in conserving Zapotec as the first language for 98 percent of the townspeople. A few families speak Spanish to their preschool children in the belief that this will be to their ultimate benefit, giving them a head start with Spanish when they begin school. (Teachers—who rarely speak Zapotec, being from other towns in Oaxaca—still complain that first-graders arrive with no knowledge of Spanish.) My next-door neighbor in San Juan is one such family. Perhaps because they own one of the few stores in town, they stress the value of dealing with outsiders. There may also be a few individuals who reject Zapotec as "uncivilized." One elderly man has not spoken Zapotec since his childhood, believing it beneath his dignity. In some Indian communities elsewhere in Oaxaca, I have heard that this attitude is pervasive to the point that most people who can still speak their native language are ashamed to do so in public. This attitude clearly reflects the arrogance of the colonial authorities of an earlier time who punished children in school for speaking their Indian language. This could have happened to San Juan, as some nearby towns have all but abandoned Zapotec for Spanish within the last fifty years. Yet San Juan and many of its immediate neighbors in this part of the Sierra Sur are proud to speak Zapotec.

But what difference does it make in the long run if the people of San Juan keep their Zapotec alive or abandon it for Spanish? One might argue that the local Zapotec language can be understood by no more than 10,000 people of the world's 6 billion, and these live in half a dozen nearby towns. One might also argue that Zapotec is too diverse—it is really a whole family of languages—to sustain a unified Zapotec ethnic force. The Zapotec in the Isthmus of Tehuántepec, that in the Sierra Norte, and that in the valley towns near Oaxaca City are as different from that of San Juan Gbëë as Italian, French, and Romanian are from Spanish.

One might argue further that it is a historical fact that Spanish is the national language of Mexico (as well as the first language of 350,000,000 people throughout Latin America and in Spain) and that even Spanish is not safe in the face of the dominance of English as the universal language of computers, global trade, aerial navigation, satellite television, etc. Thus, one's future survival will require mastery of one or more of these globally dominant languages.

One might point out that only a handful of Zapotecs have learned to read and write in Zapotec. So there is no Zapotec Shakespeare, no Cervantes, no Zapotec García Marquez nor Octavio Paz.

In defense of the local Zapotec, I would state that it is a language that has evolved in contact with the land. Most telling in this regard is the fact that the local Zapotec incorporates a rich vocabulary for local flora and fauna. San Juan speakers name more than 700 kinds of plants, 400 kinds of animals, and twenty kinds of fungi. They keep in mind a detailed map of their community and its environs, naming some 500 places within that territory.

Furthermore, this vocabulary is learned very early. One of my best teachers of Zapotec traditional environmental knowledge is Marielena Cruz, ten years old when I first met her and then just beginning primary school. During the several years of my research, she has brought many plants to show me. In just two weeks during 1999, she brought in over 300 different plants, told me their Zapotec names, how they could be used, where they grew, and when they flowered. Few of these plants have Spanish names. The Zapotec names themselves may not be of much use away from San Juan, as the plants themselves have limited distributions. Thus, if you plan to leave San Juan for a life elsewhere, you may have little use for the local language. But if you plan to live your life in San Juan, you will be impoverished without it.

The argument that one must choose either Zapotec or Spanish is seriously misleading. A child can as easily learn two or three languages as one. Once mastered, they are not readily forgotten. As master of Zapotec and Spanish one can live in both worlds: the Zapotec world of San Juan and the Spanish world outside. Furthermore, once one has learned to read and write Spanish, that skill can be readily transferred to Zapotec. Once the power of writing is widely recognized, we may see in the Sierra Sur a cultural renaissance like that under way in the Isthmus Zapotec region. There, native scholars publish a magazine in Zapotec and Spanish entitled *Guchachi' Reza* (*Iguana Rajada*) and print sensitive translations of Zapotec poetry, stories, and histories in Spanish. When many Zapotec dictionaries and grammars are published, a pan-Zapotec literature and consciousness may well evolve. With this will come a new pride in being Zapotec, a pride that does not preclude but may enhance one's pride in being Mexican and a human being. So one might hope that Zapotec will survive, striking a sustainable balance between the languages of global interaction and the languages of local attachment.

The Peasant Paradox: Rural Poverty and Limited Opportunities

San Juan Gbëë has a perilous future on the fringe of the global urban web. An endangered species can be protected by outlawing the hunting or uprooting of the species, preserving its critical habitat, and even by means of captive breeding programs or seed banks. However, one cannot preserve a culture that way. Only the people of the culture can save it, and then only if they are provided a space of their own and only if they want it badly enough to take advantage of that space.

There are always trade-offs. What is lost and what is gained in leaving San Juan? This is the choice facing San Juan's recent *telesecundaria* graduates (fig. 2.5). (*Telesecundaria* is the local middle school, grades seven through nine taught with the aid of a standard national televised curriculum.) The graduation ceremony held each July is the biggest community event of the year, bigger than the fiesta for their patron saint, San Juan. The whole town celebrates the graduates and is united in wishing them the best of futures. The priest says mass for the graduating class, one of a handful of events that warrants his presence each year. In his sermon to San Juan's first secondary-school graduating class, the class of 1997, he urged them to take advantage of their education in order to rise above the "poverty and ignorance" of their parents' lives. But must they choose between the supposed drudgery of life in San Juan—which to me does a gross injustice to village life—and the "freedom and promise" of a highly overrated future beyond the town? If the best and brightest take the priest at his word, what will be left of San Juan when the next generation graduates? Will there even be a next generation?

My neighbor's son Raúl is a poignant example of this dilemma. Raúl was a bright sixteen-year-old when he graduated with that first middle school class. He helped us as a guide and laboratory assistant over the years of our study in San Juan. His dream was to learn English (he bought language tapes and practiced late at night). He at one time dreamt of finding a job in the tourist industry at a nearby beach resort. However, his family could not afford the costs of an English-language school in the city. Besides, he was needed at home to help run the family store and work the family's land. He was clearly disappointed and frustrated at his prospects, so I was not entirely surprised to learn that early in 2000 he had set off for California, a pioneer international migrant from San Juan. He's found work near Bakersfield doing a range of farm and ranch work and seems in no hurry to return, though he calls his parents every week. He is gradually mastering English.

His friends Guillermo and Pablo have stayed in town, at least for now. Guillermo hoped to go to Mexico City to become a truck driver, but this plan was derailed when he smashed the front axle of his father's truck. Pablo apprenticed himself to a local mason and earns a bit of extra cash that way. Both have just been appointed secretaries to important town committees, the start of a lifelong career of service in town government. These young men of San Juan now walk separate roads, but who can say which of them has chosen the better path?

My First Zapotec Encounters

By the early 1990s my daughters had gone off to college, and the family concerns that had kept me close to home for fieldwork during the late 1970s and 1980s no longer held me back. I began to imagine returning to Mexico (where I had done my initial doctoral field research) to embark on a new ethnobiological study. I briefly considered returning to Chiapas, the site of my earlier studies, but the political situation was uncertain in the wake of the Zapatista uprising, and the central highland Mayan communities I had some familiarity with were crawling with anthropologists. I investigated the research possibilities in the Yucatán Peninsula, but that ground also seemed too well trodden for my taste. On a sightseeing trip in 1993, my wife, Nancy, and I drove the serpentine highway from the Pacific coast of Oaxaca up and over the Sierra Sur to Miahuatlán and on to Oaxaca City. The road climbs up from coastal tropical pastures through lush coffee plantations into pine forests reminiscent of my home here in the Pacific Northwest. Towns hung on curves in the road over steep forested slopes lost in mist, the road itself edged by riotous flower gardens, the houses of patterned wood slats unlike any Mexican towns I had seen before. I decided that one of these southern Oaxacan mountain villages would be a fine site for my next project. On the northern edge of the range, the highway drops precipitously to Miahuatlán, market town at the southern entrance to the arid central valleys of Oaxaca. In a four-hour drive of 150 tortuous kilometers, we had completed a transect of Oaxaca's great diversity of natural habitats. An indigenous community at home in this range should have developed a challenging array of traditional environmental knowledge.

I wrote my ethnobiological colleagues Gary Martin and Alejandro de Ávila, both with long-standing Oaxacan connections and founding members of SERBO, A.C., the independent nonprofit Society for the Study of the Biotic Resources of Oaxaca, my eventual academic base in the region. They strongly supported my plans. Alejandro, in a long and detailed letter, suggested a number of potential field sites, among them San Pedro Gbëë, visited by a SERBO survey crew in 1991, the next town past San Juan and my original research destination. They had been greatly impressed by the openness of the town authorities and by how well the town had conserved an extensive tract of critically endangered pine forest extending from just above the town to the highest point in the state, Cerro Nube Flan, reaching 12,350 feet (3,750 m).

On the advice of Alejandro de Ávila I scheduled a quick trip to Oaxaca just before Christmas 1994. After further consultations at SERBO, I decided that San Pedro Gbëë was the best prospect. Alejandro agreed to guide me in. He and I drove to Miahuatlán in his newly rebuilt Jeep, made inquiries over hot chocolates at the town market, then set off in the direction indicated, being careful to ignore published maps, which all proved seriously misleading as to the correct route to San Pedro. Our route—now second nature to me after more than a hundred round trips— passed through a string of villages: El Zapote, San Ildefonso, San Pedro Amatlán (aka San Pedrito, little San Pedro, as it is smaller than San Pedro Gbëë), San Cristóbal Amatlán, head town of a large *municipio* extending to the borders of San Juan. Here we forded a stream and started to climb up and around the piney slopes of Cerro Yirot. We gave a local woman a lift to the next town, San Agustín Gbëë, and plied her with questions about the region. "Yes," she reported, "there are lions in the mountains." Halfway up we came upon the road crews and from that point on had to improvise our route, testing the Jeep's limits. We passed San Agustín well above the town, looking down at the red-roofed church and the narrow ridgetop main street. We dropped slightly to San Lorenzo Gbëë, like San Agustín an *agencia* subordinate to San Cristóbal, before fording another stream to cross into San Juan territory. More stream crossings, more pine-clad ridges, then San Juan perched on a knuckle of land looking out to the north down a long valley to Mitla and into the Tehuántepec River basin. We forged on, over a saddle behind which hid the last and largest town on the road, San Pedro Gbëë.

Alejandro's family has roots in Oaxaca, and his deep interest in the local natural and cultural histories is of long standing. He patiently provided detailed explanations of each distinctive plant we passed along the route and backgrounded the political and cultural dynamics of the local Zapotec communities. Still, the region was new even for Alejandro, as the Sierra de Miahuatlán is little known to scholars, whether archaeologists, biologists, historians, linguists, or anthropologists. Even the most basic geographical data were obscure, expert sources ignorant of the existence of Oaxaca's preeminent summit well into the 1980s. For example, White-cotton indicates that the highest elevation in the Sierra de Miahuatlán is a mere 2,120 m (1977:22); Binford repeats the error of assigning the Oaxaca high-point trophy to Cerro Zempoaltepec in the Sierra Mixe at 11,138 feet (3,593 m; 1989:1, 3).

Just a few years prior to our trip, botanists from the University of Texas collecting along the ridge above San Pedro and San Juan described 25 plant species new to modern science, including a tree lupine that crowned that high ridge. I could count on one hand the outside botanical and zoological investigators who had visited these towns (Thompson 1962; Rowley 1966; Goodwin 1969). We arrived at San Pedro's Palacio Municipal in the heat of midday, and it first appeared that the plaza was deserted. However, we soon located a *regidor suplente,* who advised us that the *presidente municipal* would return from lunch in an hour, and that meanwhile we might feel free to hike beyond the town on the "Royal Road," a mule track leading into and over the mountains to the east, eventually reaching the Isthmus of Tehuántepec by an ancient route. We subsequently learned that this route had seen caravans of Aztec *pochteca,* a caste of long-distance merchants, who demanded and received hospitality in the town (Rojas 1992:257).

The "Royal Road" entered a narrow granite defile before fording the Río Grande, here a clear, brisk mountain stream draining a canyon carved into the flanks of Cerro Nube Flan and the furthest source of the Tehuántepec River. A pair of dippers foraged along the stream, testifying to its purity, while the descant chimes of a canyon wren echoed off the rock walls. Almost wilderness, except that carefully tended fruit orchards lined the narrow river bottom and small family parties hauling cut flowers and firewood back to town caused us to pause frequently to explain our presence.

Alejandro well understood the protocol required of strangers visiting out-of-the-way Indian towns in Oaxaca. The president had returned, the *palacio* doors were open for business, and we were received with polite diffidence by the authorities. Alejandro opened with introductions and questions about the adequacy of last year's harvests, the prospects for rain, and the concerns of the townspeople, and praise for an outstanding local architectural feature of house construction, hand-hewn roof beams held firmly by pitch-pine wedges. Alejandro inquired after odd trees we had studied with binoculars, growing on a mountain side across the canyon, several in full bloom, resembling stocky palm trees topped by a tall fountain of white flowers. This proved to be a rare relative of the century plant, of the genus *Furcraea.*

We were welcomed, and our proposal to return to initiate a long-term study of local knowledge and use of plants and animals taken under consideration. As San Pedro (and San Juan) see very few outside visitors, accommodations for travelers are nonexistent, excepting the hospitality of local families. The president directed us to the house of a widow who would serve us lunch and see us on our way back to the highway.

My next visit was the following August, in the rainy season, driving a rented VW bug and accompanied by my wife, Nancy. Our first challenge was to slither through a flooded stretch of road just outside Miahuatlán, the muddy water of uncertain depth. We kept afloat to the far side and encountered no further difficulties until just past San Lorenzo on the final approach to San Juan, where we found the road crews at work building the road beyond. They cheerfully waved us on, but we abandoned the vehicle soon after at the top of a steep rise paved with large, sharp-edged rocks in a stew of mud. We continued on foot. A good thing, too, as it set to raining hard and a road cut just above washed out before we got back from our six-mile hike through San Juan to San Pedro and back.

The San Pedro authorities and a good-sized crowd of the curious received us enthusiastically. We brought as an introductory gift a colorful poster of Oaxacan wildlife from SERBO. They eagerly named in *el idioma*, that is, their local Zapotec language, each plant and animal illustrated. The rain abated long enough for Nancy and me to hike back to our precariously parked car, and after a harrowing descent past the road crews, we regained the highway, limped into Oaxaca, and celebrated with a special-value car wash and a dinner downtown. The people of San Pedro were exceptionally courteous, friendly, and open to our return; we found the vistas of these mountains in the crystal air after the rains captivating, and the promise of getting to know the people and their land intriguing. Our work was cut out for us: write a successful grant proposal, formalize our collaboration with SERBO and UNAM, then read everything ever written about the region.

The Project Gets Under Way

NSF funding and a sabbatical leave in hand, properly visa-ed and permitted, Nancy and I moved to Oaxaca in July 1996 for the year. Two University of Washington graduate students with experience in the region, Jennifer Sepez and Thomas Murphy, came for the summer to assist.

Both have since completed their doctorates and moved on to successful academic careers, quite apart from my Oaxacan research. Yet I suspect they will not soon forget that first summer.

I also hired a young Mexican biologist, Donato Acuca Vásquez, splitting his time with SERBO. Donato was born and raised in Oaxaca. His maternal grandmother was a Zapotec Indian from near Mitla. Donato had earned the equivalent of a bachelor's degree from the Instituto de Biología at the prestigious Universidad Nacional Autónoma de México (UNAM). Without his passion for the work, his irrepressible good humor, his deep connection with the rural people, and his knowledge of local realities, my project might well have been stillborn. (Tragically, Donato died of an attack by a swarm of Africanized "killer" bees in February 1998 while collecting for SERBO in an isolated tract of the wild Chimalapas rain forest of eastern Oaxaca.)

In early July 1996, Donato, Jennifer, Tom, and I set out in our project vehicle, a brand-new, Mexican-made, fire-engine red VW bug (of the traditional design) nicknamed *el bicho rojo* "the red bug," a close approximation of the Mexican abbreviation for Volkswagen, *el bocho* (fig. 2.7). By the summer of 1996 the road project had reached San Juan, so, with the exception of mud slides on steep hillsides that required well-timed and prayerful acceleration, our trips into the Sierra de Miahuatlán became almost routine. Yet our initial plan to set up shop in San Pedro underwent a key setback as we rounded a curve just past the plaza at San Juan to find a wide trench bisecting the route beyond. The road crew estimated the work *might* be completed in a month, but with the rains, the road beyond to San Pedro might be impassable until Christmas. We retreated to San Juan and asked the authorities whether we might camp there while considering our options. The local consensus was that we were foolish to want to work in San Pedro in any case, as they were a bunch of thieves, and that we would be well advised to make San Juan our base of operations.

Our first night in San Juan was memorable. As night fell a small crowd of young men had gathered around our "camp" in the shelter of the *corredor* of the church, trying to teach us how to say "hello" in Zapotec (**diûzh** [< Spanish *Diós*]), poring over our bird guides, offering names in Zapotec and Spanish, asking where we came from and why we had come.

An excited, somewhat disheveled and edgy middle-aged man took us in tow, introducing himself as a member of the Comisariado de Bienes

Comunales, and insisting that we come with him to his home for dinner. This was our first encounter with Cándido Cruz Hernández and his wonderful family, four generations of independent women plus Cándido. They taught us a great deal about their lives and their land. Cándido himself has at times been possessive of us (as a resource to be controlled and exploited, perhaps) and, rarely, unnervingly unpredictable, but the women of his household have been gracious and keenly intelligent, from five-year-old Griselda to ninety-year-old Signorina. Over the first eight years of my project, I watched the youngest grow from wide-eyed children to mature young women.

Dinner was set before us on a misshapen table beneath the soot-caked ceiling of the wattle-and-daub kitchen. The women worked over the fire, molding and pressing the pancake-like, supersized tortillas favored in the region, which are made of their own corn, varying from yellow to "black" (bluish-gray when ready to eat). They toasted these tortillas before our eyes on the *comal* and served them with a soup of black beans flavored with spices from their garden; for their special guests they added a few chunks of chicken, perhaps a crisp peach or apple in season, a slice of squash or avocado, with hot chilies on the side.

Tom, Jennifer, Donato, and I settled into our sleeping bags in the church corridor as the buzz of chatter in the plaza faded into sleep. The rain quit and a cool breeze slipped down off the mountain. Ah, the tranquility of a village far from the noise and tension of the highway and the city! But then, seemingly not long past midnight, a terrific clangor directly overhead. We shot awake, fearing the roof was collapsing on us. However, it proved to be just the cracked and tinny church bells announcing a 5:00 AM service (sound clip 2.5). Then, at full volume, a scratchy recording projected into space from loudspeakers mounted on the roof of the Palacio Municipal, of Pedro Infante, Mexico's answer to Bing Crosby, crooning his beloved if dated rendition of "Las Mañanitas," the Mexican birthday anthem (likely recorded on disk in the 1950s (sound clip 2.1). There followed announcements of birthdays, school committee meetings, obligatory work projects; then Pedro Infante again singing, this time "Las Golondrinas." Clearly, the point was that one should not sleep late, as there was work to be done. I wandered off to relieve myself as the dawn broke, Venus rising brilliant over **Guì-glàg,** the mountain across from San Pedro, where Alejandro and I had spotted the stand of rare

Furcraea in bloom on our first visit. Over a camp breakfast snack we entertained a cluster of young men, too old for school, too young for polite reserve, eager to invite us to go hunting or, with their expert guidance, to go in search of rumored gold statuary hidden in mountain caves some hours above town.

We had our audience with the municipal president, a somewhat intimidating presence, taking nothing lightly and questioning us carefully as to our plans. Municipal presidents serve three-year terms and receive no salary (at least in San Juan at present) other than some reimbursement for the expenses of travel on the town's business. It is not a title fought for but a duty accepted, perhaps grudgingly, with misgivings, when called to serve by the communal assembly. The president in 1996 was C. Hermilo Silva Cruz, just turned forty, called to the office when his predecessor abruptly aborted his term, unable to deal with the pressure (fig. 2.8). Hermilo is, through and through, a *campesino* (for which the English term *peasant* is a seriously inadequate translation), and proud of it. Yet, with just a fourth-grade education, he is also an extraordinarily intelligent, highly principled, and motivated man, and a very competent linguist.

We presented *el presidente* our written proposal, and Donato proceeded to elaborate on our goals, methods, institutional connections, and intentions vis-à-vis collaborating with the people of San Juan on mutually beneficial projects. Hermilo was noncommittal but he clearly appreciated our affirmation of the value of Zapotec indigenous language and environmental knowledge, their ethnoscience. We proposed to return within the week to discuss the matter further and left our business cards identifying the SERBO office in Oaxaca as our base of operations. A few days later Hermilo and a contingent of San Juan officials appeared at SERBO headquarters in downtown Oaxaca to verify our claims. Donato met them and, with Sylvia Salas, SERBO *presidenta*, and Leo Schibli, SERBO's computer whiz, they got the grand tour of SERBO's GIS lab, herbarium collections, and project reports. Their doubts allayed, the San Juan authorities called a town meeting (*asamblea comunal*) on the occasion of our next visit, and our project was formally authorized, with a grant of permission to stay in town, to collect plants and insects, and to capture birds for study, but not to kill them. In exchange we promised to bring in experts on arboriculture and to help arrange workshops in San Juan to enhance local tree fruit production. In Hermilo's words, "We will share our 'science' with you, if you will share yours with us."

Hermilo's term ended in 1999. He was succeeded very ably by C. Florentino Hernández Hernández, a young teacher called home from his position at a secondary school in Tuxtepec in northern Oaxaca (fig. 2.9). Florentino worked closely with me to review a draft booklet I had put together on local medicinal plants. He also proved highly effective in bringing outside resources to staff a medical clinic in San Juan, to add a *Telecobao* postsecondary school in town, and to oversee the construction of a municipal sewage system, now in place. During his term the town negotiated an agreement with a local timber company allowing the first commercial timber harvests from San Juan forests since 1983. The contract promises local employment, reforestation of areas recently burned by forest fires, new roads, and eventually (perhaps) a local wood-processing operation. Income from timber sales is to be invested in community improvements, such as the new kiosk in the plaza completed as his term ended in 2002.

The next president, C. Hilarion Hernández Santiago, was a merchant called home from his business in the Isthmus of Tehuántepec to serve the town. He seemed less sympathetic to our efforts on behalf of cultural and linguistic conservation and more interested in economic development. He was succeeded in 2005 by C. Higinio Hernández Hernández, Florentino's younger brother and town secretary during Hermilo's term. All four presidents I have had the opportunity to deal with have been dedicated to their town and conscientious in their efforts on behalf of its people.

What the Census Shows

In 2000 the Mexican federal government, through its Instituto Nacional de Estadística, Geografía e Informática (INEGI), conducted the twelfth decennial general census of population and housing. Cadres of census takers fanned out to every city, town, village, and *ranchería* in Mexico to record details of the lives of each citizen and family. While the reliability of past censuses may certainly be questioned, it is clear that their sophistication is increasing progressively. However, analyses of long-term trends that rely on comparisons over decades must be taken with a grain of salt.

TABLE 2.1. "Economically active population" in San Juan Gbëë by employment sector

Sector	Year 2000	Year 1990	Difference*
Primary	318 (76%)**	65 (28%)**	x 2.71
Secondary	49 (12%)**	5 (2%)**	x 6.00
Tertiary	42 (10%)**	160 (69%)**	x 0.14
Total economically active	416 (45%)***	232 (26%)***	x 1.79
Total populations	932	898	x 1.03

* The ratio of % for the year 2000 divided by % for the year 1990, except for the last row, where the ratio of the total population recorded in 2000 is divided by the ratio of the total population recorded in 1990; ** % of total economically active; *** % of total population.

In part this is due to inherent ambiguities in certain census questions. To cite just one example, a count is made of the "economically active population," classified as employed in the "primary," "secondary," or "tertiary" economic sectors (for definitions, see INEGI 1990:648). (Data reported for San Juan from 1990 and 2000 are compared in table 2.1.)

Clearly, the actual figures did not change significantly during this period of time, only the interpretations of the questions by the census takers. (As I understand the distinction between "primary," "secondary," and "tertiary" economic sectors, only a bare handful of San Juaneros are employed in any but the primary sector, i.e., agriculture.) Nevertheless, many data are less subject to interpretation and thus may be relied upon with considerable confidence.

In addition to the official census summaries, I had the good fortune to obtain a copy of a census of San Juan conducted in 1981 by the staff of the newly established (ca. 1979) Instituto Mexicano de Seguro Social (IMSS) clinic in San Pedro. This census reports individual data. Unfortunately, one entire street appears to have been missed in this tabulation. Thus, the 1,018 individuals counted may underreport the town's population, in my estimation, by some 10 percent. If so, San Juan's recent population decline, representing a loss of nearly 25 percent of the 1970 population, occurred for the most part during a single decade, that of the 1980s (table 2.2). That this decade is the period of Mexico's oil boom and subsequent bust (cf. Collier and Quaratiello 1994; Rus, Hernández Castillo, and Mattiace 2003) is perhaps no coincidence. The town's population stabilized between 1990 and 2000, growing slightly. However, the impact of inter-

TABLE 2.2. Population trends in San Juan Gbëë

Population	2000	1990	1981	1970
Total	932	898	1,018*	1,154
Male (%)	406 (43.6)	388 (43.2)	529 (52.4)	
Female (%)	526 (56.4)	510 (56.8)	480 (47.6)	

* Data incomplete; likely ca. 10% undercounted.

national migration just beginning with the new millennium remains to be seen. Just a single international emigrant was known among the 1,018 persons counted in 1981.

One of my most knowledgeable and intelligent consultants is a young man now in his early thirties, Pánfilo Santiago Cruz (fig. 2.10). In 1998 I offered to hire him to review with me the 1981 clinic census, person by person, to learn their current whereabouts and fate. He agreed with enthusiasm, which never flagged during the more than twenty hours we spent reviewing the data.

The results are telling. First of all, the sex ratio among the 1981 respondents is 52.4 percent male, 47.6 percent female, a statistical wash but exhibiting a slight trend opposite to that of more recent censuses. By 1990 that ratio had shifted dramatically to 43.2 percent male, 56.8 percent female, a shift that held steady during the subsequent decade. It is thus clear that San Juan's population decline during the 1980s is attributable almost entirely to male out-migration. If the sex ratio in 2000 had been 50:50, as is the normal expectation, the town's population then would have been 1,052 rather than 932 (1,020 rather than 898 in 1990), reducing the population decline from 25 percent to about 10 percent.

Pánfilo was able to specify where those migrants had gone meanwhile. Of 1,018 respondents in 1981, Pánfilo had no idea about just 21; 119 had died. Of the 878 still living whose whereabouts were known, just 405 (46.1 percent) still lived in San Juan. Where were the rest? Pánfilo's incredible memory proved that this migration was strikingly localized; just six were reported to have left the state of Oaxaca or its immediate vicinity, including a single migrant to the United States and two to Baja California. Miahuatlán, now a scant two-hour bus ride from San Juan and the major regional market town—astride the highway between Oaxaca City and the Pacific Coast at Pochutla, a highway completed in the late 1960s—

attracted 129 San Juan emigrants (14.7 percent of these 878). The mountains and Pacific Coast towns to the southwest drew another 52 migrants (5.9 percent), while Isthmus of Tehuántepec cities—including Arriaga and Tonalá in neighboring Chiapas—accounted for an additional 243 migrants (27.7 percent). Finally, the city of Oaxaca and nearby central valley towns were now home to 31 San Juan emigrants (3.5 percent). These regional urban centers together account for 455 (51.8 percent) of the 878 still alive in 1998 who lived in San Juan in 1981 and whose whereabouts were known.

It is important to note, however, an apparent paradox. While over half the town's resident population was lost between 1981 and 1998, the total population of the town dropped just 20 percent. A portion of this loss was no doubt replaced by the 301 children born in San Juan since 1982 (the 2000 figure for those eighteen years and older), while just 119 of those counted in 1981 are known to have died (which should be adjusted upwards by approximately 10 percent to account for the known underrepresentation of that census). Yet I suspect that many of those Pánfilo identified as now living outside San Juan may actually be cases of "circular migration," that is, people continually coming and going, funneling cash and other resources earned in the money economy outside of San Juan back "home" in support of family and community.

San Juan Gbëë at the Millennium

The 2000 census provides a more recent snapshot of the town. Notable statistics include the percentage of native Zapotec speakers, 98.6 percent, virtually unchanged since 1970. Of the population five years and older, 21.9 percent are reported to be monolingual in Zapotec. Curiously, this percentage actually increased since 1990, when just 17.9 percent were so reported. However, I suspect this reflects a greater willingness on the part of respondents to admit their limited Spanish. The true percentage of monolingual Zapotec speakers may be considerably higher than even 21 percent, especially given the ambiguity of defining "monolingual."

Who are these few non-Zapotec speakers in San Juan? No doubt they are among the 19 residents (of 932) recorded as not born in San Juan. First of all, the schoolteachers, all of whom (excepting one kindergarten teacher from nearby San Pedro) are from elsewhere in the state and either

TABLE 2.3. School attendance in San Juan Gbëë, by age, in 2000

Age	5	6–14	15–17	18–24	Total
Yes	8 (61.5%)	158 (97.5%)	27 (62.8%)	7 (5.9%)	200 (59.5%)
No	5	4	16	111	136

speak a different indigenous language or, more likely, are Spanish monolinguals. Second, I know of only three women who have married into San Juan, which remains strongly endogamous. Rosa is one of these (fig. 2.11). She was born and raised in Veracruz state, is a Popoloca speaker, but met and married León, who was working at the time near her hometown. She has borne him two sons and a daughter. He returned with her to San Juan to maintain his claim to his land here, which he would have forfeited had he failed to pay the required annual tax assessment. Rosa has learned but a few words of Zapotec during her twenty years in town but is fully accepted as a citizen by the municipal authorities. I suspect but cannot prove that most children born to San Juan families "in exile" will learn their local Zapotec, given the strong tendency to marry *paisanos*, that is, a man or woman from one's own hometown, and given the frequency with which most "exiles" return to visit or to stay for extended periods helping with the work of the home and milpa. This is certainly the case in San Lucas Quiaviní, a Zapotec town close to Oaxaca City, that has "exported" some 800 people to Los Angeles, where they have maintained their linguistic and cultural ties to their hometown (Munro and Lopez 1999).

San Juan Gbëë has long been recognized in the region for its dedication to education. Local historian Basilio Rojas holds San Juan up as "an example for the entire district, the whole state, for the entire nation" with respect to its long-standing support of its local school. In 1954 San Juan had the only municipal school in Oaxaca, supported by a voluntary tax on its citizens (Rojas 1992:255–56). San Juan's primary school (plus the *jardín de niños* 'kindergarten') is well attended. According to the 2000 census, 158 of 162 (97.5 percent) children between six and fourteen years of age attend (table 2.3). The town's 64 percent adult literacy rate in 2000 testifies to this long-standing investment in formal education (table 2.4). Since 1995 San Juan has added both a *Telesecundaria* (in 1994) and a *Telecobao* (in 2001), each housed in a new school building. These

TABLE 2.4. Literacy in San Juan Gbëë, in 1990 and 2000

	2000: Age 15+	2000: Age 6+	1990: Age 15+	1990: Age 6+
Literate	426 (63.4%)	558 (66.9%)	300 (51.0%)	482 (60.9%)
Illiterate	246 (36.6%)	276 (33.1%)	288 (49.0%)	309 (39.1%)
Total	672	834	588	791

provide six more years of educational opportunity within the community. By 2000, sixty-six San Juan students had completed secondary training while another seventeen were in the process; seven had gone on to postsecondary instruction (table 2.5). It remains to be seen whether the availability of postsecondary schooling will promote a "brain drain" as the brightest and/or most ambitious young people leave for challenges not available in a small, somewhat isolated, subsistence-oriented village, or if these young people will find innovative ways to apply their technical expertise within the town. I imagine a day in the not-too-distant future when San Juan, and perhaps the great majority of Oaxacan villages, boast their own *centros de computación*, with banks of computers, a satellite hook-up to the World Wide Web, and their own Web page promoting their distinctive history, and perhaps marketing the finely crafted *gabanes* (ponchos) and *rebozos* (shawls) woven by local women on their backstrap looms.

Nevertheless, it seems inevitable that Spanish, and eventually English, will be routine linguistic alternatives in San Juan as literacy (in Spanish) becomes more general. In 2000 63.4 percent of those fifteen years old and older were counted as literate, versus just 51.0 percent in 1990. However, literacy need not displace Zapotec as a medium of expression. One native son, Meinardo Hernández Pérez, works full-time with the Summer Institute of Linguistics (SIL) in Mitla to develop written materials in the local Zapotec. He is supported in this effort by the expresident Hermilo Silva and a handful of other young San Juaneros who have mastered the art of writing their own language.

The 2000 census speaks also to the material well-being of the people of San Juan. I have no data on annual per capita cash incomes but suspect they would average just a few hundred U.S. dollars per household, if that. By such a measure—often relied upon by economists to rank

TABLE 2.5. Level of education in San Juan Gbëë, persons 15 years of age and older, 2000

None	Some primary	Primary complete	Some secondary	Secondary complete	Post-secondary
257 (38.5%)	116 (17.4%)	204 (30.6%)	17 (2.5%)	66 (9.9%)	7 (1.0%)

Average years of schooling for persons 15 years of age and older in 2000 is 3.50.

"third world" countries in terms of poverty levels or degrees of "under-development"—the people of San Juan are "poor." This impression is reinforced by the census tallies of *bienes electrodomésticos*, that is, "electronic goods," owned by San Juan householders (table 2.6): of 181 "private households," thirty-five own radios or cassette recorders, eight own televisions (but before 2003 there was no reception!), two own refrigerators, one a telephone, and one owns a private vehicle. On the other hand, 94 percent of households own their own homes outright, a statistic that we in the United States might envy. These private homes are not luxurious, certainly, as each room is shared by 3.27 individuals, just 26.8 percent have paved floors, and 47 percent a private latrine (table 2.7). However, 97.3 percent have piped water within their compounds and 86.9 percent have electricity. The water comes directly from capped mountain springs and is quite likely safe to drink from the tap. The power grid was extended to virtually every *asentamiento* 'settlement' in Oaxaca during the oil boom years. Reports of indigenous towns in Oaxaca lacking these two key amenities must represent isolated cases.

The lack of sewage treatment remains a serious problem, though the pipes were laid and the septic system completed in 2002. Few families have, to date, paid to be connected to this system. Finally, nearly all (98.3 percent) households rely on local firewood for heating and cooking. This practice appears sustainable, but there are known health risks linked to wood smoke. In short, one should not romanticize life in San Juan, but one should not demonize it either. If the town were to wither from a grand exodus for wage-labor opportunities elsewhere, much of real value would be lost. Conditions in the ramshackle squatter suburbs of Oaxaca City—the destination of many of those who leave their home villages—are far less healthy.

Finally, the 2000 census reports that 92.2 percent of the townspeople

TABLE 2.6. Commodities, San Juan Gbëë private households (N = 183), in 2000

Radio/cassette player	Television	Refrigerator	Telephone	Private car or truck
35 (19.3%)	8 (4.4%)	2 (1.1%)	1 (0.5%)	1 (0.5%)

TABLE 2.7. Household amenities, San Juan Gbëë private households (N = 183), 2000

	Wood fuel	Private latrine	Piped water	Sewage link	Electric power	Paved floors
Yes	175 (98.9%)	86 (47%)	178 (97.3%)	5 (2.7%)	159 (86.9%)	49 (26.8%)
No	2	97	5	178	24	134

profess to being Catholics, while 7.2 percent hold to some other faith, primarily the local evangelical Protestant congregation, who recently completed their own *templo* in San Juan after some years of worshipping in private homes. Three individuals professed to no religion.

The phenomenal success of evangelical Protestantism in Latin America during the last few decades is well documented (Stoll 1990; Annis 1987). The motives for rejecting traditional Catholicism—which in indigenous towns is typically very much homegrown, with significant incorporation of pre-conquest beliefs and practices (cf. Vogt 1970; Greenberg 1981)—are complex. The consequences are often radical, dividing communities into warring religious factions or leading to a mass exodus of Protestants—willing or otherwise—from their home villages in search of new lives elsewhere. The division between traditional Catholic (that is, of the village-based, syncretic Catholicism that has developed during the five centuries since the Spanish conquest and which has become deeply integrated into the social, political, and economic life of these communities) and evangelical Protestant is particularly acute in Mayan communities of highland Chiapas and Guatemala. By contrast, the people of San Juan appear to have struck a balance, upholding the interests of their community as more important than religious loyalties. The fact that C. Hermilo Silva, an articulate and outspoken Protestant, was chosen as municipal president, is an indication of this religious tolerance. I even know of husbands and wives of competing faiths.

This is not to claim that there are no hard feelings over religious issues between San Juan Catholics and Protestants. There was initial (and perhaps persistent) suspicion with regard to my motives, that is, whether I was a Protestant missionary in disguise, as the only *"gringos"* to have spent any time at all in San Juan were Roger and Marilyn Reeck. He is an SIL linguist, and she is the daughter of missionaries. They came to San Juan in the early 1970s, when it might take two days by truck in the dry season to make the trip from Miahuatlán. They raised their young daughters in San Juan and generously provided medical and dental services (admittedly as amateurs) when access to modern medicine was practically nonexistent. Roger Reeck mastered the local Zapotec language, and my halting attempts at conversation **ló ditzè** 'in Zapotec' are all too often judged against Roger's standard. The Reecks were forced to leave in 1978 when then-president of Mexico López Portillo, responding to accusations of SIL involvement with the CIA in Peru, decreed that foreign missionaries would no longer be allowed to live in indigenous communities or to hold permanent resident visas.

The Reecks still visit San Juan nearly every year—on "vacation" from their current missionary posting in Honduras—and are actively supportive of the efforts of Meinardo and others literate in Zapotec to develop language materials that promote Zapotec literacy (with and without a religious message) (fig. 2.12). The Reecks are respected, but also—by some Catholic partisans at least—criticized for having introduced Protestantism to the community. It is unclear to me, however, how key their role was in fostering the local evangelical congregation, as San Juan Protestants prefer to take credit for having converted fellow villagers themselves. In any case, the evidence is clear that indigenous Protestantism is by no means largely expatriate in inspiration but offers a meaningful alternative to indigenous individuals who have, for example, suffered from alcoholism or economic and political marginalization, or who resist the "expatriate" domination of non-native Catholic priests, whose message all too often is a thinly veiled attack on local community values and traditional culture.

Though the priest empowered to offer the sacraments to the San Juan faithful is based in San José Lachiguirí, some three hours distant by car, his presence seems tenuous among San Juan Catholics. Our friend and neighbor Pedro Miguel Zurita is a devoted lay leader at the San Juan church (fig. 2.13). If we fail to find him at home or working his fields, he will be at the church, working with youth groups, organizing and conducting services, offering prayers—broadcast over the church's loudspeaker, in a mixture of Spanish and Zapotec. He travels periodically to Oaxaca for religious training, so is not entirely free to interpret Catholic doctrine by his own lights. The church building is maintained—recently repainted in brilliant but subtly contrasting yellow, orange, and pink tones—under the direction of the *fiscál* and his committee of local citizen volunteers.

The Fiesta de la Santa Cruz

Pedro is undeniably a devout Catholic—he has earned the nickname **Pxòz Bêd** 'Father Peter'—but also strongly supports the semiannual celebration of the Fiesta de la Santa Cruz, May 3 and September 14. Hermilo, by contrast, is dismissive of this ritual as a pagan survival, as indeed it is. The celebration is not an organized affair; rather, each family prepares a picnic lunch, gathers flowers and candles as offerings, and hikes up the trail to the summit of Cerro San Isidro (**Guìc-dzùb** 'head of the climb' in Zapotec), a small (2,250 m) but prominent peak guarding the approach to town from the west (fig. 2.14). Nearing the summit the trail cuts through a thicket of manzanita and sumac with scattered low oaks above a saddle supporting a stand of "rock pines" (*Pinus teocote*) on thin gravelly soils. The summit offers a clear vista in all directions. The summit ridge runs some 500 m east to west, from a cross shrine sheltered by a *palapa* looking down to the town to a "sacred grove" of oaks (*Quercus castanea*) at the west end (fig. 2.15). In the center is a small, stone-lined cistern, the "door to the house of **Ngùzì** 'Lightning'," the Zapotec deity in control of the rains (the local Zapotec variant of "Cocijo"). It is said that this cistern once flowed with spring water to support the town, then known as Santa María de los Ángeles, until the people were forced to move to their present location (1690 AD), the well having gone dry because certain mysterious "priests" stole the sacred stones from the well.

Men and women offer flowers and candles, and burn copal incense at the cross shrine and at Lightning's door, while the children play within the sacred grove, building stone houses, clearing miniature milpas, and tending pinecone cattle, goats, and chickens. In May one prays for rain, to "open the door"; in September, for the rain to cease, "closing the door." Teenagers may provide a popular music accompaniment, lugging their tape decks to the summit. The feel of the celebration is of a light-hearted family outing, though the need to control the rains is quite serious. The "play" enacts the good life, traditional Zapotec style (fig. 2.16).

Yet these days not everyone participates. Not too long ago it was expected, or demanded, of everyone. Roger Reeck recounted how he had been pressured to join in but had declined. Some people suggest that this decline in civic engagement may have caused the rains to have become less dependable than formerly. If the rains are tardy, unresponsive to the prayers offered May 3, the ritual is repeated two weeks later on El Día de San Isidro Labrador, patron saint of farmers, the saint memorialized in the Spanish name of the peak. Thus, the celebration is part of the local traditional "Catholic" practice.

I first stumbled upon this ritual in San José Lachiguirí during our first summer in Oaxaca, having read a notice announcing that the Fiesta de la Santa Cruz was to be celebrated there September 14. Nancy and I decided to explore the road to San José, as it was on a branch track off the road to San Juan. San José is an important town, because it is the base of operations of the local priest. San José is 12 km and 300 m below San Juan, and we arrived at noon on a hot late summer's day. We drove into the plaza in the noon glare and found the town center nearly deserted, curiously silent for the day of a major fiesta. We inquired in the one small shop still open and were told that everyone had gone up to the top of the mountain Cerro de Cántaro, literally, "Jug Peak," named for a large vase-shaped depression on the summit. We arrived at the foot of the trail up the peak—a small but prominent and largely barren summit adjacent to the town, much like San Juan's Cerro San Isidro—as the celebrants were descending, straggling down in small groups, among them the town's brass band, complete with tuba and drums. It seems the San José observance was somewhat better organized than that in San Juan. Many of the women carried bunches of a striking tall grass with a plume of purplish seed heads (possibly *Muhlenbergia robusta* (Fourn.) A. Hitchc.).

I know little of the details of this celebration in San José, but the date is the same as for San Juan, and the focus on a water source on the summit of a nearby peak is strikingly reminiscent of what I witnessed in San Juan. Relevant background comes from yet another indigenous community in southern Oaxaca, Santiago Yaitepec, a Chatino village that was the site of James Greenberg's ethnographic studies of religious fiestas there during the 1970s (1981). Greenberg describes "special events . . . associated with the fiesta of Santa Cruz: [including a] pilgrimage to the house of the rain god to bring the rains":

> The procession to bring the rains, on May 1, is at the heart of this fiesta. This pilgrimage has its logical complement in the fiesta of the Virgen del Rosario on October 5 when an almost identical procession goes to leave the rains. Whereas the procession to "bring" the rains goes first to *ki'ya chko,* "the house of the rain god," and then to *tu xkwa,* a spring, which is his "door" (symbolically opening it), the procession to "leave" the rains reverses the order: it closes the "door" and then "leaves" the rain in the house of the rain god.
>
> Prayers offered to the rain god atop *ki'ya ka'yu* ["five mountains"] take the form of imitative magic. Each family buries an offering of bread and chocolate and lights a candle in a rock-lined hole in the center of the peak's round pine-covered knoll. Then, by building miniature corn cribs, hitching posts, and salt licks for pinecone "mules" and "cattle," they pray for the things they want and need—like domestic animals and a good harvest.
>
> People also "play" in the house of the rain god . . . they clear their "corrals" and fill them with pinecone "animals," plow their miniature fields, make hitching posts and salt licks, build corn bins, and erect little houses. (Greenberg 1981:120–21)

It is striking how widespread is this practice, with just minor differences in dates and observances. I have heard accounts of very similar practices in Central Mexico also. It seems likely to have been a widespread pre-Spanish Mesoamerican ritual.

Other Fiestas

Much has been written about Mexican fiestas. Particularly well known are the highland Maya communities in which men (and their wives) compete to sponsor an annual fiesta cycle (a *cargo*) that may require an investment of the local equivalent of several years' income to honor a saint, hosting the entire town at a series of feasts. The social and political *functions* of this "cargo system" have been exhaustively debated (e.g., Cancian 1965; Greenberg 1981:2–22). San Juan enjoys its fiestas, but they seem much less elaborate in concept and execution than among the Maya, for example. The Fiesta de la Santa Cruz is an informal affair (more so in San Juan than in San José Lachiguirí or Santiago Yaitepec), requiring no special expense or organizational effort. Likewise, the famed celebration of Todos Santos in San Juan almost escaped our notice.* There was a midnight service—actually more like 2:00 AM—under a cold, bright moon, sparsely attended; then sometime the following morning, families laid flowers on the graves of their ancestors, but there was no public procession and no festive communal gathering at the cemetery, as has drawn so much attention elsewhere. Yet the cemetery is a ritual focal point for the community, the scene of elaborate memorials marking the *novena* and *el acabo del año* processions to the graves of family (fig. 2.17). Christmas and New Year's are the occasion for *posadas*—sponsored by particular families or even by such institutions as the clinic, the school, and the municipal administration.

The most popular and elaborate local fiestas are rather secular in spirit, though ostensibly religious. The Fiesta del Patrón, that is, San Juan, takes place June 24 (but it lasts three days). This unfortunately often coincides with soaking rains that inhibit somewhat the horse races (fig. 2.18), a newly revived "tradition" in which riders at full gallop attempt to grab a live chicken suspended from a rope tied across the finish line, pulling off its head in the process. When the chicken supply is low, riders attempt to catch a key ring at full gallop on the tip of a ballpoint pen held at arm's length (a variant of the brass ring). Basketball tourneys and all-night dances following an exhilarating (and expensive) fireworks display are sponsored jointly by the town government and a committee of emigré volunteers noted for their commercial success in Miahuatlán and else-

---

* Todos Santos is also known as the Day of the Dead. Actually, the Day of the Dead, "All Souls Day," is November 2; All Saints Day, or Todos Santos, is November 1; while our secular celebration of Halloween, literally, "All Hallows' Eve," is the day before, October 31, harking back to the ancient Celtic rites of Samhain. This "Catholic" observance involves a temporal displacement of Aztec/Mesoamerican worship of Mictecacihuatl, the "Lady of the Dead" [King 2004: http://www.mexconnect.com/mex—/travel/jking/jkdayofthedead.html].

where. It is said that the *chicatanas*, giant flying ants (**miôb**, *Atta* spp.) emerge for their annual mating flight on El Día de San Juan, adding a culinary spice to the festival dinners.

Another elaborate communal celebration is El Primer Viernes, "The First Friday," of Lent, that is. Local towns take turns hosting a three-day party on subsequent Fridays throughout the Lenten season. I had imagined that Lent would be a time of quiet reflection and disciplined abstinence. On the contrary, the exuberance of *Carnaval*—timed as one last fling *before* Lent—is here celebrated throughout the run up to Easter. San Juan's main street becomes a mini–regional market (lacking a regular market worthy of the name—Miahuatlán's Monday *tianguis* dominates local commerce); guests are housed in the homes of acquaintances, in the schools, or in spare rooms in the Palacio Municipal. The centerpiece of this celebration is a religious procession, a *convite*, through the streets of town, led by the priest making one of his rare semiannual official visits. Laurel leaves are scattered along the route; altar boys swing incense to perfume the track; the procession stops regularly to bless particular shrines. Then the fun begins, the *jaripeo*, or rodeo, in a stadium and ring built especially for the occasion. The "bulls" are mostly oxen released from their plow yokes to allow young men to demonstrate their balance and daring (fig. 2.19). Hired bands play the night away.

Curiously, I believe the communal celebration that engages the townspeople most is an entirely secular and modernist ritual, the *clausura*, or graduation ceremonies for the kindergarten, primary, and secondary school programs. These events are organized jointly by the teachers and "Los Padres de Familia," parent committees, and are jointly sponsored by the town administration and a *padrino*, or godfather, of the graduating class. The *clausura* in 1997 was special, honoring the first class to graduate from the town's *Telesecundaria*. San Juan's most famous native son, the highly successful popular musician Oswaldo Cruz López, came home to serve as *padrino*, bringing his band, his massive array of electronic amplification equipment for the dance, and a professional video crew to document it all. His sentimental attachment to his hometown is memorialized in his ballad "San Juan, mi tierra de nubes" (sound clip 2.2).

Preparations for the *clausuras* are elaborate: graduating students must make or purchase special clothing: for the boys black slacks, a stiff white dress shirt, and tie; for the girls a "prom dress"—clothes they may never wear again. The kindergarten grads learn to waltz, while primary and secondary students enact patriotic speeches from Mexican history. National pride is very much in the forefront with flags, salutes, and military drills (fig. 2.20). Yet at the center of honor and attention are the children, their parents standing proudly on the sidelines as the teachers put the graduates through their paces.

As with the other major celebrations, the priest is called upon to attend and to offer a special mass for the graduates (the Catholic graduates, at least). My Spanish is not perfectly fluent, but I could get the drift of the priest's sermon, directed at the secondary school graduating class. I paraphrase: "Education is the key to a better life. Do you want to live as your parents do, in ignorance, toiling in the dirt? Education will free you from that fate!"

I can't say whether the students were listening closely to the priest's message. I hope not, as I hope the evidence I put forward in this book—of lessons taught me by those same "ignorant" *campesinos* the priest despised—will prove how false is that deprecation of their parents' lives and will inspire a renewed respect for traditional knowledge, not only among scholars but also in San Juan itself.

Usos y costumbres

San Juan is a "sovereign" indigenous town, self-governed by customary practices (*usos y costumbres*), legislated by a general community assembly (*la asamblea general comunitaria*), and enforced by the "Honorable Municipal Government" (*H. Ayuntamiento Municipal* [fig. 2.21]) through its three primary institutions. First is the executive, or *cabildo*, headed by the *presidente municipal*, with certain judicial powers exercised by the *síndico municipal*, which is charged with enforcing municipal decrees (*ordenanzas municipales*). The administration includes as well a town mayor (*alcalde constitucional*), a secretary, and a half-dozen "councilmen" (*regidores*), each with specific administrative responsibilities (e.g., *regidor de justicia, regidor de hacienda, regidor de salud*), as well as *suplentes* for each officer, delegated to stand in for their respective officials in their absence. Assisting these officials are the *mayores* and *topiles* who make themselves available for routine tasks in the service of the *cabildo*. For example, a *mayor* might escort a witness to the *palacio* to testify in a dispute; a *topil* might be responsible for turning on the streetlights each evening.

The second institution of the local government is the Commission for Communal Property (Comisariado de Bienes Comunales), a twelve-person committee responsible for assuring the integrity of the community's property, most notably, the communal lands. In the notorious incident immortalized in the *corrido "Dos pueblos conocidos"* (sound clip 2.3), the party from San Juan ambushed by their rivals were of the *comisariado*, sent to clear the municipal boundary, a communal work project typically performed once every three years. The *comisariado* is also responsible for authorizing the sale of land within the *municipio*, whether from the community to individual citizens or from one citizen to another, and oversees harvests of community natural resources, most notably timber.

The third core institution of the local government is the Council for Vigilance (Consejo de Vigilancia), another twelve-person committee, charged with maintaining "peace, tranquility, harmony, and respect among the inhabitants." In addition, there are school committees (*Padres de Familia*) and a committee serving as liaison to the medical clinic. All these administrative *cargos* are staffed by volunteers; no one is paid for their work on behalf of the community. In addition, all adult citizens (*ciudadanos*) are required to perform periodic community work (*tequios*), under penalty of a fine.

A schedule of fines was posted in 2002, affirmed unanimously by the assembly, over the signatures of the *presidente, alcalde,* and *síndico* (fig. 2.22). The fines ranged from $80 pesos (ca. $8 U.S.) for "scandalous behavior in the public streets" to $5,000 pesos (ca. $500 U.S.) for "falsifying documents" and for "dispossessing land without cause." Participation in community activities while drunk warranted a fine of $150 pesos (ca. $15 U.S.), while "contamination of public areas" (littering?) could also cost $150 pesos. The penalty for "improper discharge of firearms" was left to the discretion of the municipal authorities, while "homicidal threats" were subject to federal law (i.e., "*a la ley*").

Note especially the penalties for failing to perform community work (*"incumplimientos a los tequios"*), $100 pesos (ca. $10 U.S.), and failure to attend community assemblies (*"inasistencias en las ambleas"*), a $100 peso fine for men, but just a $30 peso fine for women! This last provision indicates that San Juan *usos y costumbres* do not accord precisely equal legal status to men and women, a criticism of local autonomy raised by human rights activists and other critics of indigenous sovereignty in Mexico. It is true that men "customarily" control municipal offices. To the best of my knowledge, there is no formal prohibition on women serving in any of the town's administrative posts, up to and including the municipal presidency. However, I know of no instance, in recent San Juan history at least, of a woman serving a major municipal *cargo*. Yet this gender bias is not the consequence of the system of *usos y costumbres*, as some have alleged, but rather reflects the influence of cultural values widespread in Mexico, and beyond.

Fieldwork in San Juan Gbëë

I have been fascinated to observe this example of participatory democracy, so unlike my experience of community political action in the United States, and in many ways more truly "democratic." Yet my work plan directed my attention elsewhere. My first and most essential task was to learn the local flora and fauna, which meant learning the Zapotec and Latin names for each local plant and animal species and variety (see chap. 4). We shuttled between San Juan—eventually leasing a "comfortable" compound in San Juan next door to the town's "commercial hub," Silvino and Vírgen's store (fig. 2.23) and telephone service—and Oaxaca, several times each month. While in San Juan I concentrated on plant collections, pressing and drying five examples of each for deposit at various Mexican herbaria. Meanwhile, Donato collected insects and netted birds, sometimes working well past midnight to preserve and catalog these finds. We attempted in each case to get one or more local "experts" to name each plant or animal in Zapotec—transcribing these names as best we could given the phonological complexities involved—and to teach us about each organism, where and when each might be found, how each might be used, and their ecological roles.

We enlisted local people whenever we could in our collecting efforts. Two of Cándido's and Roselía's daughters, Inez and Justina, collected plants during our absence, as did Pedro Miguel Zurita. Inez and Justina documented many garden plants, while Pedro ranged far afield for little-known species. Neighborhood kids would knock on our door to present us with captives ranging from a weasel—which soon escaped to live another day—to snakes, horned lizards, and scorpions, in hopes of a few pesos' compensation.

Once I had gained some control over the local flora and the relevant Zapotec nomenclature, I stumbled on the idea of offering a small bounty to children who would bring me a bag full of leaves and flowers and teach me their names and uses. I made it clear that I wanted *different* plants, not duplicates. My best customers at first were Cándido's and Roselía's youngest daughter, Marielena, who was twelve at the time, and her sidekick, Lilia, her then seven-year-old niece. This was a type of "rapid ethnobotanical appraisal" (Martin 1995:3), as I had to process each bag of 20 to 50 plants quickly, scribbling the names and uses as well as my on-the-spot scientific determination. There was no time to preserve vouchers—and in most cases the sample was no more than a scrap of foliage—but these data can be used to substantiate naming conventions and to discover new plants and extend our knowledge of the uses of familiar species. These "rapid appraisals" impressed me deeply. I was amazed at the scope, detail, and accuracy of the botanical knowledge of local children, some as young as six or seven. I subsequently designed a plant trail (what I called in Zapotec the **nèz guìzh,** literally, 'plant trail') to test more systematically this "precocious acquisition" (Hunn 2002) of botanical knowledge, as is detailed in chapter 8.

While the majority of my botanical explorations were within an hour's walk of town, or within a radius of approximately three kilometers, Donato and I also were guided to the farthest corners of the *municipio* in search of unusual habitats and species of limited occurrence, from the grove of Montezuma bald cypress (*Taxodium mucronatum*) at the Santa Catarina Quioquitani bridge, to the mist-wrapped summit of **Guì-cxò-bèe** 'Rough-stone Mountain'.

The people of San Juan belong to this beautiful, rugged landscape, and it belongs to them. It has provided for virtually all their material and spiritual needs for over 1,000 years. Their roots go deep in the landscape, while I, as their guest, can only appreciate from a distance the rich diversity of their lands. To the people of San Juan falls the right and responsibility to defend it.

CHAPTER 3

Ló Liù Sànfwân / The Land

An Introduction to the Fields, Forests, and Woodlands of San Juan

The Road to San Juan Gbëë

THE HIGHWAY FROM Oaxaca City out past the airport is a NASCAR rally of taxis, buses, cars, and trucks jockeying for advantage, dodging *topes* (speed bumps), belching fumes, careening south under a canopy of eucalyptus. Our usual plan for a stay in San Juan involved a stop at *Gigante* on the bypass next to McDonald's to stock up with food and other supplies to last a week, then out past the airport, through the black-pottery tourist town of San Bartolo Coyotepec, through the military checkpoint with fingers crossed, past the shantytown at the *entronque* that has grown up in the past decade exploiting the economic spin-offs of the huge municipal landfill nearby. The left fork here is ours. The highway snakes over a low saddle, then down past San Martín Tilcajete, famous *alebrije* town (where they make those evocative carvings of fanciful animals), then to Ocotlán, first city on the route. Ocotlán was home to the noted "primitivist" painter Rodolfo Morales until his death in 2001, as well as the Aguilar family, whose whimsical ceramic sculptures charm. Morales is a fine example of the best in civic engagement by the artist, as he invested his income generously to renovate Ocotlán's multidomed Dominican church and to establish a school for aspiring artists, now a museum in his memory. Past Ocotlán the highway runs straight through an expansive plain with scattered columnar cacti, particularly *Stenocereus treleasei*, and an endemic century plant, *Agave karwinskii*. On to Ejutla, second city en route, its market famous for goats. We take the shortcut to the south edge of town, past the "Hotel 6" (the only authorized Motel 6 franchise in Mexico; actually a converted hacienda, but one doesn't say "motel" in this part of Mexico, as it's code for "one-night stand"). Then the *cancha de pelota*

Mixteca, a long, narrow clearing where local aficionados of this version of the ancient Mesoamerican ball game practice. The road snakes through a confusion of low hills; we see our first oaks, the blue-leaved *Quercus glaucoides*, lush riparian groves of mesquite (*Prosopis laevigatus*) and guamuchil (*Pithecellobium dulce*), trees characteristic of the floodplain soils of the central valleys but which dislike the cool heights of the foothills and thus are scarcely known in San Juan. At last Miahuatlán appears, sprawled before the rising ridges of the Sierra de Miahuatlán.

This is the district capital; its full name is Miahuatlán de Porfirio Diáz, after the notorious paleoliberal dictator and hero of the war of liberation from the short-lived French occupation. The Monday market here has expanded dramatically in the past decade, engulfing nearly the entire center of the city in a chaos of stalls. Absent a private car, one searches here for the local buses to San Juan and San Pedro that depart from in front of La Farmacia Cristal. San Juan maintains a hostel here for municipal authorities on business trips or just a safe place to leave one's bundles until the buses depart. By 2003 Miahuatlán could claim ATMs and Internet cafés, unimagined just ten years ago.

From the Highway 175 bypass, one hangs a left at a street unobtrusively signed San José Lachiguirí 48, San Pedro Mixtepec 47. Our landlady Rufina's shop is just off this street. We usually stop to chat, pay our rent, and get caught up on the doings of her daughter, Lucila, a recent law-school graduate. Rufina's brothers are lawyers and judges in Oaxaca; the whole family proved too successful for San Juan, though Rufina still visits on occasion to oversee her rental property and to visit her elderly father.

Two kilometers east of Miahuatlán the road forks. To the left the "low road" runs through San Luís Amatlán to San José Lachiguirí and beyond to San Pedro Martír Quiechapa. Beyond San Pedro Martír the road degenerates badly; otherwise, one could cross through the Yautepec district to join the Pan-American highway halfway to the isthmus, but you would be traveling along a notorious drug route.

The right fork winds past Cerro Gordo 'Fat Hill', an isolated knoll with mysterious caves supporting a sparse arid woodland. The road here is bordered by living fences composed of several species of columnar cacti and the endemic century plant (*Agave karwinskii*), distinguished by its substantial trunk. It is a favorite for "artisanal" mezcal production. In season one sees the *piñas* (that is, the "heart" of the century plant, left after the leaves have been trimmed) readied for the ovens, and you pass a smoking earthen mound a bit farther along, where the *piñas* are being cooked.

The next settlement is El Zapote, just across the ford of a sandy wash bordered by irrigated plots of vegetables and the primary commercial mezcal century plant, the *espadín* (*Agave angustifolia*).

Beyond El Zapote the road climbs back onto the plateau, then turns north along the rim of an eroded canyon above lush cultivated plots lining the stream at the bottom. These belong to San Ildefonso Amatlán, first of the Amatlán villages. Scattered Michoacán pines (*Pinus devoniana*) cling to the canyon rim. This is a striking pine, growing far from its relatives in the higher mountains, with a widely spreading crown like an acacia on the East African savanna, with very long thick needles and huge cones. On the east edge of San Ildefonso is a stand of **sotol** *Dasylirion serratifolium*, used to make decorative *estrellas*, or stars, for the church at Christmas. Beyond San Ildefonso we cross a series of barren hills leading down to the bridge at San Pedro Amatlán, also known as San Pedrito 'little San Pedro', in contrast to the big San Pedro Gbëë. The creek is lined here by stately bald cypress and a profusion of cultivated fruit trees that give the town a tropical air.

Our road winds on through the arid valley to San Cristóbal Amatlán, like San Pedrito, known for its hand-woven palm products, *petates*, and sombreros. Women walk along the road busily weaving. This palm, *Brahea dulcis* (*yàg-xìn*), is the only palm species native to the higher elevations in Oaxaca (fig. 3.1). San Cristóbal weavers now buy palm leaves from near Sola de Vega, fifty kilometers to the west. It is said that *Brahea dulcis* once grew on the Cerro Yirot, an isolated mountain just east of San Cristóbal, but perhaps the species was overharvested here some years ago. San Juan petty traders, like my friend Cándido Cruz, still purchase *petates* in San Cristóbal and San Pedrito for resale at Pacific beach communities to earn a few pesos.

Past San Cristóbal the road climbs across a slope of the characteristic Amatlán white caliche earth—a common building material here, but not supportive of lush vegetation—before side-hilling into an open pine-oak woodland of Oaxaca pines (*Pinus pseudostrobus* var. *apulcensis*) and an oak with broad leaves, dark green above, silvery below, striking at night in our headlights (*Quercus liebmanni*). The pines are spared when fields on these steep slopes are planted to wheat, but their lower branches are lobbed off—*ocoteado*—for their pitchy wood, or *ocote*, which makes excellent kindling. The view back to the west is expansive (fig. 3.2).

The road tops out at 2,230 meters on an open slope offering a clear view across the canyon to San Agustín Gbëë (fig. 3.3), the first of the Gbëë towns, notable for the fact that the townspeople abandoned their distinctive Zapotec language en masse in favor of Spanish in the 1960s. Our route continues east through rock pine (*Pinus teocote*) woods mixed with the cup-leaved oak (*Quercus conzattii*) on hillsides of shallow exfoliating granite soils alternating with grassy flats on to San Lorenzo Gbëë. Here the tiny plaza is dominated by a massive oak and an empty jail. Just beyond, at the bridge, we enter San Juan territory, crossing what appears to be a heavily eroded slope with a few scattered, low prickly pear cacti (*Opuntia nejapensis*), then into another rock pine stand, where we like to pull over for a photo opportunity, a panorama of the cliffs of San Andrés and mountain profiles in endless succession to the far horizon (fig. 3.4). Though this is San Juan land, nowadays it is used infrequently, mostly to pasture goats and to collect firewood.

One more creek to cross, the "Río Jordán" according to one government map, but known locally as **Guiùu-x-tán** 'Mountain Forest River'. The creek often has a pair of black phoebes patrolling for insects. At night, particularly with a moon in spring, whiskered screech-owls and whip-poor-wills add an eerie resonance, calling from the pine- and oak-covered lower slopes of Cerro San Isidro, San Juan's sacred mountain. Finally, we climb to El Portillo, we pass the timber checkpoint shack and rough spur roads right and left where a large sign in Zapotec—**Rley no ziaad to** "We are happy that you have come"—may welcome visitors, then down past the last kilometer of "suburbs" to the town proper.

The View from San Juan Gbëë

The road to San Juan provides perspective on the contrast between valley towns, such as the Amatlanes, and the hill towns, which here share the name *Gbëë*, a historic imprint of the colonial system of ecclesiastical administration at a time when the headwaters of the Tehuántepec River system were subject to the Corregimiento de Nexapa (Rojas 1992:256). The hill towns typically perch on an exposed ridge or shelf, a bit of relatively flat land ringed by steep mountain slopes, cliffs, and canyon walls. These towns are regularly situated nearly astride the 2,000-meter contour line, which roughly demarcates the pine-oak forests above (Rzedowski 1978:263–313) from the tropical deciduous woodland below (the *selva baja caducifolia* of Miranda and Hernández X. 1963; the *bosque tropical caducifolia* of Rzedowski [1978:189–203]). As a consequence, it seems the hill towns are more diverse floristically than those of the valleys, and more sparsely populated.

This major ecotone encompasses also a mosaic of more or less natural habitats, including thorn forest (the *bosque espinoso* of Rzedowski [1978]), a shrubby stunted woodland (the *matorral xerófilo* of Rzedowski [1978]), short grass flats, riparian woodland, tiny patches of marsh vegetation, a unique cliff-face flora, and, of course, the anthropogenic ruderal communities alongside roads, trails, and fences (including "living fences" of magueyes, cacti, and trees that root easily from cuttings) and the weedy communities that dominate fallow fields (*acahuales*) in various stages of regeneration. Finally, there are the family gardens (*huertos familiares*) scattered across the town (see chap. 7).

Every day I spent in San Juan I would take a walk from town into the countryside, often with a guide to educate me as to the plants and animals along the route, usually with a set of garden clippers and a plastic garbage bag, which I would fill with samples of new and interesting plants. Donato might come along with a butterfly net, and a knapsack packed with plastic vials of alcohol, insect killing jars, and tweezers. A three- or four-hour hike left us sweating and exhausted but excited by our discoveries. Each hour collecting required at least another hour or two to sort, annotate, and prepare the collections.

The village of San Juan is at the center of the *municipio*. It is surrounded by a zone of intensively cultivated milpas, as described in chapter 5. Beyond the cultivated lands is "the bush," *el monte*, or, in Zapotec, **dán**. Trails (**něz**) lead from the center out through the fields (**dòoz** early in the cultivation cycle; **wgàa** when the corn is mature), then into and through these forest zones, above and below the town, until one arrives at the next human settlement. The town (**guièdz**) is protected from evil influences by a ring of cross shrines (**crûz**) beside each trail departing the town. These may be decorated with fresh flowers as an offering (fig. 3.5).

The town sprawls across a central, horseshoe-shaped ridge, capped on the higher eastern extremity by the plaza with the church in pride of place, next to it the basketball court with the Palacio Municipal on the right, housing for teachers opposite. The plaza is still known as **Dán-yàg-blëë**, literally, 'manzanita [*pingüíca*] forest', for the shrubby *Arctostaphylos pungens*, a dominant *matorral* species of gravelly slopes. Today there is not a single such shrub to be seen within half a kilometer of the plaza, yet the name preserves a record of the habitat as it was over 300 years ago!

The covered market at the foot of the short climb to the plaza sits in a saddle in the U-shaped ridge, drained to the north from a muddy patch called **Ló-gódz** 'at the marsh', which blooms with a delicate white lily (*nlěch-běz* 'fox onion', *Nothoscordum striatum*) in summer. The valley here is too fertile for houses and is given over to cornfields in the growing season but converted for the rodeo at Primer Viernes (fig. 3.6). The trickle of water from this valley bisecting the town drops over **Ró-ctà** 'cliff edge' to join the Fox River (**Guiùu-bèz**) that drains the amphitheater between the west end of the town ridge and El Portillo at the foot of Cerro San Isidro. The intersection at **Ró-ctà** is marked by a cross and the crumbling ruins of what had been the *cacique*'s blockhouse. The *cacique* ran the town with the aid of his private army through the 1950s. A few old-timers regret his passing, nostalgic for the influence he wielded on the local stage in San Juan's name. Most are thankful to have gained effective control of their town government and enjoy the enhanced sense of community that came with a fairer distribution of wealth and power.

My house sits above **Ró-ctà** on the northwestern extremity of San Juan's central ridge, on Benito Juárez Street (the street names are almost never used) where it levels off a bit on the climb to the bus stop at the intersection with the main street that leads past the market and up to the plaza (see figs. 3.7, 3.8). My neighborhood may be known as **Bârì-làdz-ptŏots** 'barrio of the coral bean tree'. Indeed, there are coral bean trees (*Erythrina americana*) here, also known as *tzompantli*, from the Aztec word for the skull racks of Tenochtitlán, the Aztec capital, built to display the heads of sacrificial victims. From my patio I could watch black-vented orioles feeding in the clusters of scarlet trumpet flowers of this tree, which, like a number of showy tropical deciduous trees, flowers before the leaves appear. Coral bean trees are often planted from cuttings in fence rows, though they grow wild here as well. Children have their own name for the tree, **yàg-pĭp,** which is onomatopoetic, imitating the piping sound of the toy whistles kids make of the flowers, which are also edible.

The Hike to the Cliffs of San Andrés

The street that leads northwest from the intersection at **Ró-ctà** drops past Zhey Juan's house (fig. 3.9; at the time of his death, in 1999, he was the town's most senior citizen, age ninety-five), stepping over the roots of a large oak of a species of uncertain affinity in the local taxonomic scheme. I am quite certain it is *Quercus obtusata,* not so rare but in several respects intermediate in character between two abundant oak species, *Quercus castanea,* with its small, pointy-elliptical dark green leaves and hard smooth blackish bark, and *Quercus glaucoides,* with larger lobed bluish-green leaves and pale gray, corky bark.

Below this oak, past a steep rocky stretch of trail, you cross **Guiùu-bèz** 'Fox River', really just a creek, so-called because a family of foxes had its den just above the ford. Every evening a parade of young boys, or perhaps a woman or girl, will pass the ford coming into town herding their flocks of goats with maybe a few sheep, or driving the family donkey home loaded with firewood. Past the ford the trail climbs a sandstone staircase at **Ró-quiè-bèl̲** 'edge with rocks in a line' to a cross guarding this portal of the town.

The trail here is bordered by a tight row of a century plant used for fiber (**dòb-guièdz** '*ixtle* maguey', *Agave angustiarum*), now rarely processed but in the recent past, the primary source of *ixtle* cordage. It is one of the more distinctive species of the genus here, unique for its tight spike of flowers on the tall *quiote* raised at the end of its life (thus of the subgenus *Littaea*) and narrow, arcing, olive-green leaves (see figs. 3.10, 3.11, 3.12). Scattered among these are other much larger individuals with broad gray-green leaves and the occasional candelabra inflorescence (these are predominantly *Agave americana* var. *oaxacana,* but with the occasional *A. seemanniana* and *A. salmiana*). The wide leaves of these century plants serve as a crude message board, young lovers announcing their intentions in words scratched into the leaf (fig. 3.13). *Agave americana* var. *oaxacana* and *Agave salmiana* are the preferred species for extracting *aguamiel,* the sweet sap produced in quantity by "castrating" the plant at the point of flowering. This *aguamiel* is fermented to make *pulque*, a sweetish, slimy, slightly intoxicating brew the subject of legend in Mexico for millennia. In San Juan they prefer to drink *tepache*—known in the local Zapotec as **nziù**—on special occasions such as wedding feasts (*fandangos*). *Tepache* is, as I understand it, a distinctly flavored, lightly fermented drink made from the juice of a special montane pineapple cultivar, fortified perhaps with *pulque* and seasoned with such spices as cinnamon. The sweetness of **nziù** is balanced by tossing into the mix the bitter bark of a thornless *Acacia* (**yàg-lè**, *A. angustifolia*). A species of *Stevia* (**guièe-nziù** 'tepache flower'), a shrub noted for producing chemicals many times sweeter than cane sugar, is symbolically associated with this drink but not used directly in its preparation. Both these plants are harvested above town in the pine-oak forest zone.

The trail now climbs around the head of a gully where someone has planted bananas and *carrizo* reeds, then into the shade of an isolated *Quercus castanea* that offers a fine view of San Juan against the backdrop of its southern mountain perimeter. The sounds of the town carry easily across the intervening valley below **Ró-ctà**: church bells, the cacophony of competing loudspeakers, each promoting a different taste in music, the shrill announcements of incoming telephone calls at Silvino's store, the bitter complaints of sexually frustrated male donkeys, turkey chatter, and hints of human conversation.

Farther afield the trail cuts deeply into the exposed sandstone bedrock at a place called, with telling irony, **Làdz-guièr** 'pine flat' (fig. 3.14), now a bare rock ledge bordered by a short grassy flat on the right and shrubby oak and manzanita chaparral up the slope to the left. Not much farther we cross a series of gullies: first **Psê-nìs-lày** 'Holy Water Gully', then **Psê-guiùu-nquǐts** 'White-water [i.e., lime-saturated] Gully', then **Psê-nrǒ** 'Large Gully'. These gullies shelter rich fern gardens and are favored by foraging goats. Next we arrive at **Lèts-dán-lbàa** 'Forest Tomb Town', an area of cultivated fields at the junction with the track from El Portillo that skirts the east base of Cerro San Isidro. This junction is also marked with a cross. The "tomb" alluded to in the name refers to the site of the burial ground of one of San Juan's predecessor settlements, called Santa María de los Ángeles, abandoned in favor of the present townsite in 1690.

There are several variant accounts of this historic move from the foot of Cerro San Isidro to the current site. Basilio Rojas apparently visited San Juan in the course of researching his historical geography of the Miahuatlán district, published posthumously in 1992. He reports that:

> In the chronicles of this town of San Juan, one finds reference to the fact that the town was authorized in 1690 [as memorialized on a bronze plaque at the Palacio Municipal] to move to the site where the town is now found, on account of the fact that the older place that served as the town seat, called **Guieguesube** [**guìc-dzùb** 'head of the climb', that is, Cerro San Isidro], had become very unhealthy. . . .
>
> As actions of this sort could only be accomplished by the Indians with the express permission of the vice-regal government, we tried to confirm the foregoing, but unfortunately our search ended without issue, as we were unable to find the facts relative to this point in the National Archives. (my translation from Rojas 1992:256–57, with bracketed notes)

I was told by several people in San Juan that the move was necessitated by the dessication of a spring on the summit of Cerro San Isidro, alleged to have been the site of the earlier town, though it seems strange the town would have perched on a mountaintop. But then consider Monte Albán. This spring was on the very summit where the rock cistern called the "door to the house of Lightning" is now. It dried up because sacred stones were stolen from it by "priests," a familiar theme in legendary accounts of the early days of the town.

Another quite different but not contradictory story relates that an old woman, foraging at the present site of the plaza, saw a light shining in the brush, investigated, and found an image of San Juan. The townspeople took this as a sign that they should build a church at that spot and settle around it. That would explain the adoption of San Juan as patron in lieu of Santa María de los Ángeles. In any case it seems reasonable to believe that this resettlement was motivated by the failure of the springs that supported the earlier town, perhaps a consequence of deforestation over previous centuries.

Our trail takes us farther north and at the same time further into the past, as we shall see. Beyond the cross at **Lèts-dán-lbàa** we leave Cerro San Isidro behind and follow a wide-open ridge toward a low hill called **Guì-ndzâg** 'Fatigue Mountain', just above **Làdz-ptsiêdz** 'Irrigated Flat' (fig. 3.15). The hill is named for the rigorous climb to this point from the Río Peña 300 meters below on the trail to San Andrés Gbëë located behind the cliffs of that name.

Early in 1998 a young man exposed a tomb here during preparatory winter plowing. He cautiously removed stones from the mouth of the tomb—a shallow horizontal structure—and saw that it contained a human skeleton and some old ceramic pieces. He covered it and reported his find to the authorities. Not long after, at my invitation, Dr. Marcus Winter, staff archaeologist with the Oaxaca office of the Instituto Nacional de Antropología e Historia, visited the town to investigate the mysterious caves I had "discovered" the year before on the nearby San Andrés cliffs. These caves were set high on the sheer face of the cliffs but were neatly enclosed by low adobe brick walls, some still clearly painted red and white, others with balconies supported by wooden beams (figs. 3.16, 3.17). Townspeople knew of the caves but averred no one had ever climbed into them, a not inconsiderable challenge, as the mouths were ten meters and more above the base, and the base was guarded by a tangled thorn jungle.

The town administration appointed a committee to show Dr. Winter these and other sites of antiquarian interest, with the understanding that the town would carefully guard their archaeological patrimony until such time as the INAH might fund a systematic archaeological investigation and, perhaps also, the establishment of a community museum to house the artifacts recovered.

We went first of all to a ridge at the foot of **Quiè-gbëë**, the 'Moon Cliff' for which the town is named. Dr. Winter inspected a small temple platform here, with its plaster flooring still intact, and noticed from that vantage point the outline of a classic Mesoamerican ball court, at that time being plowed in preparation for planting (fig. 3.18). Dr. Winter's survey of the ridge crest north of the ball court turned up abundant post-Classic pottery fragments. We stood on a miniature Monte Albán! But then, one can't walk ten meters anywhere in Oaxaca without stepping on a pre-Columbian site, and INAH's resources are severely limited, so when San Juan will learn more of its ancient history is anybody's guess. It is certain, however, that the immediate area has been densely settled for well over 1,000 years.

Back at the tomb on **Guì-ndzâg** Dr. Winter affirmed the likely post-

Classic age of the burial, judging by the accompanying ceramics. He recommended sealing the tomb for future study. Local elders noted that **Guì-ndzâg** was the site of a predecessor village to Santa María de los Ángeles, where the ancestors of today's San Juan settled after splitting from their San Pedro kin with whom they had lived at **Làaw-guièdz** 'old town', a site deep in a canyon at the junction of the Río Grande and the Río Calabazar at the foot of the little Monte Albán ridge, a site we will visit shortly.

Below **Guì-ndzâg**, taking the left fork, our trail descends abruptly past fallow fields, pastures, and patches of deciduous thorn forest to the ford at the Río Peña. This stream drains the mountains behind San Lorenzo, then passes beneath the base of the San Andrés cliffs. Across the stream at the base of these cliffs are terraced fields, the terrace walls likely built before the Spanish conquest, yet still farmed today (fig. 3.19). Incredibly, Zhey Valentín, San Juan's only blind person, blinded at eighteen by disease, would walk, guided by a grandchild, down to his fields here, spend the day cultivating, then return that evening, climbing up and over "Fatigue Mountain" en route. He followed this routine until, in his late sixties, his replacement hip gave out.

The cliff base above Valentín's fields is now heavily overgrown by thorn scrub, favorite lair of the black-tailed rattlesnake. Beneath this jungle Dr. Winter discovered level platforms constructed along the cliff base (fig. 3.20). With ladders the caves would have been accessible but clearly also readily defended against raids by one ambitious warlord or another. Although there is no clear historic or prehistoric evidence of warfare in this immediate region, it is known that a powerful militaristic state based at Tututepec in the Mixteca de la Costa raided in this direction centuries before the Spanish arrived (Whitecotton 1977:91–97). Thus, the need for defensible positions is understandable, though Dr. Winter reported that he had seen nothing quite like these cliff dwellings anywhere in southern Mexico.

We could follow our trail from here around to the northeast to arrive at the contemporary village of San Andrés, but instead we will retrace our steps to the summit of **Guì-ndzâg** and take the right-hand road from there through a stand of magnolia-leaved oaks, at a spot appropriately named **Dán-yàg-rèdz** 'Magnolia-leaved Oak Forest', where our trail overlooks San Juan's lone "lake," **X-làgûn-Dây** 'Medardo's Lake', a muddy puddle cupped in a ledge above the canyon of the Río Grande, said to harbor the occasional turtle (fig. 3.21). This trail descends at an easy pace north-northeast toward the road into Santa Catarina Quiè Gdán, which branches off the road from San José Lachiguirí, climbs over the northeast shoulder of Cerro Ydori, then bisects San Andrés before crossing the Río Grande on the lower margins of San Juan. Our trail drops past a rocky outcrop that offers an inspiring view into the maw of the canyon of the Río Calabazar just above "Old Town" and across to Santa Catarina, perched like San Juan on a level ridge that juts out from the forested mountains above (fig. 3.22). Curiously, this outcrop is called **Quiè-mǎw** 'Macaw Cliff', and Zhey Uc (that is, Don Eucario), who cultivated a plot of land nearby, affirmed that military macaws (*Ara militaris*) used to visit the area regularly in fall to feed on the wild cherry crop (*Prunus serotina*).

Just below this rock the trail passes the *mojón*, or boundary stone, at the frontier with Santa Catarina. At this low, hot edge of San Juan one may find species that occur nowhere else in the *municipio*, such as the giant barrel cactus **bìznâgr-ngòl** (*Ferrocactus latispinus* var. *greenwoodii*) (fig. 3.23); two columnar cacti characteristic of pristine *selva baja caducifolia*, the old man cactus, **yàg-bdzì-tǒop** 'white-headed *pitahaya*' (*Pilosocereus chrysacanthus*), with its white topknot (fig. 3.24), and *Pseudomitrocereus fulviceps*, **yàg-bdzì-nròob** 'great *pitahaya*', which reminds me of a golden-capped rocket on the launch pad (fig. 3.25); and a prickly pear, *Opuntia pilifera*, **yàg-biǎa-tǒop** 'white-headed prickly pear tree', with a distinctive crest of long, tangled white hairs (fig. 3.26).

With Zhey Uc to Santa Catarina through *Dán ptsȅë* 'Hot Country Forest'

One of my favorite country walks out of San Juan begins below the church at Eucario's *rancho* just northeast of town. When Zhey Uc was in town—he regularly visited a son who lived in Salina Cruz in the Isthmus of Tehuántepec—he spent long hours chatting with his burro and enjoying the commanding view north across his fields past Cerro Cántaro to distant Cerro Nueve Puntos ('Nine Summit Mountain') near Mitla (fig. 3.27). When he was a young man, he led mule trains down the long valley of the Tehuántepec River to the isthmus towns to trade *petates* from San Luís Amatlán for salt fish. I hired him one day to guide me as far as Santa

Catarina Quiè Gdán, which perches at the level of San Juan on the ridge opposite. To get there involves a vigorous four-hour trek, fording en route two streams deeply incised in the intervening canyons. The trail cuts through fields, pasture, riparian woodland, rocky outcrops, and the rich diversity of relatively undisturbed *selva baja caducifolia*, before climbing again into the oaks and pines to catch sight of the church at Santa Catarina.

The trail is bordered by neat stone walls and a living fence of oak, coral bean, copal trees, fiber century plant, a mulberry or two (once important for local silk production), the tree morning-glory (the leaves may cure headaches), and a small tree of the Euphorbiaceae, *Jatropha cordifolia*, that has odd woody seeds that children fashion into tops. Also conspicuous in these fence rows and scattered across the adjacent fields are *guaje* trees, protected and cultivated for their edible seeds, which are picked from the elongated reddish pods that cluster on the higher branches. This tree is the namesake of the city of Oaxaca and taxonomic focal point for a variety of local trees and shrubs of the Fabaceae.

At the cross on the trail leaving San Juan there is shade and often a cool breeze blowing down Wild Squash Canyon from the high summits to the southeast. Then we drop sharply past Chepíl Flat (**Lètz-pxìizh**) to Sandy-Clay River (**Guiùu-lĕ**) where it is joined by Guava Creek (**Guiùu-buì**), the continuation of Fox River that drains the southwest edge of town. The ford is usually just a few inches deep, and one can dance across from rock to rock, except after a hard rain. There are odd boulders here that look for all the world like giant skulls (fig. 3.28). The river is lined with familiar riparian trees, representing Mexican species of widespread North American genera, such as alder, willow, and dogwood. The narrow canyon is lush with ferns.

Our trail now angles up the far slope bearing south on exfoliating granite soils in full sun (fig. 3.29). Eucario leads me into the spiny world of the *selva baja caducifolia*. Here it is cut over and heavily grazed by foraging goat flocks under the care of young boys from town. The genus *Acacia* is prominent, as are columnar and prickly pear cacti, and century plants.

There is a variety of century plants along our route, some planted as fencing, others in fields to retard erosion, while others grow wild. We have already met **dòb-guièdz** 'rope maguey', *Agave angustiarum*, which, as the Zapotec name indicates, is a traditional source of fiber for rope. A second smallish species is **dòb-bè** 'oxalis maguey', *Agave potatorum* (fig. 3.30), reputed to make the best mezcal (but since San Juan is not a mezcal-manufacturing town, it is not much used). The association with **guièe-bè** 'oxalis flower' is intriguing. It has been reported that the oxalic acid in the herb assists in breaking down the complex indigestible starches in the maguey *piña* ("pineapple") when it is baked, converting them to sugars. The sweet *piña* may then be eaten, or the sweet juices extracted in a homemade press or *palenque*, fermented, and distilled to make mezcal (Sánchez López 1989). The leaves of this maguey are very broadly lanceolate with prominent hooked spines perched atop "nipples" on the leaf margins.

We pass a few individuals of **dòb-mpiè** 'pulque maguey' (*Agave salmiana*), with its broad, twisting, gray-green leaves, planted on the margins of a milpa. The owners of these magueys wait for the huge central bud to begin to elongate (after seven to twenty years). They "nip it in the bud," carve out a bowl in the center of the rosette of leaves to collect the *aguamiel*, harvesting several liters every few days for some months before the plant exhausts its chemical energy reserves. Mixed with this species are some that are equally massive but with narrower, straighter, light-bluish leaves. These are a secondary source of *pulque*, **dòb-dzìn** 'honey maguey' (*Agave americana* var. *oaxacana*; see fig. 3.31). While *A. salmiana* is most likely a pre-Spanish introduction from Central Mexico, *A. americana* var. *oaxacana* is a native.

Finally, we meet *Agave marmorata*, **dòb-pcuêl**, literally, 'corn-husk maguey', a maguey *"que crece sólo,"* that is, a truly wild species. It has large, broad leaves, characteristically sandpaper-surfaced (fig. 3.32). These leaves are used medicinally to "heat" feet swollen from a sprain or twist. To alleviate the pain of childbirth, the leaf is burned as a fumigant. (Fray Juan Caballero [1998:75] cites the sixteenth-century Zapotec term *Tóba cuéla* from Cordova, which is clearly cognate, as referring to *Agave potatorum*.) *A. marmorata* is striking in flower; the *quiote* holds up flat sprays of golden flowers against the gray-green backdrop of the *selva baja caducifolia* (fig. 3.33).

Our trail sidehills past a grand isolated *cardón* cactus, *Stenocereus pruinosus* (fig. 3.34), the least common of the three species one may see near town. It has a half-dozen sharp-edged, prominent ribs, and showy white tubular flowers at the crown of the stems that give way to sweet, red, golf-ball–sized fruits that must be harvested with sticks, given the height of the crowns. These fruits are called **bdzì** in Zapotec, *pitahayas* in Spanish. The columnar cacti generally are thus **yàg-bdzì** '*pitahaya* tree'.

As you approach this *cardón*, the trail ducks beneath the shade of a tree that looks something like the Brazilian pepper tree (*Schinus molle*) that is so widely established throughout the Mexican highlands. But it's not a pepper tree, though it is of the same family, the Anacardiaceae, and that should be a warning to the unwary. However, on my first encounter with this tree, I failed to note the resemblance and forgot that poison oak, that bane of my childhood in southern California, belongs to the same family. I reached up and grabbed a branch, intending to prepare a voucher specimen. Pedro, my guide, tried to warn me, but too late. The next morning I woke to an odd tightness on the skin of my face and soon could scarcely see for the swelling. I suffered intense itching and blistering on all the most sensitive surfaces of my skin. A painful introduction to **yàg-lăadz** 'hives tree', known in local Spanish as "*hinchahuevos*," a crude allusion to the 'swollen testicles' one may suffer from the contact dermatitis induced by even second-hand contact with the defensive chemistry of *Pseudosmodingium multifolium* (fig. 3.35). One should also beware of **lăadz-guiùu**, the more familiar poison ivy (*Toxicodendron radicans*), the vines of which might be found in the lower riparian zone. Despite my strong allergic reaction to *Pseudosmodingium*, I have seen young boys clambering about in its branches, and the wood is said to be useful for fence posts. My mishap is fondly recalled by my San Juan friends, who miss no opportunity to tease me about it, bringing me branches of similar plants, such as *Fraxinus purpusii* and *Pistacia mexicana*, sometimes called **xín-yàg-lăadz** 'relative of *Pseudosmodingium*', to watch my reaction.

A short way past the poison tree we arrive at a saddle on a long, flat ridge (**Rò-dán-gbĕ̈ĕ**) and the junction with the trail from San Pedro. The trail on to Santa Catarina cuts sharply around the ridge and drops beneath **Quiè-gbĕ̈ĕ** 'Moon Cliff'. Local legend recounts how the distant ancestors of San Juan, San Pedro, and San Lorenzo founded a common town at the sign of a white, moon-shaped rock high on this cliff.

At the saddle a tributary trail stays on top of the ridge, angling due north past an odd, squarish hill. Dr. Winter, the INAH archaeologist, immediately recognized the "hill" as a temple platform, the top surface a plaster pavement. A glance off the edge revealed to his practiced eye the remnants of a classic late Monte Albán ball court, now nearly invisible beneath second growth and the initial stages of milpa cultivation. North along the entire length of the ridge we found a dense scattering of potsherds and further evidence of "palace" floors. The western slope of the ridge is in milpa cultivation, but with the benefit of pre-Columbian stonewall terraces. In truth, this was the ancient hilltop redoubt capital of a Classic-period city-state—the founding settlement of which their legendary origin story speaks—whose descendants no doubt are the contemporary citizens of San Juan and neighboring towns.

The eastern escarpment of this "temple ridge" is too steep for farming and supports an extensive, little-disturbed tract of *selva baja caducifolia*. One prominent tree on this ridge is the kapok tree, or *ceiba*, modest relation of the great Mayan tree-of-life, *yash-te* (*Ceiba pentandra*). Our *ceiba* is *yàg-miòong* (*C. acuminata*). Football-shaped fruits hang from the branch tips and when mature split open to release a cloud of kapok fibers. These were once used as cotton. A few wild figs grow here, in the company of two striking, if nearly useless, trees of the Fabaceae, which have been given memorable names: 'iguana-tail tree' (*Senna galeottiana*) and 'sun's toy tree' (*Conzattia multiflora*).

Within 500 meters of this ridge one may distinguish seven species of copal trees (*Bursera*), American relative of the sacred myrrh of the Middle East (fig. 3.36). The pitch of another species not found in San Juan is burnt as a ritual offering.

Toward the north end of the ridge of the Classic period ruins, one may scramble over a low wall at the boundary between San Juan and Santa Catarina. Property ownership in this area is fluid, as parcels may be bought and sold from members of one community to neighbors across the line (subject to the approval of the Comisariado de Bienes Comunales of the responsible community). It is possible that in this way community boundaries may flex in response to shifting demographic fortunes.

Beyond this wall the trail snakes steeply down the nose of the ridge through a dense thicket of shrubs. My young neighbor Raúl and I hiked this trail one morning, to explore the caves below. These thickets are diverse, but several sumac species (*Rhus* spp.) are characteristic (figs. 3.37, 3.38). The sour orange seeds of these sumacs are chewed to ease the discomfort of canker sores. The Anacardiaceae are well represented here.

In addition to the sumacs are two trees that mimic the poisonous *hinchahuevos* tree, the Mexican pistacio (*Pistacia mexicana*) and a species of ash (*Fraxinus purpusii*). These are found in close association with the true *hinchahuevos*. On this descent I located a small population of a curious shrubby oak that did not seem to match any known species. Yet it has a local Zapotec name, **yàg-pxù-làs,** literally, 'slender/small glaucous-leaved oak', for the resemblance of the leaves to miniatures of *Quercus glaucoides*. Mexico's leading expert on oaks, Dra. Susana Valencia Avalos, checked the specimen in 2004 and matched it to a species, *Quercus sebifera*, previously collected far to the northeast in the Tehuacán-Cuicatlán Valley toward the border with Puebla (fig. 3.39).

The trail steepens, then cuts across a final low cliff into the deep canyon where the two streams join. On the left rushes the stream that heads on **Quiè-cxòbèe,** then flows as the Wild Squash River between San Juan and San Pedro, the same stream we had crossed just below town. On the right is the Río Grande, which drains the high forests of San Pedro. Here it is a swift clear stream a half-meter deep, augmented by a substantial flow of crystal cold water emerging from a nearby fissure in the cliff. At the mouth of the cave from which this stream emerges, Raúl and I found the remains of an incense offering, burned to petition the spirits of this spring.

We are at **Làaw-guièdz,** literally, 'Old Town', the site of the ancient town where the people of San Juan and San Pedro once lived together as a single community. All that remains are several substantial pyramid-like mounds of river cobbles five meters tall, clearly foundations of ancient structures. As a sign of the purity of the water here, we flush a dipper (*Cinclus mexicanus*), an odd gray bird of river rocks that plunges into the current to harvest bugs from the bottom. Another fond reminder of the mountains back home.

The canyon widens a bit farther downstream. Along the right bank we find a complex of wooden troughs on stilts, an aqueduct for irrigating riverside orchards and gardens. Cultivated here are avocados, mangos, custard apples, bananas, sugar cane, a tall reed nearly a bamboo cultivated for its utility as light fencing, and a single coffee tree (fig. 3.40). San Juan, located in the rain shadow of the Sierra de Miahuatlán, is too dry for coffee. Thus, the town has been spared not only the influx of wealth coffee may bring but also the internal conflicts and violence that plague coffee towns on the south slope of the Sierra (Hernández Díaz 1987; Greenberg 1989).

Our destination is the ruined mill of the old *cacique* who dominated the town through intimidation until the mid-twentieth century. His men once ground wheat here and baked bread in limestone ovens. Today wheat is the special product of San Agustín, down the road, and bread is baked by a few enterprising women in San Juan with purchased wheat flour. Tortillas, however, remain the overwhelming favorite.

It is not much farther downstream to the new bridge for the road into Santa Catarina via San Andrés from San José Lachiguirí. This is near the low point of San Juan territory. At the bridge are several massive *ahuehuete* trees, Montezuma bald cypress (*Taxodium mucronatum*) (fig. 3.41), the species of the famed giant at Santa María del Tule just east of Oaxaca, among the largest and oldest of living things.

With Cándido and Pánfilo into *dán guì* 'Mountain Forest'

Today there is a graded, all-weather dirt road linking San Pedro and San Juan with the district capital and regional market center, Miahuatlán. This road was improved in 1995. Before, the truck route out of San Juan led up through the pines to the ridge crest, then via the mountain meadow at La Nevería, over the shoulder of Cerro de la Sal, to La Cieneguilla and on west to Mexican Highway 175 south of Miahuatlán. Climbing up this "old road" out of sight of San Juan, one passes a cross at a saddle called **Rò-dán-guièdz**, literally, 'the lip [between] forest and town'.

I vividly recall my first hike up the "old road" in July of 1996. At Cándido's invitation we joined his family on a trip to inspect their milpa, which he assured us was just thirty minutes' walk from town (fig. 3.42). It proved rather to require a brisk hour's hike, gaining over 200 meters elevation. "We" were myself, my Mexican colleague Donato, and my two graduate-student assistants Jennifer Sepez and Tom Murphy. The Cruz family included Cándido, his wife, Roselía, four of his five daughters (one was living that year in Pochutla, on the coast), and two granddaughters, Lilia and Griselda, the children of Cándido and Roselía's widowed eldest daughter, Inez. The milpa was in the tender stage called *dòoz*. I tried my

Roselía Hernández, her daughters Justina and Inez, carrying her daughter Griselda on her back, and their animals en route to the milpa, August 17, 1996.

hand at weeding (fig. 3.43), but likely did more harm than good, as it was not at first apparent what was crop and what was weed. Cándido was intensely proud of the milpa and led us and the younger girls in search of edible and medicinal herbs and ornamental flowers at the forest edge and down past the small cascade in the stream at the lower border of their field, tossing out ethnobotanical commentary at a fast clip.

Cándido got a small campfire going in front of his *rancho*, where we sheltered from the periodic showers and ate toasted tortillas with beans. Meanwhile, the two youngest planted their own "milpa" under the shed, of flowers (fig. 3.44).

Cándido's milpa had been recently carved out of the forest; it was near the upper margin of regularly cultivated lands at 2,250 m; beyond and above is forest. The spindly "rock pines" (*Pinus teocote*: needles medium length, three to a bunch; small persistent cones) and massive, spreading

Michoacán pines (*Pinus devoniana*) common along the main road on the approach to town here give way to the primary pine forest species, tall Oaxaca and Douglas pines (*P. pseudostrobus* var. *apulcensis*, *P. douglasiana*). The Oaxaca pine has fine, light green needles (five in a bunch) that droop from the tips of the branches and large cones with distinctive projecting spines on the basal scales. It is the preferred species for harvest by timber companies and is often "shaved" of its lower branches for firewood. The Douglas pine (another five-needle pine with smaller elliptic cones) dominates large tracts of forest between 2,300 and 2,600 m, with some individuals attaining remarkable size, for example, 4 m circumference (1.3 m diameter) at breast height (fig. 3.45). Beneath the Douglas pine canopy one occasionally encounters a stand of the more delicate-leaved *Pinus leiophylla*, characterized by deciduous needle sheaths.

Scattered Mexican white pines (*P. ayacahuite*) appear at 2,300 m and are somewhat more numerous above, to 2,800 m. They are distinctive with their long pendant cones clustered at the branch tips and fine short needles in fives (fig. 3.46). These alone among the local pines are distinguished nomenclaturally from the pine generic, **yàg-guièr**. Most often the white pine is called **yàg-grètâd**, a name derivative of Spanish *grietada* 'creviced, fissured'. However, Hermilo Silva, guardian of authentic Zapotec nomenclature, declares that the proper term is **yàg-là**. The wood of this pine is prized by the people of San Juan for house beams and other construction projects.

As the pines increase, the oaks thin out and shift from one set of species to another. Along the old road past **Rò-dán-guièdz** are examples of all the major Zapotec oaks: **yàg-xìid**, *Quercus castanea* (fig. 3.47); **yàg-zhòg**, *Quercus conzattii* (fig. 3.48); **yàg-pxû**, *Quercus glaucoides* (fig. 3.49); **yàg-rèdz**, *Quercus magnoliifolia* (fig. 3.50); even **yàg-lbìis**, *Quercus acutifolia* (fig. 3.51), in shaded canyons. On closer inspection one may note variations on these basic oak themes: **yàg-xìid-mběe**, *Quercus obtusata* (fig. 3.52), which resembles both *Q. castanea* and *Q. glaucoides*, with leaves more the color and texture of *Q. castanea* but lobed more along the lines of *Q. glaucoides*. At the *barranca* at the turnoff to Cándido's milpa, below the road is a fine example of **yàg-rèdz-bêy**, which, however, is not an oak at all, but the native ash, *Fraxinus uhdei*. It's not clear to me why the ash and the oak should be so closely linked in Zapotec, as local people are well aware that **yàg-rèdz-bêy** has no acorns.

As the pine canopy closes, at about 2,300 m, *yàg-zhòg* is replaced by *yàg-zhòg-diè*, *Quercus crassifolia* (fig. 3.53), with quite similar large, oval, thick, cupped leaves, white felty beneath rather than rusty, as in *Q. conzattii*. Finally, deep in the mountain pines the *yàg-lbìis* give way to a different oak with the same name, *Quercus laurina*, a massive tree of the pine understory, with dark, glossy laurel-like leaves.

We scrambled to the ridge behind Cándido's milpa and met another trail that climbs farther into the pine forest. This trail left town past another cross, one set above the *panteón*. Following this trail, we ascended the ridge past the water tank, to the wet meadow at **Nìs-l-quièdiè** (2,650 m), then beyond to **Quiè-yádòo** 'Church Rock' (fig. 3.54), **Làdz-guièer** 'Crater Flat' at the foot of **Quiè-vèntân** 'Window Cliff', then descended to the west to the town's primary water intake at **Làdz-lgâzh** 'Fir 'Flat' (2,760 m) at the head of a lush mountain canyon (fig. 3.55). As the name suggests, there is at the water intake a fine stand of *Abies guatemalensis*, the Guatemalan balsam fir, *yàg-lgâzh*, mixed with stately Douglas and Mexican white pines and massive laurel-leaved oaks (*Quercus laurina*) and a few *Quercus peduncularis*, *yàg-pxù-yěets* 'yellowish *Quercus glaucoides*'. This humid canyon comes close to being cloud forest, and one may find the occasional *manita-de-león* tree, *yàg-lâs*, *Cheiranthodendron pentadactylon*, with its bizarre red-clawed flower cups (fig. 3.56). These host an array of exotic hummingbirds, even the odd Aztec thrush. A fierce forest fire swept the crests above this canyon in April of 2000, incinerating the dry wood of a corral along the trail in the bottom of the canyon. But the forest in the canyon refused to burn.

On a ridge to the west of **Làdz-lgâzh** one rainy July day, Pánfilo Santiago guided Donato and me in search of mushrooms (*měy*). Our student assistant that summer, Oscar Barrera, videotaped. We collected thirty species in just a few hours and recorded names and uses for twenty distinct varieties. Pánfilo demonstrated his technique for distinguishing edible from poisonous *Boletus* and *Amanita* species, peeling a bit off the cap and noting how the color of the flesh changes.

Above the water tank, beyond **Quiè-vèntân**, is a dangerous tract of forest, not because of the occasional cougar, bobcat, or ocelot one could conceivably encounter trekking the high ridges, but because of an outstanding territorial dispute with San Juan's neighbors to the south. At issue are 14 km^2 of valuable pine timber, as well as the right to hunt and travel without fear of attack through the area. A murderous encounter in 1990—memorialized in a well-known ballad, "Dos Pueblos Conocidos"—keeps the people of San Juan on guard and fearful of climbing to the ridge crest.

The disputed territory extends from **Quiè-cxòbëë**, literally, 'Rough-Textured Rock', descriptive of the distinctive dark volcanic stone at the 3,700-m summit, west to **Quiè-zêd** 'Piedra de Sal'. The intervening area, mostly above 3,000 meters, is said to be clearly marked as pertaining to San Juan on a colonial land-grant map, but San Juan's southern neighbors have more direct access via the ridgeline road and now have de facto control.

These high forests are nearly pure stands of *Pinus hartwegii* (fig. 3.57). Tough, fire-resistant pines clothe the ridges east to Oaxaca's highest summit, Cerro Nube Flan (3,750 m). Periodic crown fires have raged along these ridges (e.g., 1988, 1999), creating a habitat mosaic that supports a rich mountain flora.

The ridge road cuts through the 1988 burn in plain view of the people of San Juan if they should look up from the town plaza. This road then bends south down the far slope of the range to reach several isolated Zapotec communities in the *municipio* of San Juan Ozolotepec. As the descent begins, the road passes Rancho Conejo, a satellite community of San Pedro established by several pioneering families some fifty years ago when there was an active timber mill here. The Rancho Conejo families survive without electricity or piped water, hauling their water from the aptly named Río Frío just below their *ranchería*. They are an independent bunch that subsist on potatoes, a cultivated *Oxalis* tuber (*gù-bè*) imported from the Andes, and a commercial crop of oregano (*Origanum vulgare*), supplemented by hunting the forested wilderness that stretches unbroken eastward for fifty kilometers. This forest tract is likely the best-preserved high montane forest in Mexico and a refuge for a diverse indigenous fauna.

Cerro Nube Flan is literally "Custard Cloud Mountain," a picturesque colonial name that is likely an unintended corruption of Cerro Nuevo Flandres, "New Flanders Mountain." The local Zapotec name for the peak is **Guì-nguliá** 'Caterpillar Mountain'. My colleague Donato Acuca and I "summited" this peak just past my fifty-fourth birthday after a four-hour scramble from the road above Rancho Conejo. An open forest cloaks the highest ridges, as timberline at this latitude is another 1,000 feet higher. To reach the highest point, we waded up a gradual slope through waist-high wildflower gardens, through understory thickets of a giant lupine (*Lupinus jaimehintonianus*), showy red and purple penstemons, and multicolored bush lobelias.

The landscape took me back to my early days hiking the Sierra Nevada wilderness in California, as many of the plants were of familiar Rocky Mountain genera. Even the birds seemed like home: band-tailed pigeons, flickers, hairy and acorn woodpeckers, red crossbills, Steller's jays, ravens, and kestrels among the residents, joined by late-wintering Townsend's, hermit, and Audubon's warblers. Near the summit three white-tailed deer bolted away over the ridge, and a rare zone-tailed hawk cruised to the west.

At the highest point of the long summit ridge we found a small stone altar with remnants of candles and copal incense burned to petition the spirits of these high places (fig. 2.6). We searched the immediate vicinity but never did find the "holy lake" our friends at Rancho Conejo had spoken of. It is likely a marshy spring hidden below the crest and, like most natural water sources in these mountains, the dwelling place of *duendes*, guardian spirits, who care for the spring and may abandon it if offended. Townspeople reported that as the cause of the dessication of one of San Juan's two water sources in the aftermath of a major forest fire in April of 1999.

In the summer of 2001 Pánfilo guided me and a group of botanists from the Washington State Native Plant Society led by Mark Egger, *Castilleja* aficionado, to the nearby summit of **Quiè-cxòbëë**—the highest point in the *municipio* of San Juan and perhaps a match in elevation to Cerro Nube Flan. We had come in search of rare Indian paintbrushes. We were not disappointed, as we were able to locate two species and an additional form endemic to this single high ridge (see the *Castilleja* summary in chapter 7). One was a rare endemic (*Castilleja nivibractea*) known only from this high ridge.

CHAPTER 4

Lè / Names for Plants and Animals

Gbëë Zapotec Plant Names

PLANT NAMES REWARD careful scrutiny, revealing much beneath the surface. Obviously, they *name* plants; that is, they refer to or denote specific categories of plants. These categories range widely in specificity from a particular color variety of some cultivated flower, for example, **guièe-gèrân-nìzhniê** 'red geranium' (*Pelargonium zonale* variety), to highly generalized groups up to and perhaps including the entire plant kingdom (plus some lichens and mosses), for example, **guìzh** in one sense. These categories are open-ended, as there may be an unlimited number of individual plants named by each. Clearly, the human mind must recognize a particular instance of a category by reference to some mental *rule* or pattern-recognition "program." At this point we can say little or nothing about the underlying mental processes that make naming possible, except that they work with extraordinary speed (e.g., 300 milliseconds, as in the "P-300" neural response [Rao et al. 1997]) and efficiency, if with somewhat less than perfect accuracy—misidentifications do occur. Furthermore, children master these recognition routines at an early age with little explicit instruction. In short, learning names and learning to use names to describe the natural world is deeply rooted in our human nature, much as is the larger task of learning to speak and understand a human language.

The names themselves are endlessly fascinating. They may be simple and entirely arbitrary labels, such as "oak" in English or **bàz** in Zapotec, which is prototypically the fern *Phlebodium aureolatum*, noted in San Juan for its value in treating dysentery. Or they may be complex evocative metaphorical terms such as "Jack-in-the-pulpit" (*Arisaema triphyllum*) in English or **rlăal x-pëëd-á** 'drops-its-children', for the air plant (*Bryophyllum pinnatum*), a South African ornamental flower cultivated in San Juan gardens (fig. 4.1). The name describes how this plant reproduces by "dropping" buds that form along the flower stalks.

Most Gbëë Zapotec plant names, however, not only name (and often describe) the plant but also indicate the life-form category or categories to which it belongs, thus making explicit the larger conceptual structure in which each plant category is embedded. This naming convention is, of course, quite like the binomial names of modern biological nomenclature, following Linnaeus; for instance, *Homo sapiens* is the species *sapiens* 'wise' of the genus *Homo* 'human'. Binomial names are also frequent in vernacular English, as in "black oak," "mule deer," and "deer tick." Zapotec examples include **zhób-ngǎs** 'black corn' and **bliòo-nìzhniê** 'red *Tillandsia*', for a species of this mostly epiphytic bromeliad genus. Note that Zapotec nominal stems generally precede their modifiers, as in Latin but contrary to English word order.

Gbëë Zapotec carries this process a step beyond scientific Latin, using more often than not a *trinomial* where we might expect a binomial name, the third and initial element of the name specifying the life-form, such as **guièe-cŏb-guìin** 'chili pepper marigold' (*Tagetes patula*), composed of **guièe** 'flower', **cŏb**, an otherwise meaningless element, which combines as **guièe-cŏb** 'marigold', of which there are several named subcategories or folk specifics, for example, as noted above, 'chili pepper marigold', named metaphorically for the distinctive red bases to the petals of this marigold species.

It should be clear at this point that Zapotec plant names are rarely truly *arbitrary* labels, despite the fact that the arbitrariness of words has been taken as a fundamental characteristic of human language since at least Saussure (1996). While it is true that there is no *necessary* connection between the name itself and the concept or "thing" named—that is, one can only very rarely infer the identity of that which is named from the name itself—plant names nevertheless are often highly informative about the plant named. In other words, most plant names have *descriptive force* (Hunn 1996), which, as Berlin has noted (1992:255–59), may serve to facilitate learning names and remembering relevant properties of the plants named.

I cite below a series of examples to illustrate the variety of Gbëë Zapotec plant names, organized following the lexeme typologies of Conklin (1962) and Berlin (1992), but highlighting certain peculiarities of the local Zapotec nomenclature.

(1) Simple primary names:
   (a) Distinguishing life-forms or other highly abstract categories:
      yâg* 'tree/shrub' (also 'firewood', 'post') (*tone normally shifts to low when prefixed);
      guìzh 'herbaceous plant' (also 'trash');
      blâg 'distinctive large-leaved plants' (also 'leaf');
      ncuàan 'medicinal plant' (also 'poison' or 'edible herb'/'*quelite*');
      dòb 'agaves and similar plants'.
   (b) Distinguishing folk generics:
      gbày literally, 'broom', in particular several species of *Dalea*;
      gù 'potato', *Solanum tuberosum* (also, 'edible tuber');
      nìt 'sugar cane', *Saccharum officinarum*;
      zhïits 'pineapple', *Ananas comosus*;
      rrûd 'rue', *Ruta graveolens* (< Spanish *ruda*).
   Note that these simple names may function solely as plant names or may be *polysemous*, with multiple but allied referents. In such cases even simple terms have descriptive force in that their use to name a plant calls to mind their alternative meanings. For example, *gbày* 'broom' and *gù* 'potato' (which also means 'edible tuber' in general, of which the potato is a prototypical example) indicate how the plants are used.
(2) Complex primary but unproductive names look superficially like binomial names but are constructed quite differently; they name folk generic taxa and are composed of two or more elements, but none of these elements names a superordinate taxon:
      guièts-nîz 'spiny corncob', the prickly poppy, *Argemone mexicana*;
      lùdz-mdzìn 'deer's tongue', ferns of the genus *Elaphoglossum*;
      ngùd-dăm 'ball/fruit of the great horned owl' *Lycianthes* spp.;
      x-càa-mèr-gòl 'tom turkey's testicles' *Erythrina montana, E. sousae*.
   Such names may incorporate elements borrowed from Spanish:
      guìc-chîv goat head, < Spanish *chivo*, the fern *Polystichum speciosissimum* that grows from a root stock resembling a goat's head;
      x-còrôn-rêy king's crown, < Spanish *corona, rey* with the Zapotec possessive prefix *x-*, *Amaryllis belladonna* and/or *Bomarea hirtella*.
   Pseudobinomials are a special case of unproductive complex names that mimic binomials, such as "silverfish" in English, which, unlike "goldfish," is no fish:

dĭp-rên, literally, 'blood grass', the native wild clover, *Trifolium amabile*, which is not a kind of **guìzh-dĭp** 'grass'.

(3) Complex primary, but productive names, that is, true binomials, may name folk-generic or folk-specific taxa. Note the occasional Spanish loan embedded in the name:

blàg-wê *Wigandia urens*, 'leaf' plus an unanalyzable constituent, a folk generic;

bzhăazh-nquĭts 'white moss', Spanish moss *Tillandsia usneoides* (actually, an epiphytic bromeliad, not a true moss), a folk specific;

dób-bè 'Oxalis agave', *Agave potatorum*; oxalis plants may be cooked with the agave heart of this species in the production of mezcal;

guièe-dzîl 'orchid', includes a variety of orchids as subcategories, a folk generic;

guièe-dzĭng 'hummingbird flower', inclusive of a range of plants with red tubular flowers attractive to hummingbirds, a folk generic;

guìzh-dĭp 'grass', including many grasses, rushes, and sedges, a folk generic;

lbè̤-bziàa 'bean vine', *Phaseolus vulgaris*, a folk generic; often abbreviated as **bziàa**, which refers specifically to the seed pods;

ncuàan-dzéb 'fright medicine', inclusive of a range of subcategories, a folk generic or a nontaxonomic grouping based on common utility;

spìnòsî-làs 'small/slender *espinosilla*' *Loeselia glandulosa*, a folk specific;

x-quìzh-bziĕ 'flute's herb', *Phytolacca icosandra*; in this instance the life-form name is possessed, literally, 'its herb of the flute', which remains obscure;

yàg-bziă, literally, 'cherry tree', *Prunus serotina* ssp. *calpuli*, a folk generic;

yàg-x-quĭit-ngùbìdz 'sun's toy tree', *Conzattia multiflora*, a folk generic; the modifier in this case is a complex metaphorical descriptive phrase;

zhwĭs-nguăts 'black *Iresine*', *Iresine* cf. *celosia*, a folk specific.

(4) Complex primary productive names may be trinomial; these may name folk specifics or folk varietals. In a few exceptional cases trinomials appear to name folk generics. This issue is discussed below:

guièe-dâl-mrùux 'June bug dahlia', < Spanish *dalia*, a folk specific inclusive of several wild species of *Dahlia* and *Cosmos*;

guièe-dzîl-nzhíxtò 'hanging orchid', *Epidendrum parkinsonianum*;

guìzh-crùz-ró-guiùu 'cross herb [i.e., 'fern'] at the river', < Spanish *cruz*, a folk specific, the fern *Thelypteris divalis*;

guìzh-guiĕt-nì-mágùs 'female under-foot herb', *Gomphrena diffusa*, a folk varietal, a variety of this species with white bracts; the 'male' *guìzh-guiĕt-nì-mguì* has rose-colored bracts;

ncuàan-dzéb-guièel 'night fright medicine'; the prototype is the fern *Pellaea ovata*;

yàg-bdiò-mànzân 'apple banana tree', < Spanish *manzana*; a local banana (*Musa sapientum*) cultivar;

yàg-pchŭux-yâas 'black tomato bush', *Solanum americanum*.

The 'thorn trees' *yàg-guièts* present a puzzling case. I have chosen to treat this category as a named intermediate, as its several named subcategories strike me as properly understood as folk generics in their own right, despite the trinomial names applied, and the quadrinomials applied to their subheads, which I thus treat as specifics rather than as varietals. *Acacia farnesiana* is the prototype of *yàg-guièts-clâv* 'nail/spike thorn tree' < Spanish *clavo*. This species is also known as *yàg-guièts-clâv-nquĭts* 'white nail thorn tree', to contrast with *yàg-guièts-clâv-nìzhniê* 'red nail thorn tree', which is *Acacia cochliacantha* (fig. 4.2). *Acacia pennatula*, *yàg-guièts-yàaz* 'black thorn tree', is a second generic taxon of this complex. *Mimosa biuncifera* is the prototype of *yàg-guièts-nàad* 'hooking thorn tree', a third 'thorn tree' generic. The prototype may be further specified as *yàg-guièts-nàad-mòrâd* 'purple hooking thorn tree' to contrast with *yàg-guièts-nàad-ngăs* 'black hooking thorn tree', which is *Mimosa galeottii*. Finally, somewhat more loosely allied with the former species is *yàg-guièts-zhìg* 'gourd thorn tree', the ocotillo, *Fouquieria formosa* (Fouquieriaceae).

The custard apple, *Annona cherimolia* (Annonaceae), *yàg-guiél*, presents a similar case. It is a common and favorite fruit tree round about the village. However, three more tropical fruits, known primarily as market products, are named as if they were kinds of *yàg-guiél*, though they do not seem to be perceived as particularly closely allied with the prototypical custard apple. Nor are they closely related from a modern systematic botanical perspective, sharing little more than their status as native cultivated trees that bear edible fruits. These are *yàg-guiél-bêdz* 'wildcat custard apple' *Licania platypus* (Chrysobalanaceae), known in Spanish as *mezon zapote*, a Nahuatl loan; *yàg-guiél-dzìn* 'honey/sweet custard apple' *Manilkara zapota* (Sapotaceae), the *chico zapote*; and *yàg-guiél-zhôn* (*zhôn* is an unanalyzable constituent), *Pouteria sapota* (Sapotaceae), the *mamey*. It is possible that these nomenclatural equations may reflect a much earlier time, before the ancestors of the San Juaneros moved into the mountains.

A striking peculiarity of Gbëë Zapotec plant names is the frequent use of alternate and multiple prefixed life-form names (Hunn 1998). This indicates that local Zapotec life-forms do not contrast perfectly with one another, but rather are organized in partially overlapping "layers" (fig. 4.3). These prefixed life-form names occur in a nearly fixed order: *yâg* 'tree/shrub' or *guìzh* 'herbaceous plant' comes first, unless both are absent; they are mutually exclusive. Then may follow *guièe* 'flower', *blâg* 'leaf, *lbè̖* 'vine', and/or *ncuàan* 'medicinal plant'. For example, *guìzh-guièe-tĭ*, the beggar's tick, *Bidens* spp. (*tĭ* is an unanalyzable constituent). I summarize the frequencies of each combination in tables 4.2 and 4.3. Following are a series of illustrative examples:

> *guìzh-guièe-dzĭng* 'hummingbird flower herb', which may just as often be named *guìzh-dzĭng* or *guièe-dzĭng*, apparently depending on context; that is, if the plant is in full flower, *guièe-dzĭng* 'hummingbird flower' is deemed more appropriate; if without flowers, *guìzh-dzĭng* 'hummingbird herb'. I have recorded many instances of the compound prefix *guìzh-guièe-* but rarely if ever—and that most likely in error—* *guièe-guìzh-*. Thus, *guièe* is subordinate to *guìzh*, though not fully encompassed by the latter, as the example of *yàg-guièe-yăl* shows (see below);
>
> *guìzh-guièe-tînt* 'dye flower herb' or *yàg-guièe-tînt* 'dye flower tree/shrub' < Spanish *tinta*, a folk generic, *Justicia spicigera*, which is somewhat woody, and thus may be considered either *yâg* or *guìzh*;
>
> *yàg-blàg-bîdz* 'dry leaf tree', or abbreviated as *blàg-bîdz* 'dry leaf', the *jarilla*, *Dodonaea viscosa*;

yàg-guièe-rôs 'rose flower tree' < Spanish *rosa*, the several varieties of cultivated roses, *Rosa* spp., or simply *guièe-rôs* if the flower rather than the plant itself is the focus;

yàg-guièe-yăl 'frangipani flower tree' *Plumeria rubra* f. *acutifolia*, a folk generic; the flower itself is *guièe-yăl*; *yăl* is an unanalyzable constituent; two color varieties are named, *yàg-guièe-yăl-nquĭts* 'white frangipani tree' and *yàg-guièe-yăl-nguĕts* 'yellow frangipani tree'; these are folk specifics; *yàg-guièe-yăl-mâch* 'male frangipani tree', *Senecio praecox*, is a folk generic named metaphorically for a superficial resemblance to *Plumeria*.

Finally, plants may be referred to using the prefix *xín-* 'relative/kin of' for species that resemble a well-known prototype but are not sufficiently similar to be treated as an acceptable example of the named category. For example, *yàg-bèch-mbăr* 'sour knot tree' (or simply *bèch-mbăr* 'sour knot'), may refer to *Rhus oaxacana*, *R. pachyrrhachis*, or *R.* cf. *terebinthifolia*. However, *Rhus standleyi* is set apart as *xín-bèch-mbăr* 'sumac's kin'.

Comparable examples have been widely reported. In the Tzeltal Maya case, peripheral taxa are noted as *kol pahaluk sok X* 'almost the same as X' (Berlin, Breedlove, and Raven 1974). In Sahaptin, the suffix *X-wáakut* 'resembles X' plays this role (Hunn and French 1984). In Zapotec the kinship metaphor is explicit, an interesting convergence upon the Darwinian idea that biological taxonomies should represent "family trees." Berlin refers to the "basic" and "extended ranges" of categories, with such examples as these relegated to the extended range (Berlin, Breedlove, and Raven 1974:57; Berlin 1992:41); I have referred to the same situation in terms of taxonomic "core" and "periphery" (Hunn 1976).

I have chosen to treat terms with the kinship prefix *xín-* as descriptive phrases rather than as true plant names, although it is conceivable that a term of this sort might through repeated use come to be a habitual label and thus become a true name.

The Impact of Spanish

Zapotec languages are noted for freely incorporating foreign elements, particularly from Spanish, the language of colonial and church administration since 1520. Whether Zapotec is more open to borrowings than other languages is debatable, as the greater part of contemporary English vocabulary, for example, is borrowed from or otherwise derivative of many foreign language sources, mostly French (Fromkin and Rodman 1988:308–12). Yet English remains English at the core (cf. Sapir 1921:206). Mexicano, aka Nahuatl, the language of the Aztecs and their descendants in central Mexico, may now be spoken as a thorough blend of Nahuatl and Spanish lexical, grammatical, and phonological elements, the balance between the two source languages largely a function of the pragmatics of relative social status of speaker and audience (Hill and Hill 1986). San Juan Zapotec plant names freely incorporate Spanish elements (as well as a few from Nahuatl, filtered through local Spanish), often in complex and intriguing ways.

The simplest cases involve mostly introduced plants named by borrowing the local Spanish name for that plant. In several cases Spanish loans are applied to native plants, for reasons as yet unclear. Such borrowed names are typically modified phonetically to correspond to the phonological conventions of San Juan Zapotec. How this is accomplished depends on how the Spanish source name is pronounced, that is, whether the accent falls on the penultimate syllable, as is most often the case, or falls on the last syllable or some syllable before the penultimate. In the normal case, the Spanish name is truncated, the final, unstressed syllable deleted, and the vowel of the stressed syllable given a falling tone in Zapotec:

bêrr < Spanish *berro* 'watercress' (*Rorippa nasturtium-aquaticum*), a native species;
ptiôn < Spanish *pitiona* 'verbena' (*Verbena officinalis*);
rrûd < Spanish *ruda* 'rue' (*Ruta graveolens*);
àlbâc < Spanish *albahaca* 'sweet basil' (*Ocimum basilicum*);
bòrrâj < Spanish *borraja* 'borage' (*Borago officinalis*);
lùsêm < Spanish *alusema* (*Salvia lavanduloides, S. muscuroides*), native species;
gòrdòlôb < Spanish *gordolobo*, literally, 'fat wolf' (*Gnaphalium* spp.), a native species;
spìnòsî < Spanish *espinosilla*, literally 'little spine' (*Loeselia mexicana, L. glandulosa*), native species;
sàntàmàrî < Spanish *Santa María* 'feverfew' (*Tanacetum parthenium*).

Many such borrowed names incorporate a prefixed Zapotec life-form name, in a pattern characteristic of San Juan Mixtepec plant names:

blàg-pâsm < Spanish *pasmo*, a local disease term (*Cissus sicyoides*);
guièe-dâl < Spanish *dalia* 'dahlia' (*Dahlia* spp. and *Cosmos* spp.), native species;
guièe-mànzànî < Spanish *manzanilla* 'chamomile' (*Matricaria recutita*);
guìt-tàliân < Spanish *Italiano* 'zucchini' (*Cucurbita pepo* ssp. *pepo*);
guìzh-cânzr < Spanish *cáncer* 'cancer', but with a different local meaning (*Tournefortia* spp., *Cordia salvadorensis*);
yàg-drâz < Spanish *durazno* 'peach' (*Prunus persica*);
yàg-mànzân < Spanish *manzana* 'apple' (*Malus domestica*).

In a few cases, the Zapotec loan is truncated further. These may represent older, more established borrowings:

guièe-pûnt < Spanish *floripondio* 'tree datura' (*Brugmansia* x *candida*);
guièe-pânt < Spanish *agapanta* 'lily-of-the-Nile' (*Agapanthus africanus*);
yàg-brètâyn < Spanish *Gran Bretaña* 'tree tobacco' (*Nicotiana glauca*).

If the Spanish name is otherwise accented, the accented vowel again takes a falling tone, but the Zapotec loan may retain all the syllables of the original:

ârnìcà < *árnica* 'arnica', but with a distinct local meaning (*Bocconia arborescens*), a native species;
còrdèbân < Spanish *cordeván* (*Euphorbia rossiana*, *Pedilanthus* cf. *tomentellus*), native species;
sièmprvîv < Spanish *siempre viva* 'resurrection plant' (*Selaginella lepidophylla*, *S. pallescens* and/or *Sedum praeltum*);
yàg-laùrêl < Spanish *laurel* 'laurel' (*Litsea glaucescens*), a native species;
yàg-nîspèrò < Spanish *níspero* 'loquat' (*Eriobotrya japonica*).

A few Spanish loans are also commonly used as modifiers in plant names, notably such color terms as *morado* 'purple', *rosado* or *de rosa* 'pink', and *azul* 'blue'. San Juan Zapotec lacks basic color terms (cf. Berlin and Kay 1969) for these colors, though the indigenous term *nìzhniê* 'red' may be extended to cover purples, and *nguiâ* 'blue/green' may cover blues:

> *guièe-dâl-mòrâd*, for purple-flowered dahlias;
> *guièe-dâl-ròsâd*, for pink-flowered dahlias;
> *guièe-pûnt-dèrôs*, the rose-flowered tree datura (*Brugmansia* cf. *versicolor*);
> *guièe-àzûl*, literally, 'blue flower' (*Salvia cacaliaefolia*, *S. vitifolia*);
> *ncuàan-dzéb-còrâl* < Spanish *coral*, alluding to the color, 'scarlet pimpernel' (*Anagallis arvensis*, in particular, the variety *arvensis* with salmon-colored petals).

The Spanish term *Castellano* 'Castillian' is an old colonial borrowing, which as a modifier (*-xtîl*) may indicate an introduced relative of a well-known native species, often cultivated, or may be used metaphorically to single out the more "showy" variety of a species:

> *bziàa-xtîl* 'fava beans', literally, 'Castillian bean' (*Vicia faba*);
> *dòb-xtîl* 'aloe vera', literally, 'Castillian agave' (*Aloe barbadensis*);
> *guièe-bgùs-xtîl*, literally, 'Castillian zinnia' (*Zinnia* cf. *elegans*), cultivar derived from a native species, *Z. peruviana* (*guièe-bgùs*), which grows wild;
> *guìzbè̱-xtîl*, literally, 'Castillian amaranth' (*Amaranthus hibridus*, a variety with patterned leaves);
> *zhób-xtîl* 'wheat', literally, 'Castillian corn' (*Triticum aestivum*).

In a few cases a Spanish loan has been "Zapotecized" by prefixing the normal San Juan Zapotec possessive prefix *x-*:

> *x-côl-bǐch* < Spanish *cola* 'tail' and *biche* 'blue-eyed', literally, 'cat's tail' (*Acalypha* sp.);
> *x-côl-càbây* < Spanish *cola* 'tail' and *caballo* 'horse', literally, 'horse's tail' (*Equisetum myriochaetum*).

As noted, Spanish loans are frequently used to name introduced species but are also used to describe color varieties for which basic Zapotec color terms are lacking. Cases in which introduced species have been given indigenous Zapotec names, however, are quite unusual. Most appear to be early colonial borrowings. The following are two such cases:

lcházh 'garlic', cf. *ajo* (*Allium sativum*);

nlěch 'onion', cf. *cebolla* (*Allium cepa*); note that a native species of the same family, *Nothoscordum striatum*, is called ***nlěch-bèz***, literally, 'fox onion'; other similar but less closely related species (*Zygadenus mexicanus* of the Melanthiaceae and the orchids *Mesadenus polyanthus* and *Platanthera* cf. *brevifolia*) are considered to be ***guìzh-nlěch*** 'onion herb'. (This is an interesting instance where the life-form prefix is used to name a contrasting folk generic category.)

The latter case is reminiscent of a historical pattern noted by Berlin (1970) for Tzeltal Mayan, in which an introduced plant or animal gradually displaces a related native species, usurping its name. Thus, native deer come to be called "forest sheep," while sheep take the name originally applied to deer. However, we lack historical evidence to support this hypothesis in this case.

To sum up, of 4,017 instances of 543 distinct terminological elements employed in 1,693 names (including synonyms), just 663 (16.5 percent) were derived from Spanish. By contrast, 211 of the 543 terminological elements were of Spanish origin (38.9 percent). Clearly, many of the elements of Spanish origin are used only occasionally. The San Juan plant nomenclature remains essential Zapotec.

Counting Names, Counting Taxa

Ethnobiology aspires, among other things, to be a comparative science. To achieve this goal demands that we count and measure the conceptual elements within our domain (cf. Hunn 1975b) so that we may address questions such as: "How does local Zapotec knowledge of plants compare with that of a professional botanist?" "Are the taxonomies of farming peoples 'deeper' than those of hunter-gatherers?" "Are polytypic taxa largely limited to plants of high cultural salience?" "If we know the size of a plant, can we predict for it the degree of taxonomic refinement in Zapotec?" "At what age do children master 90 percent of the adult ethnobotanical vocabulary?" "Which group exhibits the more refined appreciation of their local flora, the Zapotec of San Juan or the Tzeltal Maya of Tenejapa?"

Such comparative questions require first that we inventory systematically the plants and/or animals that occur within the region by reference to their "scientific" or Latin names. These species are "available" to be recognized. This inventory of scientific taxa is relatively straightforward, at least it would be if a descriptive flora existed for the locality studied. However, no such flora exists for Oaxaca, though recent monographs cover the ferns (Mickel and Beitel 1988) and the pines (Farjon and Styles 1997), and species lists are available for some nearby regions (e.g., Acosta et al. 2003).

To test the "degree of refinement" of a local ethnoflora, we need to know not only which plants are recognized, named, and/or used, but also those plants which are not recognized, whether ignored, overlooked, or simply "lumped" with better-known species. For example, there are at least ten species of pine trees (*Pinus* spp.) native to the *municipio*, but only two major types of pines are named, with possibly two or three less well-defined subtypes sometimes noted (table 4.4). A fair assessment of the ethnobotanical "state of the art" should document the fact that the modern scientific classification surpasses the local Zapotec in degree of pine diversity recognized. By contrast, the 13 local species of oaks (*Quercus* spp.) are more carefully differentiated, the local Zapotec classification of oaks closely approximating that of modern systematic botany (table 4.5). To quantify this contrast I have elsewhere (Hunn 1999a) devised a statistic I call the Scientific Species Recognition Ratio (SSRR), which is "simply the number of basic level folk taxa used to classify the species of the sampling unit [e.g., a genus or family of plants or animals] divided by the number of scientific species in that sampling unit [recorded in the local area]" (pg. 53). Such comparisons as this raise new questions, such as why oaks should be more salient than pines for this Zapotec community.

Determining the correct Latin name for the more than 2,200 plant specimens representing over 1,000 species so far identified in San Juan has been a challenge, lacking a comprehensive flora of Oaxaca. For most plant families we must look for the closest approximation in neighboring regional floras, such as the *Flora Novo-Galiciana* (McVaugh 1983–), now approximately 50 percent complete in its coverage of an extensive region to the northwest of Oaxaca that exhibits a similar range of elevations and habitats. Floras for the Federal District (e.g., Sánchez Sánchez 1968), for the state of Veracruz, and for Guatemala (Standley 1946), and the initial volumes of the *Flora Mesoamericana* may also be consulted. Staff at the National Herbarium (MEXU) at the Universidad Nacional Autónoma de México have reviewed most of my San Juan specimens but have not been able to name them all at the species level. Doubts remain as to the precise identity of particular plants, and I suspect that a number of species "new to science" (that is, new to modern science) remain to be identified. One possible new species of orchid is being reviewed (Salazar and Hunn n.d.). The recognition and formal naming of new species is a task for regional specialists in particular genera, and such specialists are scattered around the globe.

Adding to the uncertainties here is the fact that Latin names are anything but stable, despite the Linnaean dream of a common and perfectly consistent global scientific nomenclature for living things. Scientific names are subject to frequent revision as our knowledge of the evolutionary processes that define relationships within and among taxa itself evolves. For example, three of the ten San Juan pine species have been renamed and/or taxonomically reassigned since the previous "expert" opinion was published (Perry 1991; cf. Farjon and Styles 1997). Nevertheless, with the aid of the Internet and a careful review by Mexican plant specialists, it has been possible to achieve an adequate if not perfect level of classificatory detail for San Juan plants from the modern scientific perspective. This allows the exploration of all manner of interesting leads with regard to each plant, such as their wider distributions, their provenience if not native, their known pharmacological and nutritional qualities, and records of their varied uses throughout their range.

The next step is to determine where each such plant fits within the local Zapotec classificatory system. Note that I assume that such a *system* exists and that the folk system of plant classification and nomenclature is sufficiently like that of modern science for fruitful comparison. This is not an idle assumption, but one based on an extensive series of carefully documented ethnographic studies, mostly elaborated since 1950 (e.g., Conklin 1954; Berlin, Breedlove, and Raven 1974; Hays 1974; Turner 1974; Sillitoe 1983; Felger and Moser 1985; Kesby 1986; Taylor 1987; Waddy 1988; Martin 1996; Hunn 1990; Breedlove and Laughlin 2000).

Names, Taxa, and Taxonomies

Every human language employs a vocabulary of discrete plant names. All such names—whether simple or complex—are unitary *lexemes,* their meanings not predictable from the meanings of the parts of which they are composed (cf. Conklin 1962). Thus, each requires a separate entry in the mental dictionary, and each is defined by reference to the set of biological organisms to which it refers.

The categories, or concepts, that each name denotes are *taxa* (singular, *taxon*); their organization vis-à-vis one another is a *taxonomy.* As a general rule, each individual organism recognized will be *identified* as a member of one and only one contrasting taxon, though an organism may be classified at various taxonomic levels simultaneously. Thus, a "white pine" is not a "jack pine" but is a "pine," and thus also a "tree" and a member of the "plant" kingdom. In Zapotec, an individual of the pine species *P. teocote* is simultaneously *yàg-guièr-quiè* 'rock pine', *yàg-guièr* 'pine', and *yâg* 'tree/shrub'. It is also clearly recognized as a plant rather than an animal, though no term exists for the plant kingdom per se (which is covert). Yet no tree is simultaneously a pine and a fir, no *yâg* is both *yàg-guièr* (*Pinus* spp.) and *yàg-lgâzh* (*Abies guatemalensis*).

Exceptions to this rule most often involve crosscutting higher-level categories, which may be defined with respect to incompatible properties, as, for example, a dandelion may at times be considered a "weed," at times a "wildflower," and at other times an "herb," depending on the cultural context while ignoring the affinities of "over-all morphology" that seem of primary relevance for defining the overall structure of the folk biological classification (see Berlin 1992:9 for an extended discussion).

Plant and animal names in every human language may be *translated* into scientific Latin by reference to their denotata. We leave aside for now the subtle contrasts of connotation between the meanings of a name such as "dog," for example, which denotes for everyone *Canis familiaris* but which may call to mind variously a culinary delicacy, a beloved family member, or a dangerous beast. This cross-linguistic denotative equivalence characteristic of the large majority of plant and animal names is neither obviously necessary nor an artifact of the ethnographer's craft. Rather, it is a consequence of the fact that the evolutionary process tends strongly to produce at any particular historical moment at a particular place a finite set of discrete species populations, each of which reproduces after its own kind from generation to generation, whether by sexual or asexual means. These localized (in time and space) "species" are recognized in human perception with great precision, despite the highly abstract nature of the perceptual processes responsible for this taken-for-granted—but in truth amazing—intellectual achievement. How is it that we humans can learn to distinguish a "dog" from a "coyote" or a "wolf," a "hemlock" from a "spruce" or a "fir," or one's own mother from any other woman glimpsed passing in a crowd? This is an issue for the psychology of perception, but it is a fact that is foundational for ethnobiological comparison.

Determining what is and what is not a name—specifically, a plant or animal name—is less than straightforward, as we have already demonstrated. The difficulty of making such determinations is a consequence of two things primarily. First, each language employs distinctive morphosemantic processes of word formation that give to names peculiarities characteristic of each human language. Second, words and phrases may be employed in different contexts, in the one as a name, in the other as a descriptive phrase, a semantically transparent, fully productive construction, generated for the moment, not held in memory. A well-worn English example is "bluebird," which may *describe* any bird that is blue (in which case it is written as two words and takes primary stress on "bird") or which may *name* a particular species of bird (in which case it is written as one word and takes primary stress on "blue"), individuals of which may in fact be hardly "blue" at all (e.g., females).

I continually struggle with this issue with my Zapotec data. For example, are such expressions as **guièe nquĭts** 'white flower', **guièe nguĕts** 'yellow flower', and **guièe mòrâd** 'purple flower' names, and thus countable, or productive linguistic constructions made up on the spot? These expressions may be used in a dismissive way as nonce forms invented to satisfy the ethnobiologist's incessant query, **Zhă lĕ guìzh ríi?** "What is the name of this plant?" At other times, however, the identical term (not even distinguished by stress contour as in English) clearly calls to mind much more than the bare bones the term itself suggests. Thus, **guièe-mòrâd** may refer to a quite specific plant, for example, *Pinaropappus roseus*, a weedy dandelion relative, known for its milky sap and applied medicinally to treat pimples, diaper rash, or chapped skin. Consultants may describe very specific details of the form, habitat, or use of the plant. In such cases I feel justified in treating the term as a valid name and so indicate by the use of a hyphen to connect the constituent elements of the name. However, it is not always possible to be certain that a particular usage is or is not a valid name. Often a particular term will be offered as a name by one person only to be rejected as an invention by another. In such cases one must judge the reliability of one's consultants as well as the degree of consensus on a particular usage within the community.

A name is not really a name (i.e., not countable as such) if it is idiosyncratic, if it is understood only by a single inventive speaker. This is the "cultural criterion." Understandings must be *shared* to be cultural, at least to some minimal extent, while recognizing that it will rarely be the case that everyone within a community will agree perfectly on anything. I have done my best here to include as valid plant and animal names and named taxa only those well attested for San Juan Gbëë by the standards discussed above.

Applying these standards, I recognize here 844 San Juan Zapotec plant taxa (table 4.1) and 461 of animals (table 4.7).

A Sketch of Berlin's Taxonomic Framework

The standard analytic framework for ethnobiological classification presumes that living things are classified into floral and faunal domains ("kingdoms"), each of which consists of a hierarchical taxonomic structure. (I analyze the applicability of Berlin's theoretical framework to the San Juan Zapotec data in more detail in part 2 online at www.uapress.arizona.edu/Books/bid1957.htm.) Berlin (1992) defines three to five "universal taxonomic ranks" within each of these domains. The folk generic rank is the heart of each domain, including in the neighborhood of 500 *folk generic taxa*, which represent the most perceptually salient "natural" kinds within the experience of the local community. Moving down through the hierarchy, one may find that some folk generic taxa are subdivided by *specific*, and perhaps yet further subdivided by *varietal*, taxa; moving upward one finds that the majority of folk generic taxa are subsumed by a few *life-forms*, and, in some instances, cluster to form *intermediate* taxa. The life-forms then are included in a "kingdom," which defines the "unique beginner" of the "taxonomic tree."

However, actual folk taxonomies exhibit a number of "irregularities" that require some theoretical refinements of this basic scheme. For example, it has long been recognized that some folk generics will be "unaffiliated" with any life-form. These generics are directly included in the "unique beginner," the kingdom plant or animal. This is attributed to either the perceptual aberrancy of the unaffiliated taxon or some extraordinary cultural significance of the taxon, such as might be associated with domestication (Berlin 1992). Motivated by peculiarities of a Zapotec ethnobiological classification system, I have suggested that we need to recognize that folk specific and even varietal taxa may be unaffiliated at one or more superordinate ranks (e.g., a folk specific that is directly included in a life-form or a varietal directly included in a folk genus or life-form) (Hunn 1998). These rents in the taxonomic fabric, I suggest, indicate that a formal taxonomic structure does not adequately capture the psychological reality of folk biological classification (cf. Hunn 1977, 1982).

Měy: Where Do Fungi Fit?

My analysis of the San Juan Gbëë classification of fungi motivates a further extension of unaffiliated status to life-forms with respect to the kingdom rank. The Gbëë Zapotec category *měy* 'mushroom' could be analyzed as either an exceptionally large, heterogeneous folk generic taxon or as a small life-form. Each "kind of" mushroom—approximately twenty are widely recognized—is named binomially (e.g., *měy-guìin* 'chili mushroom', *měy-yâg* 'wood mushroom'), which might argue in favor of these naming folk specifics within a single generic taxon. However, as I have demonstrated elsewhere (1998), Zapotec routinely incorporates the life-form name into the names of folk generic plant taxa, for example, *yàg-guièr* 'pine tree', *guièe-bgùs* 'spindle flower', the zinnia. Thus, there is no compelling reason to treat *měy* as other than a life-form on a par with *yâg* 'tree/shrub' and *guièe* 'flower'.

Given that the mushroom life-form exhibits a nomenclatural pattern common in the plant domain, and unlike that of the animal domain, why not simply treat *měy* as a plant life-form? The problem is that *měy* begins with *m-*, a reduced variant of *mâ* 'animal', a feature shared with a large majority of all animal names, such as *mguìn* 'bird', *mèel* 'snake', *mèedz* 'wild cats and allies', and *mrè* 'ant'. This interpretation of the initial *m-* of *měy* is further supported by the fact that a negative response to the query, "Are there mushrooms here?" (i.e., when there are none) is *"guiènd mâ"* 'there are none [animate]'. This contrasts with the appropriate response to the parallel questions: "Are there flowers here?" *"guiènd-á"* "There are none [inanimate]"; "Are there women here?" *"guiènd mé"* 'There are none [persons].'' One consultant responded to my direct question as to whether mushrooms were plants or animals that they were neither.

Mushrooms are "neither fish nor fowl," that is, they are unaffiliated with either the plant or the animal kingdom, though certainly considered to be living things: they have "life" (*guièl-mbán*) and some claim also that they "have a heart" (*rquiànié zdòo*) as do many plants, such as corn. In light of all this, I believe it makes sense to treat *měy* as an unaffiliated life-form within a covert "superkingdom" of living things.

Gbëë Zapotec Fungi

Donato Acuca and I made 124 collections of fungi in San Juan during 1996 and 1998. Most of these were determined by M. en C. Ricardo Valenzuela of La Escuela Nacional de Ciencias Biológicas del Instituto Politécnico Nacional, Mexico, D.F. These collections represented at least 49 species of 40 genera in 25 families. In August 2005 M. en C. Marco Antonio Vásquez Dávila of the Instituto Tecnológico de Valle de Oaxaca joined me on a tour of the pine forests above San Juan at 2,200 to 2,450 m elevation. We were guided by Maximiliano Sánchez and Lorenzo Mendoza of the San Juan Comisariado de Bienes Comunales. We collected an additional 70-odd specimens, which were provisionally identified by Marco by reference to an illustrated guide (Díaz Barriga 1992). Photographs of these and previous collections were reviewed in March 2007 by M. en C. Hugo León Avendaño and Biol. Alfonso Aurelio. We await positive determinations. All told to date we have recorded at least 74 species of 53 genera of 32 fungi families within the *municipio*. Consult table 4.17 and section F in part 2 for details and images. All our specimens are deposited in the ethnomicological collection at the Instituto Tecnológico de Valle de Oaxaca. Though our collections fall far short of a comprehensive local mycological survey, we now have examples of most of the named categories, including all those used as food or medicine. These uses are discussed in detail in chapter 6.

It is noteworthy that local consultants distinguish edible and poisonous varieties of **měy-lân**, *Agaricus* spp., by noting the color of the gills, blackish for the edible forms, pink for the poisonous ones. We cannot state for certain yet which species of this genus are eaten and which avoided, but as mushroom poisoning is said to be rare in the village, it seems reasonable to assume that they are conservative and accurate in their judgments. Local consultants also distinguish edible and poisonous species of the genus *Boletus*, calling the edible and choice *Boletus edulis* 'bread mushroom' and the others 'poison mushroom'. They may be distinguished by examining the color of the flesh beneath the skin of the cap. Likewise, they eat *Amanita caesarea* (**měy-yùp**), while avoiding the deadly *A. virosa* and the dangerously hallucinogenic *A. muscaria*.

One species, **měy-xquìdiè** 'powder mushroom', is used medicinally. The powdery spores are applied to wounds. The prototype of this category is the common puffball, *Lycoperdon perlatum*. However, several species of *Lycoperdon* and at least one earth star (*Astraeus hygromatricus*) are also employed in this fashion. One species is said to produce a blue dye. This is **měy-tînt** 'ink mushroom', which may be a species of the Hygrophoraceae.

Other species are well known despite being of no particular use or notoriety. These include **měy-nrùdz** 'slimy mushroom', a *Suillus* species, **měy-x-quiě-bûrr** 'donkey's-dung mushroom', noted for its substrate; and **měy-yàg** 'wood mushroom', a broad category of mushrooms that grow on dry wood. The majority of the most widely recognized folk taxa correspond to a single scientific species or to a small number of scientific species of a single genus. Exceptions to this generalization are **měy-xquìdiè** and **měy-yàg**, both of which include a number of species of several genera or families, though in both cases, the Western scientific taxa so named constitute "natural," that is, phylogenetic, groupings.

There remains a large "residual" of small and/or insignificant species that are not consistently distinguished but which may be named by reference to some superficial characteristic. For example, mushrooms may be named for a prominent color, or with respect to the size, shape, or surface texture of the mushroom, for example, **měy-làs** 'slender mushroom', **měy-nì-nôol** 'long-footed mushroom', and **měy-zhŭil** 'cotton mushroom'. Finally, there are a number of rather loosely defined categories named for substrates or hosts. Some have already been mentioned above among the more widely recognized types, but the following seem to have some currency in the local vocabulary also: *měy-dùr* 'pine needle mushroom', *měy-yâg-biâap* 'rotten wood mushroom', and *měy-yàg-lbìis* 'laurel oak mushroom'. The legitimacy of many of these expressions as true names remains unclear.

Finally, Marco spotted a cluster of a diminutive "bird's-nest fungus" (*Cyathus* aff. *striatus*), which our guides called *x-chòb-guièt-lí* 'Virgin Mary's tortilla basket'; the spore capsules look like tiny bird's eggs in a cup; raindrops rupture these capsules, dispersing the spores; it is said in San Juan that if there are just a few such "eggs," there will be little rain. This is the single instance of a fungus named without the life-form prefix.

Mâ 'Animal'

Naming Animals

It doesn't seem right to ignore the "other half" of the ethnobiological equation, the zoological domain, in this natural history. The emphasis here on plants is not arbitrary but reflects the predominant role that plants play not only in San Juan Gbëë economic life but also in their conceptual universe. Nevertheless, animals are by no means ignored or dismissed.

The Zapotec languages reflect a deep appreciation for the *animate* in nature. We see this quite clearly in the semantics of animal names, which are constructed quite differently than are those for plants. While plant nomenclature is built upon a visible skeleton of life-forms that provide a morphological foundation for most such names, animal names are constructed, by and large, on a common foundation of animacy, that is, by prefixing *m-*, *měe-*, and *ngu-*, or constructing polynomials on *má-* 'animal' with modifiers.

The prefixes *m-* and *měe-* are certainly contractions or transformations of *mâ* 'animal' but are almost always tightly bound to a stem that has no clear meaning in its own right, suggesting substantial antiquity for such names. In fact, the variant phonological forms of the introductory animate element *m-* are definitive of deep historic divisions within the Zapotec language family. It is represented as unvoiced *p-* in valley and northern Sierran dialects and by a transitional *mb-* in western dialects of the Sierra Sur Zapotec branch, which is reduced to *m-* in the Cisyautepecano group, to which San Juan Gbëë Zapotec belongs, according to Smith Stark's recent analysis (2001). Likewise, the prefix **ngu-**, which serves generally to derive agentive nouns from verbal roots, takes the cognate form **co-** elsewhere in the Zapotec family. Thus, the Zapotec god of thunder, Cocijo, is *ngùzì* in San Juan. Animal names that build upon the syllabic head term *mâ* are limited to what we might call "bugs," that is, small invertebrate animals, and are often of obviously recent coinage, if not invented on the spot. The rather few animal names that fail to incorporate these explicit animate markers are either onomatopoetic or loans from Spanish.

It must be noted that these prefixed elements are not unique to animal names—though 65 percent of all non-Spanish-derived animal names in Reeck's dictionary start with "*m*," only 36 percent of all non-Spanish-derived entries in that dictionary that start with "*m*" are animal names (Hunn 1998:45). However, the exceptions "prove the rule" and are of particular interest. I have already noted the apparent anomaly of *měy* 'mushroom'; a second example is *mgàg* 'acorn'. Both share the prefixed *m-* with most animal names. That these instances are not simply coincidental occurrences of an initial *m-* is demonstrated by the response to the question "Is there an X on the table?" when in fact there is not. The answer in these two cases is identical to the answer in the case of any animal, "***Guiènd mâ*** 'There is none [animate]', as opposed to "***Guiènd-á***" 'There is none [unmarked]', which is what we would expect to hear with reference to a plant or an inanimate object.

As we have noted, mushrooms are conceptually ambivalent for local Zapotec speakers, being considered neither plant nor animal, though biochemically speaking they are more closely allied with animals than plants. Acorns, as well as seeds in general, ***mîdz***, are granted a measure of animacy by virtue of the power of generation within them. It may be said that they "have heart" (***ràp zdòo***). Likewise, such natural "forces" as wind (***mě***), sun (***ngùbìdz***), and moon (***měë***) are "animate," if not also "persons." The agentive prefix ***ngu-*** is also more generally applicable, often marking names for deities or other natural forces or categories of persons characterized by particular activities or abilities.

Perhaps related to these semantic issues is the response I received to a questionnaire I presented to twenty-three San Juaneros that was designed to explore local concepts in somewhat more depth. In particular, the responses to such questions as these were instructive:

1. Do the following have 'heart' (*zdòo*) and/or 'life' (*guièlmbán*): snake (*mèel*), grasshopper (*nguzhánch*), maize (*guiêl / dòoz / zhŏb*), bread mushroom (*mĕy-guièt-xtîl*), organ-pipe cactus (*yàg-bdzì*), avocado tree (*yàg-ngùd-guièx*), marigold (*guièe-cŏb*), the moon (*mĕë*), wind (*mê*), rain (*nìsquiê*), rock (*quiè*)?
2. Are the following 'intelligent' (*guièlbìinî*) and which are the more intelligent: dog (*mècw*), child (*mèëd-wĭn*), sheep (*mècw-xĭil*), goat (*chîv*), mouse (*mzîn*), ox (*ngŏn nòvî*), turkey (*mèr*), frog (*mbîich*), owl (*dăm*)?
3. Should people capture white-winged doves and keep them in cages? Why or why not?
4. Are there male (*mguì*) and female (*mágùs*) of the following: lizard (*ngurăgw*), ant (*mrè*), mushroom (*mĕy*), agave (*dòb*), willow tree (*yàg-zhguiès*)?

Not surprisingly, interviewees were nearly unanimous in attributing "life" to the plant and animal examples cited. However, they were nearly as certain that "moon," "sun," "wind," and "rain" were alive (76 percent). Criteria cited to justify these judgments emphasized "movement," "light," and the "life-giving" powers of these natural elements. Movement was considered characteristic of animals, growth from seeds characteristic of plants. Nevertheless, 35 percent considered even "rock" to have "life" for its power to endure. Also salient for distinguishing animals from plants was sexual reproduction. Respondents were nearly unanimous in affirming that there were "male" and "female" lizards and ants, but with comparable unanimity rejected the notion that mushrooms, agaves, and willow trees might be "male" and "female." Clearly, the sexual life of plants—the dioecious willow, for example—is not understood in the local Zapotec ethnobiology as it is in modern botany.

Responses to the "heart" question were more variable, perhaps because the term *zdòo* may mean 'stomach' or 'liver' as well as 'heart'. Only 47 percent of respondents judged that snakes and grasshoppers possessed "heart." While 76 percent affirmed that "bread mushrooms" were alive, just 35 percent would grant that they possessed "heart." "Mushrooms" are ambiguous with respect to the most salient qualities of animals and plants, lacking seeds and the capacity to move, but nevertheless capable of growth. However, interviewees were unanimous in granting "heart" to maize, and substantial majorities allowed that organ-pipe cacti (68 percent) and avocado trees (73 percent) have "heart"—maize and the avocado because of their seeds that generate new life, the cacti because of the particularly durable "heart wood" inside their columnar trunks. González's Zapotec consultants in Talea de Castro affirmed similar beliefs about maize, that it had a "soul," one translation of the Rincón Zapotec term cognate with the San Juan term for "heart" (2001:104).

A tree with "useless," soft wood is said to have no "heart." This may be best understood as metaphor, though it may be related to the complex ontology developed by Aztec savants, in which the life essence of a person is embodied in three centers, or "souls," one in the heart, another in the head, and a third in the liver (Ortiz de Montellano 1990). However, I have no evidence that a clearly articulated philosophical system comparable to that of the Aztec elites has been elaborated in San Juan, though certain implicit common elements of belief may underlie the nomenclatural practices I have described.

I also inquired as to the "intelligence" of various animals. Substantial majorities attributed "intelligence" to all the animals named, and those who ranked animals in terms of their intelligence were generally in agreement of the following partial ordering: first, a child (of three to five years of age); second, a monkey; third, a dog; followed by goats, sheep, oxen, and mice, which were considered roughly equivalent, followed by turkeys and frogs. The Great Horned Owl was granted exceptional intelligence by several interviewees on the basis of its power to foresee future events. The relative "intelligence" of goats and sheep was a point of contention, some favoring the goat for its independence, others sheep for their inclination to follow their masters. This debate reminds me of the argument between dog and cat partisans, each emphasizing contrasting aspects of "intelligence," the cat people favoring independent problem solving, the dog people "teach-ability."

Finally, the responses to my question about whether it was appropriate to capture and keep a white-winged dove in a cage (a practice I observed in San Juan) split in terms of an anthropocentric or utilitarian moral valuation supportive of the practice (69 percent) and what has been termed a biocentric moral stance in opposition (31 percent). Those who considered it appropriate noted that the dove "sings," is "beautiful," or might be eaten. Those opposed objected that an innocent wild creature of God so confined would be sad, and this might bring "bad luck."

In conclusion, San Juaneros not only recognize, name, and appreciate the utilitarian value of the plants and animals of their local environment but readily attribute to them life, "heart," intelligence, and, selectively, moral sensibility.

Animal Life-forms

Plant life-forms include at least three "macro life-forms" and in addition several "midi" and "mini" life-forms, frequently overlapping but recognized by the consistent application of the life-form name as a plant name prefix. It is not as easy to identify animal life-forms. Potential life-form names are only sporadically prefixed to the generic names. For example, **mguîn** 'bird' occurs as an obligatory or optional element in just 19 of 69 (28 percent) folk generic bird names. Other broad zoological categories widely recognized as animal life-forms (cf. Brown 1979) are of uncertain status in the local Zapotec classification. 'Fish', **mèl**, is best considered a folk generic, given the very limited diversity of local fishes due to lack of habitat. Just one local folk specific category is recognized, though a few other specific types are known, but more as market produce than as living organisms. 'Snake', **mèel**, a term nearly identical to that for 'fish', is prefixed to the names of ten types of snakes. I have been tempted to treat it as a polytypic folk generic, but as four of these are usually abbreviated and two are further subdivided, it seemed more appropriate to consider **mèel** a small life-form (fig. 4.3b).

A further complication is a consequence of the fact that **mèel** may also mean 'worm' and is prefixed to the names of a variety of wormlike invertebrates, such as earthworms (**mèel-yù**, literally, 'earth worm'), leeches (**mèel-lèts**), millipedes (**mèel-yàas**, literally, 'black worm'), and maguey worms (a larval moth, **mèel-dòb**), as well as to salamanders and one type of lizard, both of which are called **mèel-nì** 'leg-snake'. Perhaps I should conclude that in the local Zapotec conceptual world 'snake' and 'worm' are fused as a single 'snake/worm' category, thus disregarding Linnaean classificatory principles. However, I believe such a conclusion is unwarranted, as I have no doubt that San Juaneros recognize a fundamental difference between 'snakes' and 'worms', though there is no strictly linguistic evidence to demonstrate this. I thus distinguish **mèel₁** 'snake' and **mèel₂** 'worm', the first as a mini-life-form, the second as a metaphoric element of diverse folk generic names, but not as naming a discrete taxon.

Invertebrates are known as **má-wĭn**, literally, 'little animal'. Though this term is a binomial, thus atypical of names for higher-level taxa, it seems to be widely employed to refer to insects and other invertebrates in general, and thus qualifies as a life-form. Two additional categories might be considered to qualify as life-forms, but I treat them as folk generics, albeit uncommonly polytypic. 'Spider' (**ngùdzìi**) includes perhaps twenty named subcategories, but the great majority of the subcategories named resemble folk specific or varietal taxa in their emphasis on simple ecological or morphological attributes such as habitat, size, or color (e.g., **ngùdzìi-lén-yù** 'house spider', **ngùdzìi-làs** 'small/slender spider', **ngùdzìi-ngǎs** 'black spider'). The highly distinctive tarantulas are named in parallel fashion, **ngùdzìi-zhàb** 'husk spider'. None of the spider specifics, however, is known by an abbreviated or monomial name, supporting the conclusion that 'spider' is best considered simply a very diverse polytypic folk generic. For a statistical summary of animal taxa, see table 4.7.

San Juan Gbëë Mammals

As is usually the case in folk zoological classifications, there is no clearly recognized "mammal" category (Randall and Hunn 1984; Brown 1984; Berlin 1992). Instead, virtually all large mammals (i.e., larger than a mouse or bat) are recognized as "unaffiliated" folk generics, as are large "leggy" reptiles. These are prototypical "animals" that, it would seem, do not require being set apart in a life-form of their own.

I recognize thirty-eight mammalian folk generics, excluding *Homo sapiens*. Though humans are recognized as an animate species, sharing with other such beings 'life', 'heart', 'sexual differentiation', and 'intelligence', our species is granted a unique ontological status apart from **mâ** 'animal' by virtue of possessing a 'soul'. Of these folk generics, twenty-nine correspond 1:1 to Linnaean species, of which nine are introduced domesticates. Examples include: **mèebĕ**, the long-tailed weasel (*Mustela frenata*); **mdzìn**, white-tailed deer (*Odocoileus virginianus*); **mĕcw**, the domestic dog (*Canis familiaris*); and **chĭv**; the domestic goat (*Capra hircus*). Three more correspond to two congeneric species (e.g., **mèedz-cuĭ**, ring-tails, *Bassariscus astutus* and *B. sumichrasti*), and three more to two closely allied species of different genera within a single family (e.g., **cònêf** Spanish *conejo*, rabbits, inclusive of the native cottontails, *Sylvilagus floridanus* and *Sylvilagus canicularis*, and the European rabbit *Oryctolagus caniculus* [but excluding the hare, *Lepus callotis*, set apart as **mlìan**]). Two folk generic taxa remain poorly defined. These include poorly known rare and reclusive animals, such as the smaller wild cats, **mèedz-yâg** and/or **mèedz-sìlôt**, which refer one way or another to the ocelot (*Felis pardalis*), margay (*Felis wiedii*), and jaguarundi (*Felis yagouroundi*). These species are encountered so infrequently as to preclude detailed firsthand knowledge of them. Finally, three categories of small mammals involve extensive "lumping" at the level of the Linnaean family or above, namely, shrews (**nguîit**, family Soricidae) of as many as six species of three genera; mice (**mzîn**) of up to twenty-eight species of twelve genera of three families; and bats (**nguíd-bdzîn**) with up to thirty-six species of twenty-three genera of five families (table 4.8).

An examination of mammal names indicates some explicit recognition of special relationships among certain mammal categories, which might be recognized as intermediate taxa. We have noted above the term **mèedz**, which seems to point to a rather broad collection of "fierce" or "savage/wild" predatory animals, with the cougar (*Felis concolor*) as prototype. Some five species of wild felines are so named, though the jaguar (*Felis onca*) may be known simply as **tîgr**, < Spanish *tigre*, as it is commonly known in the local Spanish vernacular. **Mèedz-bŏn** is the bobcat (*Lynx rufus*). As noted above, **mèedz-sìlôt**, < Nahuatl via Spanish *ocelote*, refers to the ocelot (*Felis pardalis*) and/or margay (*Felis wiedii*), while **mèedz-yâg**, literally, 'tree cat', is most likely the jaguarundi (*Felis yagouroundi*). **Mèedz** is extended to the ring-tails (*Bassariscus* spp., of the raccoon family, Procyonidae), called **mèedz-cuĭ**. At this point the issue gets cloudy. What are we to make of **mèedz-gŏn**, a kind of biting fly, and **mèedz-yăs**, the crayfish? Interview respondents clearly recognize these names as naming metaphorically animals fundamentally different than the prototype.

By and large, native mammals bear native Zapotec names, while introduced mammals are named with terms borrowed from Spanish (e.g., *bŭrr* 'donkey', < Spanish *burro*; *càbây* 'horse' < Spanish *caballo*), or from Nahuatl via the local Spanish vernacular (e.g., *mĭts* the house cat, *Felis domesticus*, < Nahuatl *miztli* 'cougar'). However, there are a number of intriguing exceptions to this rule. Sheep have been called "cotton dogs" (*mĕcw-xĭil*) since the sixteenth century (Córdova 1987 [1578]), while the all-important oxen are named for their work in cultivation, *ngŏn* < *ràn* 'to farm, plant' (Reeck 1991). On the other hand, the native cottontail rabbits are known only by a Spanish loan, *cònêf* < Spanish *conejo* 'rabbit', or as *cònêf-dán* 'forest/mountain rabbit' to distinguish it from the domesticated European rabbit, known as *cònêf-ró-yù*, literally, 'house cottontail'. Curiously, this nomenclatural anomaly is widespread throughout the Otomanguean family (de Ávila Blomberg 2004). Similarly, the native wild "pig," the peccary (*Tayassu tajacu*, of the Tayassuidae), is now distinguished as *ngúts-guìx*, literally, 'bush pig', while the introduced domestic pig—rarely kept in San Juan—is known simply as *ngŭts*. *Ngŭts* appears to involve the Zapotec agentive prefix *ngu-*, though the appended stem has no obvious etymological derivation.

Binomials are applied to serve several distinct semantic functions in mammal names. Firstly, to distinguish age and/or sex categories within a folk species: *bŭrr-mâch* 'male donkey' < Spanish *macho* 'male'; *ngŭts-yèen* 'baby pig'; *chìvât* 'male goat with horns' < Spanish *chivato*; *ngû-chŏp* 'four-point [buck white-tailed deer]'; *ngŏn-nòvî* 'castrated bull' < Spanish *novillo*. These categories are readily distinguished from "taxonomic" specifics by virtue of the explicit recognition by consultants of "species" as categories of plants or animals that faithfully reproduce themselves. As noted above, animals are distinguished by the recognition of "male" and "female" individuals of each species. Clearly, piglets do not reproduce other piglets, nor do castrated bulls reproduce castrated bulls.

Binomially named folk specific taxa, properly so-called, refer to "natural kinds" capable of reproducing themselves, for example, 'forest' versus 'Castillian' rabbits, *Sylvilagus* spp. (*cònéf-dân*) versus *Oryctolagus cuniculus* (*cònêf-xtîl*); [tree] versus 'flying' squirrels, *Sciurus aureogaster* (*ndzĭz*) versus *Glaucomys volans* (*ndzĭz-rsìibê*); 'black' versus 'white' skunks, *Mephitis macroura* (*mèt-ngăs*) versus *Conepatus mesoleucus* (*mèt-nquĭts*). I include as folk specifics categories that correspond not only to distinct Linnaean species but also to consistently named varieties of domesticated species, as these recognize heritable qualities, for instance, **mécw-xtîl** 'Castillian dog', a small dog breed with short legs and long hair; **ngŭts-yâg**, literally, 'pole pig', a long-snouted pig that doesn't fatten readily.

Finally, we should note that local consultants are at odds with academic zoologists in asserting the existence of two "species" of coatimundis (*Nasua narica*), **mzhìidz-yàal**, which travel in large groups, and **mzhìidz-tìb**, literally, 'one coatimundi', which are larger and solitary, claiming that they each reproduce "after their own kind." Academic zoologists report that the latter are simply old males of the species.

Of the thirty-eight mammal generics, nine are polytypic, including a total of twenty-six folk-specific taxa, for fifty terminal taxa and fifty-nine total taxa. These correspond to as many as 114 species known to occur in the south-central Oaxaca region (abstracted from Goodwin 1969). However, several species are scarcely known or known only from hearsay: spider monkey, tamandua, jaguar, brocket deer, peccary, and river otter. This represents a Scientific Species Recognition Ratio (SSRR) of just 43 percent. However, if we discount the smallest mammals, the bats, shrews, and rats and mice—a total of seventy species represented by just three folk generics—the remaining forty-four mammal species correspond rather closely to thirty folk generics, with an SSRR of 68 percent at the folk generic rank and of 105 percent for terminal taxa.

Twelve of these 114 mammals are introduced. Three are domestic rats and mice; the remaining nine are domestic animals: horse, mule, donkey, ox, sheep, goat, pig, rabbit, and house cat. Donkeys, oxen, sheep, and goats are essential to the local economy. As noted, the ox, sheep, and pig have authentic Zapotec names rather than names borrowed from Spanish.

San Juan Gbëë Reptiles, Amphibians, and Fishes

There are relatively few species of these vertebrate classes in San Juan Mixtepec, though there are no doubt considerably more than we have been able to verify to date, which is a very limited set indeed. We have recorded but one local fish species, excepting the very popular salt fish brought to town from coastal markets. Consultants speak of other small fish that live in the lower reaches of the Río Grande below town. These are known simply as **mèl**. They also speak of a blind cave fish that is said to live inside the mountain above the site of the ancient village at the junction of the rivers that drain past San Pedro and San Juan, respectively. It has no special name, however.

I count a minimum of twelve species of lizards familiar to San Juaneros, at least eleven species of snakes, six amphibians, and four fish, for a total of thirty-three species of these three vertebrate classes. They correspond to twelve folk generics (table 4.9). Two of the folk generics, however, are highly polytypic. There are at least seven named kinds of **ngùrăgw** 'typical lizard' and perhaps over a dozen of **mèel$_1$** 'snake'. I count eight monotypic generics plus twenty-six specifics within four polytypic generics. I have recorded two named varieties of a type of rattlesnake, for a grand total of thirty-five terminal taxa.

Snakes are scarce, though the authoritative reference for the poisonous snakes of the American tropics (Campbell and Lamar 1989) indicates that three rattlesnake species (*Crotalus*) and one pygmy rattlesnake (*Sistrurus*), one species of the fer-de-lance group (*Ophyracus*), and two coral snakes (*Micrurus*) might be encountered in or near San Juan. I have seen a black-tailed rattlesnake (*Crotalus mollossus nigrescens*) once below town, near the mouth of a cave in rough hot country. Besides this, neighbors brought in two small snakes, a garter snake (*Thamnophis* sp.) (fig. 4.4) and what appeared to be a black-headed snake (*Tantilla* sp.) (fig. 4.5).

Though snakes are rarely seen in San Juan, they nevertheless are widely feared. Though I have recorded quite a variety of binomial snake names of the form **mèel-X**, it has been difficult to elicit clear descriptions of these that unambiguously distinguish one from another. Examples include the garter snake noted above, which was called **mèel-nìs**, literally, 'water snake'. **Mèel-yâg**, literally 'tree/bush-snake', is a slender brown snake that climbs in bushes, not considered to be poisonous. **Mèel-gây**, literally, 'rooster snake', named for its horned brow ridges, may be the viper *Ophyracus undulatus*. **Mèel-ngòoz-mdzìn**, literally, 'deer-hunter snake', often abbreviated as 'deer-hunter', may be the boa constrictor (*Boa constrictor*). **Mèel-dòo**, literally 'rope-' or 'great-' snake, appears to be a fantastic creature, a giant snake that lives underground beneath springs and seeps, guarding these critical water sources. Some consultants, however, consider it to name an actual snake.

As noted above, a single term, **mèel**, must do double duty for both 'snake' and 'worm'. However, consultants do not consider snakes and worms to be the same kind of animal. They clearly employ **mèel₁** 'snake' and **mèel₂** 'worm' polysemously. I treat **mèel₁** as a small life-form, as several types of snakes are more commonly named as distinct folk generics; for example, **mzión** is preferred for the coral snake (*Micrurus* spp.) to the synonymous alternative **mèel-mzión**; **ngùbìdz**, literally, 'sun', is preferred to **mèel-ngùbìdz** for rattlesnakes (*Crotalus* spp.). Rattlesnakes are further differentiated by color: **ngùbìdz-yàas** 'black rattlesnake' versus **ngùbìdz-yĕets** 'yellowish rattlesnake'. The black-tailed rattlesnake we saw below town was identified as **ngùbìdz-yĕets**, descriptive of its olive dorsal ground-color. By recognizing **mèel** as a life-form, we may count **ngùbìdz** a generic and **ngùbìdz-yĕets** a folk specific, which strikes me as the most satisfactory interpretation.

Rumor has it that a species of turtle, **mȅw** (most likely *Kinosternon integrum*), has occurred in the seasonal pond known as **Lô-wgàa** 'Eye of the Milpa', aka **X-làgûn-dây** 'Medardo's Lake', north of town. I had no luck finding them there, but on one occasion I spotted a turtle crossing the road just west of San Pedro Amatlán. From the photographs it appears to be *Chelopus rubidus rubidus* of the Emydidae (fig. 4.6).

Donato and I collected one toad (*Bufo* sp.), two frogs (*Rana* sp., *Eleutherodactylus* sp.), and two salamanders (*Pseudoeurycea* sp.) during our various visits to San Juan, but we were unable to extract additional information about other amphibians. We could only conclude that the various species are uncommon, elusive, and inconsequential, though we did not doubt that a number of species could be collected by diligent effort by expert herpetologists.

Lizards, by contrast, are conspicuous and varied, with at least eleven local species. Spiny lizards (*Sceloporus*) are everywhere, from the walls of houses in town to the highest pine forests above. Three species are common in and near town. Each is distinguished at the folk-specific rank within the large, polytypic typical-lizard generic: **ngùrăgw**. The 'rebozo lizard', **ngùrăgw-băy**, *Sceleporus mucronatus omiltemanus* (fig. 4.7), is common on house walls and sports a distinctive collar suggestive of its name. **Ngùrăgw-zhòoy**, *Sceleporus espinosus* (fig. 4.8), is a stocky, prominently keel-scaled species partial to rocky outcrops and bare ground outside of town. **Ngùrăgw-bèed**, literally, 'dirty lizard', is *Sceloporus siniferus* (fig. 4.9), small and obscurely marked. Finally, **ngùrăgw-ngùzì**, literally, 'thunder god lizard', is the stunningly beautiful emerald green species found in pine forests above town and to the highest summits of the Sierra Sur. It is possible that two species are involved, as both *Sceloporus formosus* and *Sceloporus jalapae* (figs. 4.10, 4.11) match this description.

Also included within **ngùrăgw** are species of *Norops* (*Anolis*), *Ameiva*, and *Aspidoscelis* (*Cnemidophorus*). Anoles are **ngùrăgw-guìd** 'hide lizards' (fig. 4.12), aptly descriptive of their smooth, leathery skin. They splay their brightly colored throat pouches in courtship or defensive displays. Striped whiptails, slender and swift (*Aspidoscelis* sp.) (fig. 4.13), and the large, bull-headed, pale-greenish *Ameiva undulata* (fig. 4.14) are 'snake lizards', **ngùrăgw-mèel̲**. We encountered a strikingly black-and-white banded juvenile *Gerrhonotus liocephalus* (fig. 4.15), which we were told was **mèel̲-nì,** literally, 'legged-snake', a term more often applied to the notorious giant beaded lizard of the arid lowlands of the Isthmus of Tehuántepec (*Heloderma horridum*) and to the occasional local salamander (*Pseudoeurycea* sp.), though salamanders may be distinguished as 'smooth lizards' **ngùrăgw-rùdz̲**.

One may stumble upon the oddly lethargic, flattened, spine-margined horned lizard, aka 'horned toad', *Phyrnosoma braconnieri*, **mdzîd** (fig. 4.16), here at the southern limit of the range of the genus. Some say it can cure a headache: place one on your head to draw out the heat. The occasional black iguana **ngutsiĕts-ngăs,** literally, 'black iguana' (*Ctenosaurus similis*), straggles up to the lower edge of the *municipio*, where they are promptly caught and eaten. I saw a boy with one just once, below town at San Cristóbal Amatlán, but at the elevation of the lower margin of San Juan. Many in San Juan are familiar with the green iguana, **ngutsiĕts-guièl,** literally, 'lake iguana' (*Iguana iguana*), and may have encountered caimans (*Caiman fuscus*) and/or crocodiles (*Crocodrilus acutus*) on their travels to the coast and the Isthmus of Tehuántepec. Crocodilians (**mĕn**) are better known these days as **làgârt** < Spanish *lagarto*.

'Frogs' **mbîich,** whether diminutive robber frogs (e.g., *Eleutherodactylus* sp.) (fig. 4.17) or true frogs of the genus *Rana*, are distinguished from 'toads' **mèe-bĕdz̲** (*Bufo* sp., fig. 4.18), but 'tadpoles' are lumped with an odd assortment of aquatic invertebrates (see below) as **mlôol̲**. Nevertheless, it is generally recognized that tadpoles grow into frogs and toads, while other types of **mlôol̲** do not. This notable lack of interest in distinctions among small aquatic animals is best explained by the low "ecological salience" (Hunn 1999a) of such creatures in this rugged, semiarid landscape. Zapotec terms for turtles, iguanas, and crocodiles are likely passed down within a regional tradition reflecting the broader ecological base of the Zapotec linguistic stock, as there is little immediate local relevance for such terms.

San Juan Gbëë Birds

The term **mguîn̲** may be translated as 'bird'. A wide range of what are considered to be 'birds' in English are explicitly or implicitly included under that heading. However, nearly all of these are what we might call "dickey birds," that is, small to medium-sized birds that are not otherwise notable, predominantly wood warblers, flycatchers, thrushes, sparrows, and blackbirds. Examples include:

mguîn̲-guìùu, literally, 'river bird', the black phoebe (*Sayornis nigricans*);
mguîn̲-rchǔup 'whistle bird', the dusky-capped flycatcher (*Myiarchus tuberculifer*);
mguîn̲-ló-liù 'ground bird', the horned lark (*Eremophila alpestris*);
mguîn̲-pàyâs 'clown bird', the bridled titmouse (*Baeolophus wollweberi*) and Mexican chickadee (*Poecile sclateri*);
mguîn̲-quiè 'rock bird', Boucard's wren (*Campylorhynchus jocosus*);
mguîn̲-nìs 'water bird', the American dipper (*Cinclus mexicanus*);
mguîn̲-guìib-tsár 'bell bird', nightingale thrushes (*Catharus* spp.) and solitaires (*Myadestes* spp.);
[**mguîn̲-**]**bèd,** the cedar waxwing *Bombycilla cedrorum*();
[**mguîn̲-**]**bzhiàn** 'angry bird', the slate-throated redstart (*Myioborus miniatus*);
mguîn̲-dǎm̲ 'great-horned owl bird', the rufous-capped warbler (*Basileuterus rufifrons*);
[**mguîn̲-**]**wǐzh** onomatopoetic, the spotted towhee (*Pipilo maculatus*);
mguîn̲-x-còl-nquǐts, literally, 'white-tail bird', yellow-eyed junco (*Junco phaeonotus*);
mguîn̲-mòlîn 'mill bird', the house sparrow (*Passer domesticus*).

Two of the some twenty such terms are exceptions to the rule in that they refer to larger and more strikingly distinct birds, that is, [**mguîn̲-**]**pliêgw,** the northern flicker, and **mguîn̲-rlě-dzìt** 'bone-breaker bird', the crested caracara. The first is more often abbreviated as simply *pliêgw*, which is onomatopoetic. The last named is clearly a calque on the Spanish vernacular term and likely a recent invention in the local Zapotec, as caracaras are not normally encountered near San Juan. This suggests that the life-form 'bird' is focused prototypically on small birds, which has been shown to be true of "bird" in English, as well (Rosch 1978). In fact, interviewees for my survey of ethnobiological beliefs rejected the claim that vultures (*pĕch*) and chickens (*nguĭd*) were kinds of 'birds' *mguîn*. This finding suggests caution in assuming referential equivalence between life-form names in various languages solely on the basis of partial or prototypical overlap (cf. Randall and Hunn 1984).

I recognize 69 folk-generic bird taxa in San Juan Gbëë Zapotec. Of these, 14 are further differentiated at the folk-specific level into 48 specific folk taxa, for a total of 103 terminal taxa (69 + 48 - 14) and 118 total taxa, inclusive of the life-form (69 + 48 + 1). These folk categories correspond to 190 Linnaean species that Donato Acuca Vásquez and I recorded in and immediately adjacent to San Juan Gbëë (Hunn, Acuca Vásquez, and Escalante 2001) (table 4.10).

Most generic taxa (49 of 69, or 71 percent) correspond 1:1 to Linnaean species. Examples include:

> *gârs* < Spanish *garza*, prototypically the cattle egret (*Bubulcus ibis*), the only species so far recorded in San Juan. However, the category would no doubt be extended to include several additional species of herons and egrets, both white and dark-colored, that occur commonly at low elevations along the Oaxaca Pacific coast and at the Isthmus of Tehuántepec, regions familiar to most San Juaneros from their travels. In that case, it is likely the term would be modified to take account of size and color contrasts, at least;
> *líd* onomatopoetic, the American kestrel (*Falco sparverius*), a common winter visitor;
> *mèr,* the domestic turkey (*Meleagris gallopavo*); toms, hens, and pullets are distinguished, either by modifying the generic term or by applying distinctive pseudogeneric terms, for example, *nguzĕy* 'tom', *nguzân* 'hen'. The use of such distinctive Zapotec terminology recalls the prevalence of such terminological distinctions in

English for many domestic animals, for example, "rooster" versus "hen," "bull" versus "cow." Of course, the use of such sex-specific terms does not imply a failure on the part of speakers to recognize the essential unity of the "natural kind";

mtsòo onomatopoetic, the long-tailed wood-partridge (*Dendrortyx macroura*);

mriĕ, the lesser roadrunner (*Geococcyx velox*);

ngă onomatopoetic, the northern raven, known locally as *cuervo* 'crow' (*Corvus corax*);

mziùud, the bushtit (*Psaltriparus minimus*), a rare instance in which the root of a name with the animate prefix *m-* is itself meaningful, in this case derived from rziùud 'woven bag', which aptly describes the nest;

mĕcw-guiùu, literally, 'water dog', the blue mockingbird (*Melanotis caerulescens*), of somewhat obscure derivation, probably alluding to doglike vocalizations and the bird's preference for riparian habitat;

chûurr onomatopoetic, the white-throated-towhee (*Pipilo albicollis*), an abundant and characteristic ground-feeding bird of towns and fields, endemic to central Oaxaca;

mguîn-ngăs, literally, 'black bird', the great-tailed grackle (*Quiscalus mexicanus*), aptly named but not a descriptive phrase.

The rest are *underdifferentiated*, that is, they correspond to more than a single Linnaean species (Berlin 1973). Examples include:

lôr < Spanish *loro*, 'parrot', applied generally to stocky parrots of the genus *Amazona*, none of which occurs naturally in San Juan but several of which may be seen regularly in captivity or for sale in local markets;

mquí onomatopoetic, prototypically the whiskered screech-owl (*Otus trichopsis*) but likely extended to include other small owls, such as the elf owl (*Micrathene whitneyi*) and northern pygmy-owl (*Glaucidium gnoma*); possibly also the flammulated (*Otus flammeolus*) and northern saw-whet (*Aegolius acadicus*) owls, which are known in Oaxaca from the Sierra Norte; if we were to formally distinguish the prototypical core concept from the "extended range" (cf. Berlin 1992:90ff), the prototype would be in 1:1 correspondence;

cùchguêr onomatopoetic, prototypically the Cassin's kingbird, *Tyrannus vociferus*, but including without distinction other kingbird species that occur less frequently, including at least the thick-billed kingbird (*Tyrannus crassirostris*) and western kingbird (*Tyrannus verticalis*); these species vary in vocalizations; the name most closely echoes the characteristic calls of the prototype.

In most such cases of underdifferentiation (13 of 21, or 62 percent) the generics include folk-specific taxa, and most of these subcategories (23 of 37, or 62 percent) correspond 1:1 to closely related Linnaean species. For example:

pĕch 'vulture' includes *pĕch-msì-dòo* 'eagle vulture', the king vulture (*Sarcorhamphus papa*); *pĕch-rúx*, the black vulture (*Coragyps atratus*), and the unmarked prototype *pĕch*, the turkey vulture (*Cathartes aura*); alternative, older terms exist for both king and black vultures, *rên*, literally, 'blood' for the king vulture and *ngólbĕts* for the black vulture, so the current taxonomic organization is likely recent; in any case, current usage clearly reflects the perceived family resemblance among these three species;

cuı̯l onomatopoetic, prototypically refers to the western scrub-jay (*Aphelocoma californicus*), abundant near town, but includes as *cuı̯l-guì*, literally, 'mountain scrub-jay', the Steller's jay (*Cyanocitta stelleri*), the common species of pine forests above town; we may characterize the contrasting prototype as *cuı̯l*.

In other cases, the folk specifics are themselves underdifferentiated. For example:

msì, literally 'barred', a general term inclusive of most hawks, is polytypic; *msì-làg* 'small hawk' refers prototypically to the sharp-shinned hawk (*Accipiter striatus*) but may be extended to include the very similar Cooper's hawk (*Accipiter cooperi*) and even the northern harrier (*Circus cyaneus*), which is occasional in migration; *msì-dòo* 'mecate' or 'great' hawk or 'eagle' is generally reserved for the largest raptors; however, we recorded no true eagles in San Juan; the largest raptor noted was the red-tailed hawk (*Buteo jamaicensis*); however, this species was as often referred to simply as *msì*; the smaller short-tailed hawk, *Buteo brachyurus*, was also so-called; given the difficulty of observing hawks closely and their general scarcity, these folk-specific distinctions are not consistently applied;

xlútsĭ onomatopoetic, swallows (four species of three genera of the family Hirundinidae) and swifts (three species of two genera of the family Apodidae); though the two families are not at all closely related, their aerial habits make it difficult to get close views;

dzĭng onomatopoetic, hummingbirds (fourteen species of eleven genera of the family Trochilidae); all are quite small, but on close observation they may be seen to vary substantially in color, size, habitat, and seasonal patterns of occurrence; a few specific types are distinguished by some consultants, but with little consistency; for example, ***dzĭng-yá-guì*** 'mountain hummingbird' may refer to several large pine forest species, particularly the white-eared hummingbird (*Hylocharis leucotis*); the tiny bumblebee hummingbird (*Atthis heloisa*) may be distinguished as ***dzĭng-guè*** or ***dzĭng-mgòod***, allusions to its diminutive size (about half the length of several larger hummingbird species).

Thus, the overall correspondence of Zapotec terminal taxa and modern scientific species is very good. The single case of *overdifferentiation*, that is, when a folk taxon subdivides a Linnaean species, is the domestic chicken, for which at least nine distinct varieties are named. A number of these are well-known local *criollo* races or forms, such as that characterized by the absence of neck feathering, a variety recognized in San Juan as ***nguĭd-pèlûq*** < Spanish *peluca* 'wig', valued for its exceptional egg production (Jerez Salas, Herrera Haro, and Vásquez Dávila 1994:49).

As has been widely reported (Hunn 1977:94; Berlin and O'Neill 1981), bird names are very often onomatopoetic. Twenty-two of our sixty-nine generic bird names are clearly onomatopoetic, and an additional five may be. Another five names allude to characteristic vocalizations of the birds named. Of particular interest are cases in which the name is *interpreted* in Zapotec (and in one instance in Spanish!), rather as in English "whippoor-will," "killdeer," and "bobwhite." For example, the white-tipped dove (*Leptotila verreauxi*) announces by its name, ***guiès-ró-yù*** 'pot by the door'. The greater pewee (*Contopus pertinax*) repeats its name, ***pèdrĭt*** < Spanish *Pedrito* 'little Peter', then offers advice: "***pèdrĭt, dzĕ, dzĕ, buì yù***," that is, "***pèdrĭt***, slowly, quietly, go home." Clearly, vocalizations are of outstanding prominence in the identification of birds, as they are more often heard than seen.

San Juan Gbëë Invertebrates

I list in the Ethnofauna (part 2) all the names I have so far recorded for categories of invertebrates. This listing is provisional in that it is particularly difficult to distinguish valid named taxa from ad hoc descriptive terms for invertebrates. More systematic work is required to clarify the correspondence of these terms to the locally occurring scientific taxa. Though I collected nearly 500 invertebrate specimens, these were the primary responsibility of Donato Acuca. After his death I made a special trip to Oaxaca to review his notes but was unable to find notes on a number of specimens, nor was I able to connect Acuca's notes and specimen numbers with my own field notes. Thus the invertebrate fauna remain poorly documented. Since 2002 E. Miriam Aldasoro Maya has begun more systematic ethnoentomological studies in San Juan, which should clarify and elaborate on this inventory.

Nevertheless, I am confident that well over 100 generic taxa are recognized in San Juan Gbëë Zapotec (table 4.11). To determine the exact number will require a more careful analysis of the taxonomic status of a number of terms with names of the form *má-* ['animal' +], as many such expressions are descriptive inventions (table 4.12). Some so-called, however, are clearly valid named taxa, while others may prove to be so on further analysis. A few examples will illustrate this problem: *má-nëëg* ['animal' + 'thirst'] names various species of cicada (Homoptera: Cicadidae); the name is widely if not universally recognized for these insects. Similarly, *má-dòozhêr* ['animal' + 'scissors'] refers to earwigs (Dermaptera: Forficulidae). Somewhat less certain is the term *má-nìs* ['animal' + 'water'], which is commonly used to refer to dragonflies and damselflies (Odonata). However, it may also apply to a wider range of superficially similar insects of streamsides and ponds, such as lacewings and adult antlions (Neuroptera). Expressions of this type are also commonly used to name species by reference to a host plant, for example, *má-bziàa* ['animal' + 'bean'] for a variety of small, colorful beetles that eat the leaves of cultivated beans (*Phaseolus vulgaris*). It is not yet clear whether the term is restricted to a certain group of beetles that parasitize beans or whether it may be applied to any insect found in association with bean plants. Less certain yet are terms that likewise specify a host plant but give no indication that the association is of any particular cultural significance, for example, *má-ló-guièe-tĭ* ['animal' + 'on' + 'sticktight'] or even *má-ló-guièe-tĭ-nguĕts* ['animal' + 'on' + '*Bidens aurea*']. Such terms are not counted as established taxa but are listed in the Ethnofauna as nonce forms (NON) pending further evidence of the consistency with which they may prove to be used. Finally, we have several dozen descriptive expressions applied at the specific rank to butterflies alone (*pàlòmít*, adult lepidoptera inclusive of skippers and most moths), most if not all of which are on-the-spot inventions: for example, *pàlòmít-àzûl* 'blue butterfly'; *pàlòmít-biòg* 'brown and yellow moth'; *pàlòmít-càfê* 'tan butterfly/skipper/moth'; *pàlòmít-càfê-nìzhniê* 'red butterfly'; *pàlòmít-càfê-nquĭts* 'tan and white butterfly'; *pàlòmít-càfê-pînt* 'brown, patterned butterfly/moth'; *pàlòmít-càfê-ró-yù* 'tan butterfly of town'; *pàlòmít-chòb-còlôr* 'two-colored butterfly'.

Based on the categories we believe deserve recognition, there are 123 folk generics, of which 27 are polytypic, including between them perhaps 126 folk-specific taxa. There are just two valid varietals. These invertebrate folk generics are distributed very unevenly across the spectrum of scientific taxa. Five folk generics (all monotypic) refer to local species or groups of species of the four phyla Platyhelminthes, Nematomorpha, Mollusca, and Annelida. The remaining 118 refer to Arthropoda, of which 105 refer to animals within the single arthropod class Insecta, while 13 refer to non-insect arthropods, such as those of such classes as Crustacea, Myriapoda, and Arachnida. The great majority of the folk-generic insect taxa (94 of 105, or 90 percent) refer to species or groups of species of seven orders, the Orthoptera (16 generics), Hemiptera (13 generics), Homoptera (8 generics), Coleoptera (20 generics), Lepidoptera (14 generics, of which 11 are categories of larvae), Diptera (7 generics), and Hymenoptera (16 generics).

It is arguable that the invertebrates constitute a "life-form." Though *má-wĭn* ['animal' + 'child/small'] may be used to refer very generally to small animals, most of which are arthropods of one sort or another, the term would not be used for most larval forms—which are most often labeled *mèel* 'snake/worm'—neither for mollusks nor worms. A further complication is that *má-wĭn* may also be used to refer to juvenile vertebrates. The root *má-/mĕe-* 'animal' is not restricted to invertebrates, though as the head of compound generic terms it is most often encountered in that context. (Thirty-five invertebrate generics [28 percent] incorporate **má-/měe-** as the head of the name.) Several such examples have been noted above. Note that **má-gùs** 'female' and **má-bguì** 'male' apply to animals of all sorts, including humans. The vertebrate-invertebrate boundary is not clearly defined. Thus, there seems but weak justification for treating invertebrates as a life-form.

A number of insects, particularly Orthoptera, but also larval and/or adult Coleoptera, Lepidoptera, and Hymenoptera, are collected for food. At least seventeen species of invertebrates are edible or produce edible by-products, such as honey (table 4.13). At least nine species have medicinal applications (table 4.14), while six others have miscellaneous uses, in technology or as charms (table 4.15). However, it is the negative impacts that are most prominent. A number of species bite or sting, some are ill omens, while others are pests of crops or livestock (table 4.16). In all, forty-eight invertebrate categories thus warrant special recognition.

Measuring Invertebrate Taxonomic Correspondence

The exercise of measuring the correspondence of folk to scientific classification is particularly difficult, if not impossible, for invertebrates, as comprehensive inventories of local invertebrate faunas at the level of the Linnaean species do not exist and are not likely to be developed in the foreseeable future. We may, nevertheless, consider the distribution of folk taxa across invertebrate phyla, classes, and orders and compare these distributions with those of other communities and with global or regional species tallies. By this means we may assess local cultural emphases.

A second difficulty in any statistical analysis of invertebrate classification is a consequence of the extraordinary abundance of invertebrate species in most local environments, combined with their small size. Thus, invertebrate classifications may focus on a relatively small number of particularly well-defined and culturally salient types, naming these unambiguously, while applying essentially descriptive terminology with limited consistency to large residual groupings. This is the case with San Juan Zapotec. Some 80 folk generics are well attested, while another 29 are less certainly recognized. Only some 25 folk specifics are unambiguously distinguished, while another 74 might ultimately be substantiated but are questionable on current evidence. I will focus here on the 105 well-attested generic and specific invertebrate taxa.

A quick glance at table 4.11 shows that three of the 26 insect orders (cf. Borror and White 1970) account for 54 of 108 (50 percent) of our insect generics: Orthoptera (broadly defined to include grasshoppers, crickets, mantids, phasmids, and roaches), Coleoptera (beetles), and Hymenoptera (including ants, bees, and wasps). These three orders are highly diverse, including among them 417,500 of the world's estimated 703,500 insect species (59 percent). Three additional orders, Hemiptera (the true bugs), Lepidoptera (butterflies and moths and their larvae), and Diptera (the flies) add 34 folk generics, to total 88, or 81 percent of insect folk generics and 89 percent of all insect taxa named in San Juan. Of course, these six orders encompass 91 percent of the world's insect species. Thus, they are recognized in San Juan roughly in proportion to their global representation.

Lepidoptera and Hymenoptera are classified nearly in proportion to their global species totals, while Coleoptera and Diptera are relatively underdifferentiated. San Juan Hemiptera and Orthoptera stand out for the disproportionate detail of their classification relative to their fraction of global insect species totals. In San Juan a variety of grasshoppers and katydids (six types total) are culinary treats, while in Mexico generally these two orders provide numerous edible species.

CHAPTER 5

Dòoz / The Milpa

San Juan Gbëë Agriculture

ONE STRIKING FACT about San Juan Gbëë is that no one is overweight. Nor are they tall by contemporary U.S. standards. My wife is 5′ 3½″, but in a crowd of San Juan women she stands nearly a head above them. Are we to judge the San Juan diet insufficient on this basis? Standard nutritional assessments used by the local clinic staff involve plotting heights and weights of children by age on a graph marked with percentile curves. Too low on the curve, and a child is judged *desnutrido* to the first, second, or third degree. Based on such evidence, Dr. Miguel Ángel Esparza, in charge of the IMSS clinic in San Pedro during the early years of our work in San Juan, was concerned that many local children were undernourished, if not seriously malnourished. His staff tracked children of the three local towns that were his responsibility, San Pedro, San Juan, and Santa Catarina Qui Gdan. In some of the more serious cases he provided dietary supplements to the parents, including several families in San Juan.

The doctor's fears struck me as inconsistent with my own experience. I knew that of the three local town populations under his care, at least the people of San Juan incorporated a great variety of foods in their daily meals, in addition to the core staples, maize and beans. While they ate meat in quantity mostly on special occasions, as at community-wide festivals and at weddings—for one of which seven goats and two sheep were slaughtered—they relished also a wide range of fruits both cultivated and wild, *quelites* (edible weedy greens), culinary spices, and wild edible plants, not to mention a variety of grasshoppers, a species of giant ant, wasp larvae, and, on occasion, small game. I had seen no evidence that the diet lacked variety, nor that it was deficient in any particular nutrient, though I could not judge whether food was available in sufficient quantity for all at every season. An adequate assessment of the adequacy of the local diet will have to wait for a systematic dietary survey.

Aside from the doctor's concern about local children's growth rates, it has been suggested that certain common San Juan medical complaints might suggest malnutrition, in particular the widespread concern for illnesses such as *espanto* (aka *susto*, ***dzéb***), and for *manchas* (***běy***), white spots or blotches on the face and arms, a frequent symptom of *espanto* (likely the condition we know as vitiligo), as well as for *fuegos en la boca*, that is, canker sores, all of which might be symptomatic of specific dietary deficiencies (see chap. 6). On the other hand, men, women, and children in San Juan are more vigorous physically and certainly no less acute in their mental life than contemporary citizens of the United States.

The question of the adequacy of the local diet—past, present, and future—must be understood in terms of the local subsistence economy, in terms of local agricultural science and its practical application. The term "subsistence" is virtually a curse in the mouths of modern experts in rural development. It is usually phrased as "bare subsistence," as if meeting basic dietary requirements is a trivial matter, a primitive first step toward more sophisticated consumerism. I will argue that the people of San Juan are *rich*, not poor, in that the basic physical requirements of food, clothing, and shelter for themselves and their families are by and large assured by two things: their collective control of adequate land and their traditional knowledge of how to make a living from that land. This should remain the case so long as the past and present balance between the local population and its land base remains within certain limits. The future of San Juan, however, depends as well on how the community and its people engage with regional, national, and global political economies. Key elements of that engagement involve the export and import of labor and its products, which may well induce significant and rapid changes in the local subsistence economy and thus the diet. In this chapter I will sketch my understanding of the local subsistence system and discuss the community's involvement with external markets.

San Juan Gbëë Agriculture in Context

Nearly every resident of San Juan Gbëë depends for most of his or her food on subsistence agriculture supplemented by animal husbandry. Hunting and gathering of wild food plants is of minor importance, though gathering of forage plants for domestic animals and collecting firewood are major subsistence activities. Essential agricultural tools, such as plows, are constructed of local native trees, while local timber and quarried stone are still important as building materials for houses. There is heavy dependence on garden cultivars and gathered wild plants as medicines (chap. 6). Some families earn cash by selling fruit grown in home gardens and orchards; others market goats supported on communal pasture lands. Wage labor is limited to part-time employment on road projects and construction for community or private buildings. Four or five families operate small stores in their homes. Civic authorities serve without salary. Salaried positions are limited to schoolteachers and clinic physicians, both transient, short-term residents.

In short, San Juan is a peasant community heavily dependent on its collective land for most of life's necessities, but engaged with regional markets for certain agricultural commodities, labor, and consumer goods to a not insignificant degree. Evidence suggests that this situation has changed little since before the conquest, when San Juan was a key node on a trade route linking central Mexico with the Isthmus of Tehuántepec (Rojas 1992:257). As noted above, ruins near San Juan suggest continuous occupation of the area since at least the Classic period, that is, 200 BC to AD 750 (Winter 1997), while oral histories support the view that the contemporary citizens of San Juan are the direct descendants of the preconquest population of the region. This is not to say that San Juan's subsistence system has changed little since the conquest. On the contrary, though the major food crops are native cultivars, agricultural technology employs ox-drawn plows of European origin, while animal husbandry, with the exception of turkeys, depends on Old World domesticates.

Recently, more profound changes in the indigenous subsistence system are evident. San Juan lost 30 percent of its population between 1970 and 1990 (though the population had recovered somewhat by 2000), most emigrants settling in nearby cities and towns. This emigration is often temporary or partial, with emigrant families or family members returning frequently to maintain agricultural production on San Juan lands. This pattern of migration has been called "circular migration." The long-term stability of this balance of subsistence production and market engagement by the members of the "greater San Juan Gbëë" community, inclusive of those involved in this circular migration, is uncertain. In any case, emigration is not motivated by a shortage of agricultural land in San Juan.

The Role of Traditional Environmental Knowledge

The subsistence economy depends on a widely shared body of traditional environmental knowledge focused on the local land and its plant and animal resources. This knowledge has not yet begun to deteriorate under acculturative pressures. I will summarize this knowledge with respect to the following categories:

1. milpa agriculture,
2. home gardens and orchards (see also chap. 7),
3. animal husbandry,
4. gathering of wild plants and fungi,
5. hunting,
6. use of local materials in manufacturing,
7. harvest of medicinal plants (see chap. 6), and
8. harvest of ornamental plants (see chap. 7)

An Inventory of San Juan Gbëë Edible Plants

(Table 5.1. San Juan Gbëë cultivated food plants, native; Table 5.2. San Juan Gbëë cultivated food plants, introduced; Table 5.3. Cultivated food plants known in San Juan Gbëë but grown elsewhere)

I have recorded 145 species of plants, both cultivated and wild, that are considered by at least some San Juaneros to be edible. Fifteen of these species include recognized varieties, which is often the case with important cultivated plants. These 145 species encompass 184 total named varieties. Thus, 13.6 percent (145/1,064) of recorded plant species are considered edible, while 25.7 percent (184/717) of locally recognized plant taxa are considered to be edible.

I have recorded 101 species of cultivated food plants (inclusive of 138 named varieties) recognized in San Juan. However, 20 of these (inclusive of 21 varieties) are not grown in San Juan but are known from visits to neighboring communities or from the Miahuatlán market. Thus, 81 species (inclusive of 117 varieties) are grown in San Juan.

Sixteen edible plant species (11.0 percent) are weeds of gardens, fields, and roadsides. The edible plant total includes in addition twenty-eight species that grow wild (19.3 percent), that is, **lò dán** 'in the forest/bush'.

Sixty-seven of the edible plant varieties have been introduced since the Spanish conquest (36.4 percent). With regard to the part of the plant consumed, nearly half of all edible plant varieties are harvested for their edible fruits (79, or 42.9 percent), pulses (19, or 10.3 percent), or grain (8, or 4.3 percent); nineteen varieties of edible plants (10.3 percent) have edible "roots," that is, bulbs, corms, tubers, etcetera; 45 (24.5 percent) provide edible stems, leaves, or flowers, or the entire plant is eaten as a potherb. Thirty-one of the edible plants (16.8 percent) are used as seasonings, while thirteen (7.1 percent) are used in the preparation of alcoholic beverages, such as mezcal, *pulque*, and *tepache*, and teas, or simply as a source of water for thirsty travelers.

Dietary staples may be defined as foods eaten on a more or less daily basis in significant quantities year-round. These are all indigenous cultivated plants, mostly of the milpa: maize or corn (*Zea mays*), a single species with six named varieties (figs. 5.1, 5.2); common beans (*Phaseolus vulgaris*), a single species with nine named cultivars (figs. 5.3, 5.4); and squashes (*Curcubita pepo* [fig. 5.5], *C. ficifolia* [fig. 5.6], and *Sechium edule* [fig. 5.7]), including six varieties of four species. Small quantities of fava beans (*Vicia faba* [fig. 5.8]), introduced peas (*Pisum sativum* [fig. 5.9]), and sorghum (*Sorghum vulgare*) may be planted in the milpa with the native cultigens. Wheat (*Triticum aestivum*) is rarely planted in San Juan, but wheat flour and bread baked from it are familiar, as it is grown in neighboring San Agustín Gbëë and baked in San Juan. Chilies (*Capsicum annuum* and *C. pubescens* [fig. 5.10]) are available at all seasons, as they are cultivated in home gardens, where they are irrigated by hand. Though the total quantity of chili fruits consumed is small, their contribution toward meeting minimum daily requirements of vitamins A and C is likely substantial.

The local inventory of edible plants may be organized in terms of where they are found. As we have already noted, the key staples are the primary milpa cultivars. The milpa is a plowed field sowed at the onset of the rains (in May most years), and harvested in October, November, and December. Milpas may be located in town but are more often at a distance of 1 to 5 km from the house, occasionally farther still. Milpas are maintained on a short fallow rotation, cultivated for two or more years in succession. Soil fertility is maintained primarily by applying organic supplements (*abono*), in particular, goat dung mixed with a bed of plant material (figs. 5.11, 5.12). The milpa is then fallowed ("rested") for an approximately equal period, then brought back into cultivation by a controlled, nighttime, downslope burn, or simply by plowing under the weeds and grasses grown up during the fallow.

Home gardens (*huertos familiares*) are a second site for the cultivation of edible plants, though food plants share space in home gardens with a variety of medicinal and ornamental plants (see chap. 7). Home gardens are tended daily, watered by hand, and fertilized by recycling kitchen wastes. A wide range of condiments, many of introduced species, are ready to hand year-round in these gardens (fig. 5.13).

Species primarily of Eurasian origin of the celery and mint families stand out, such as anise, dill, coriander (fig. 5.14), and parsley of the Apiaceae; *hierba buena*, basil (fig. 5.15), oregano, rosemary, and thyme of the Lamiaceae. Native potherbs and condiments such as a variety of chilies, husk tomato (fig. 5.16), and amaranth, are also prominent, all shaded by a mix of native and introduced fruit trees, such as *nopales*, *guajes* (fig. 5.17), avocados (three local varieties; figs. 5.18, 5.19), figs, bananas (three local varieties; fig. 5.20), pomegranates, loquats, apples (fig. 5.21), peaches (three local varieties, fig. 5.22), and six species of citrus trees (fig. 5.23). These fruit trees and other water-loving species are also grown in irrigated orchard plots in the canyons of the larger local streams. These might be termed riparian orchards, as distinct from the household gardens. Though of strictly limited extent, they are especially productive and produce the bulk of the fruit grown for sale.

A third source of edible plants is the milpa weeds, or *quelites*, and plants established in "living fences" that guard many cornfields. Several delicate *Oxalis* species (fig. 5.24) appear with the first maize sprouts, followed by lamb's quarters (*Chenopodium album*), epazote (*Chenopodium ambrosioides* [fig. 5.25]), amaranth (*Amaranthus hybridus* [fig. 5.26]), *pápaloquelites* (*Porophyllum tagetoides*), and several weedy annuals of the tomato family, such as *hierba mora* (*Solanum americanum*) and *vishate* (*Solanum nigrum*), wild husk tomatoes (*Physalis undatus*), and *Lycianthes*.

Hedgerows and living fences supply *palo de chile* (*Salmea scandens* [fig. 5.27]) and several species of century plants (*Agave*) that at the end of their lives offer tender *quiotes*, *aguamiel*, and, if allowed to bloom (e.g., *Agave angustiarum*), edible buds and flowers (fig. 5.28). Likewise, coral bean trees (*Erythrina americana*), guajes (*Leucaena* spp.), custard apples

(*Annona cherimolia* [fig. 5.29]), *nanches* (*Byrsonima crassifolia*), and guavas (*Psidium guajava*) are planted along field margins. Columnar cacti and tall prickly pears provide fruits in season. Fields in fallow (*acahuales*) abound with wild mustard (*Brassica campestris*, *B. nigra*), *verdolaga* (*Portulaca oleracea*), *Phytolacca icosandra* [fig. 5.30], and *chepiles* (*Crotalaria* spp. [fig. 5.31]).

Finally, there are edible plants that grow "wild," that is, with little or no help from humans, intended or otherwise. These are plants of forests, *matorral*, meadows, cliffs, and marshes. Examples include: *Agave potatorum*, *Bidens* cf. *lemmonii*, *Tagetes filifolia*, *Rorippa nasturtium-aquaticum*, *Hechtia* spp., the barrel cacti, some columnar cacti and prickly pears, a wild squash (*Cyclanthera langaei*), nut sedge (*Cyperus* cf. *esculentus*), *Comarostaphylis glaucescens*, *Acacia angustifolia*, *Phaseolus coccineus*, *Litsea* sp., *Encyclia* spp., wild cherry (*Prunus serotina* var. *calpuli*), blackberries (*Rubus* spp.), and false oregano (*Lippia* spp.). These are harvested opportunistically, for the most part, by boys tending goats, by hunters, travelers, or women seeking firewood or medicinal herbs. They may be eaten on the spot or brought back in quantity for the evening meal.

Milpa Agriculture

Most agricultural production is on plots managed on a short-fallow rotation. Most plots are within an hour's walk of the town center (at 2,050 m), though some plots near the northern lower border of San Juan (at 1,650 m) require a two-hour walk. Within this zone, most plots are privately owned (*"terreno privado"*) and worked either by the owner with the aid of family members or by share-cropping (*a medias, a tércios*), a common practice with no stigma attached.

Plots are worked on slopes up to 25° (fig. 5.32). Some fields utilize what appear to be pre-Columbian terraces, as little new terracing is under construction. Stone walls or, more often, living fences (*"cercas vivas"*) of *Agave* spp. (fig. 5.33), *Bursera* spp., columnar cacti, or other woody plants divide plots and help retain the soil. Valuable trees may be spared in midfields, such as *Plumeria rubra* or mulberry (*Morus celtidifolia* [fig. 5.34]). A family must cultivate approximately 2 ha of land (5 acres) for basic food-crop production, a figure close to that reported for other southern Mexican indigenous communities (Casas, Viveros, and Caballero 1994:83; González 2001:164; Rus and Collier 2003:58). Individuals without adequate private land may open plots on communal lands (by "slash-and-burn"), which may be up to three hours' walk above the town (to 2,500 m) in communal forests (figs. 5.35, 5.36).

Except on limited streamside plots and orchards and in home gardens, there is no irrigation. However, deep in the canyon of the Río Grande I was shown streamside plots irrigated by means of a clever series of wooden troughs, sometimes bridging the stream or conveying the water around sheer rock walls. Pedro Miguel Zurita, always interested in innovation, had gone so far as to purchase plastic irrigation pipe but had abandoned the effort because of the cost of purchasing the water from the community system. However, by 2004 the town was developing a systematic irrigation scheme.

Soil fertility is maintained by applications of animal manure and crop by-products (*abono, lo sobrante, el rastrojo*, or in Gbëë Zapotec **guìzh-diè**) and short-fallowing as needed. There is limited use of chemical fertilizers (fig. 5.37). Crop pests are mostly managed by hand tilling to destroy root-boring insect larvae (e.g., the *gallina ciega* or **mtsàn**, larvae of june beetles [*Phyllophaga* spp.]), or, in the case of birds, by setting up "scarecrows" (*espanta-pájaros* or **ngutséb**) in their fields, which may be as simple as stringing cassette tape across a field, which vibrates in a light breeze. Commercial insecticides are rarely applied.

The Agricultural Cycle

The typical agricultural cycle near the village may involve an initial plowing in January or February, to turn under stubble and animal dung spread on the fields after the harvest. A second preliminary cultivation (by plow or by hand tools) just before the rains serves to expose insect larvae and to loosen the soil. The primary plowing and planting is timed for the first solid spate of rain marking the onset of the summer monsoon in May or June. Rituals to petition for rain are performed twice in early to mid-May on the summit of Cerro San Isidro, a prominent hill one km west of town, for the Fiesta de la Santa Cruz, May 3, and the Día de San Isidro (patron saint of farmers, which gives this hill its Spanish name), May 15 (see chap. 2). In some years the summer rains may not begin in earnest

Mother and son plowing; Primitivo Cruz and Irena Zurita work together to plow and plant the milpa, June 15, 1998.

until early to mid-June or later. This may seriously affect agricultural outcomes for the year. One response is to emphasize planting at higher elevations and to select fast-maturing maize varieties, such as "rabbit corn" (*zhób-cònêf*).

San Juaneros own some thirty-six teams of oxen (*yuntas*, **něz-ngŏn**, literally, 'a road of oxen'), but these are the property of particular men, and there are many without. The available teams are shared in exchange for provisioning of the animals or, more often, rented. The going rate in 2004 was reported to be $250 pesos (U.S. $22) per day, or $200 pesos (U.S. $17.50) for a half-day. Oxen are not raised in San Juan but must be purchased outside. A team costs $4,000 to $7,000 pesos (U.S. $364–$636).

Martina Romero, wife of Eucario Hernández, planting corn and bean seeds, June 16, 1998.

Oxen begin work at age two and may continue to pull plows for fifteen or more years. Owners name their oxen and are clearly fond of them. Farmers may also simply do without the plow, cultivating as they did before the Spanish conquest using the *coa* or hoe, now tipped with iron (fig. 5.38). This tool is used, in any case, to cultivate odd corners of a field not readily reached by the plow, as well as in weeding.

Plowing and planting are most often done simultaneously by two people working together, one manipulating the plow, the other following, dropping seed in the newly opened furrow (*surco*) (figs. 5.39, 5.40, 5.41, 5.42, 5.43, 5.44). Such teams may consist of a man (working the plow) and his wife (placing the seed), a boy and his father or mother, or a brother and a sister, two brothers, cousins, or *compadres* (who may alternate tasks). It is unusual for women to plow and plant alone; the few cases were the subject of some critical commentary.

On the subsequent pass, the plow opens a new furrow while covering the seed in the previous one. Plowing is across the slope, conserving water and minimizing erosion (though I have noted exceptions). Individuals

León Hernández working with his oxen, Bonito and Alegre, June 28, 2002.

may practice their own cultivation styles, which seem to be quite self-consciously elaborated. Local agricultural practice is the subject of much discussion and critical evaluation and thus is dynamic, within broad "traditional" constraints.

Planting should be completed within two weeks of the onset of the rains. A typical planting scheme is to plant 2 to 4 kernels of seed corn at 50 to 80 cm intervals along a furrow. Furrows are 50 to 80 cm apart. Thus, seed is planted on a 50 to 80 cm^2 grid at densities that may vary between 3 and 16 seeds/m^2, averaging ca. 70,000 seeds/ha. Spacing is in part a function of elevation, as seeds are planted farther apart above town than below. The number of maize seeds planted at each point may depend on the specific goals of the farmer, as fewer seeds favor larger cobs and stronger stalks while more seeds produce more leaves, which may be used to feed domestic stock.

Most cultivators plant the larger bean cultivars between the maize, such as **bziàa-guiès,** a large black bean, or some variety of **bziàa-dùuzh,** string beans, as these produce vines long enough to reach and climb the adjacent cornstalks. However, others may plant two bean seeds with the corn or alternate beans, squash, and corn at 50-cm intervals or plant beans two weeks later to prevent the beans from pulling the corn over.

The basic unit of measurement of volume, weight, and land area is the *almud* (*mûd*), a Spanish term of Arabic derivation. An *almud* of seed is typically measured in a small wooden box said to hold 4 kg of seed (= 4 liters). (González measured a sample of *almudes* in Talea del Castro and found that they averaged 4.20 kg [2001:78]). A kilogram (or a liter) is thus called *tìb cuârt* in Zapotec, from Spanish *cuarto,* as in *un cuarto de un almud* 'a quarter of an *almud*'. Four *almudes* of corn seed are judged sufficient to plant one hectare of land. However, since maize kernels vary in size and planting intervals also vary substantially, it is clear that the local system of land measurement cannot be directly translated into our familiar units of area, such as hectares or acres, nor can we calculate planting densities precisely on this basis. The local system seems perfectly well suited to judging how much seed to plant to feed one's family. Thus, Hermilo Silva estimates that he will need to plant ten *almudes* to be confident of having a sufficient maize harvest to feed his large family (himself, his wife, three teenage children, and two a bit younger) for the coming year.

González reported that yields in Talea de Castro ranged from 1,210 to 2,016 kg/ha (2001:164), a return on seed planted of 75–150:1. He also calculated daily consumption for maize in the form of the large local tortillas (0.17 kg per tortilla) for adult males, adult females, children aged six to fourteen, and children five and under (2001:155). (A small sample of San Juan tortillas averaged 0.125 kg and 25 cm in diameter, a bit smaller than those of Talea.) I have prorated these averages with respect to the proportions of the San Juan 2000 population. The average is very close to 700 grams per person per day.

The USDA nutritional values database (http://www.nal.usda.gov, June 5, 2004) cites for corn tortillas "ready-to-bake" an energy value of 2,220

Emiliano Miguel loading maize for transport home from his father-in-law Eucario's milpa, December 18, 1996.

calories/kg and 5.7 percent protein (based on a moisture content of 44.1 percent). Thus, 700 grams of tortillas per person per day translates to 1,540 calories, or ca. 75 percent of the UN FAO recommended daily requirement averaged over this population, and 39.9 grams of protein.

This figure for the protein content of maize must be adjusted downward somewhat, given that the amino acid profile of maize protein is unbalanced and that significant fractions of certain key amino acids, such as leucine, are bound in indigestible compounds insoluble in water. Yet it has been shown that the nearly universal Mesoamerican practice of soaking maize in limewater prior to grinding the *masa* frees a large fraction of these bound amino acids, more than doubling the available protein

(Katz, Hediger, and Valleroy 1974). Given the fact that tortillas are routinely eaten with beans, which helps balance the amino acid profile of maize, it is likely that the local diet is more than adequate both in terms of calories and protein.

Corn sprouts within one week of planting. After three to four weeks, mounds are pushed up to support the young cornstalks. At this time the weakest plants may be removed, and those left moved so that they are separated by 5 cm to allow them to "breathe." The first weeding (*limpia*) takes place after 3 to 4 weeks (figs. 5.45. 5.46, 5.47). A second weeding is required when the corn flowers. Green corn on the cob (*elote*) is usually harvested in October, depending on the time of planting and the cultivar planted. The smallest ears are removed at this stage to leave just one to two per stalk to develop fully. (Beans may be ready for harvest by November.) Stalks are bent over approximately two weeks before harvest to facilitate drying, then harvested in December and January (figs. 5.48, 5.49). Fields 200 to 400 m below town are planted later but harvested earlier. Higher fields may be planted first and harvested last, as rainfall and soil moisture vary directly with elevation, while temperature and insolation vary inversely. Most individuals cultivate two or more fields at different elevations and of varying soil types, ideally dividing one's plantings evenly between higher and lower fields to compensate in advance for the uncertainties of local rainfall.

The ripe ears are packed in large baskets, then packed home on the backs of donkeys and stored in the house until needed. Shelling the corn is a continuing task of the women of the household (figs. 5.50, 5.51).

San Juan Gbëë Cultivars

(Table 5.4. Corn varieties named in San Juan Gbëë; Table 5.5. Specialized San Juan Gbëë corn terminology; Table 5.6. Bean varieties named in San Juan Gbëë; Table 5.7. Squash varieties named in San Juan Gbëë)

San Juaneros express a strong preference for "creole" varieties of corn and beans. Many have experimented with commercial seed varieties promoted by CONASUPO (Compañía Nacional de Subsistencias Populares), the government trading enterprise that maintains a small store in San Juan, but judge local cultivars to be superior in their adaptability to local conditions, in taste, and in nutritional value, but most of all in their known qualities and predictable responses to changing conditions. Five local maize cultivars are widely recognized, as listed in table 5.4 (fig. 5.52), along with terms for commercial varieties and allied species that fall within the extended range of the term *zhŏb*. The most frequently planted are *zhób-nquĭts*, a general-purpose "white" variety, and *zhób-ngăs*, a local "black" variety (fig. 5.53) planted most often above 2,200 m and particularly appreciated for making "black tortillas." In some Oaxacan villages black maize is considered an inferior variety. Not so in San Juan, where it is particularly esteemed (fig. 5.54). This variety is also known as *zhób-bziòw*, the modifier *bziòw* a color term peculiar to maize. Similarly, "yellow maize" may be named *zhób-nguĕts* or *zhób-ngôo*, the latter term particular to maize and considered somewhat archaic. These special terms are indicative of the unique value of maize in San Juan life. "Rabbit corn" (*zhób-cònêf*) is a fast-growing variety that matures in four months (i.e., produces green corn ears or *elotes* in that span of time) when just over one meter tall and which is well adapted to higher elevation fields. Many fields near town were planted in "rabbit corn" in 1998 to compensate for the late onset of the rains. Pedro planted a few individuals of this variety among his "white corn" in 1997, to provide a few early-maturing ears and, perhaps, to compare the performance of the two varieties.

All of San Juan's varieties would most likely be classified by corn specialists as belonging to a single "race" of maize (that is, "conico") or at most two (Steven Brush, pers. comm.). The racial classification of maize has been the subject of much research and debate (Anderson and Cutler 1942; Wellhausen, Roberts, and Hernández X. 1951; Doebley, Goodman, and Stuber 1985; Sánchez, Goodman, and Stuber 2000). However, this racial variation is described on a scale of evolutionary differentiation of little relevance at the village level. It is generally agreed that there may be some sixty "races" of maize native to Mexico (cf. Sanchez, Goodman, and Stuber 2000:45), but if the half-dozen varieties recognized in each village —mostly named with respect to the color of the seeds—are in fact genetically distinct from one another, and, as is most likely, also genetically distinct from the similarly differentiated varieties in neighboring villages, the number of genetically distinct local cultivars of maize in Mexico would number in the thousands. González (2001:120) reports that "more than 20,000 varieties of maize exist in Mexico and Central America."

The primary nomenclatural distinction is drawn by color: black, white,

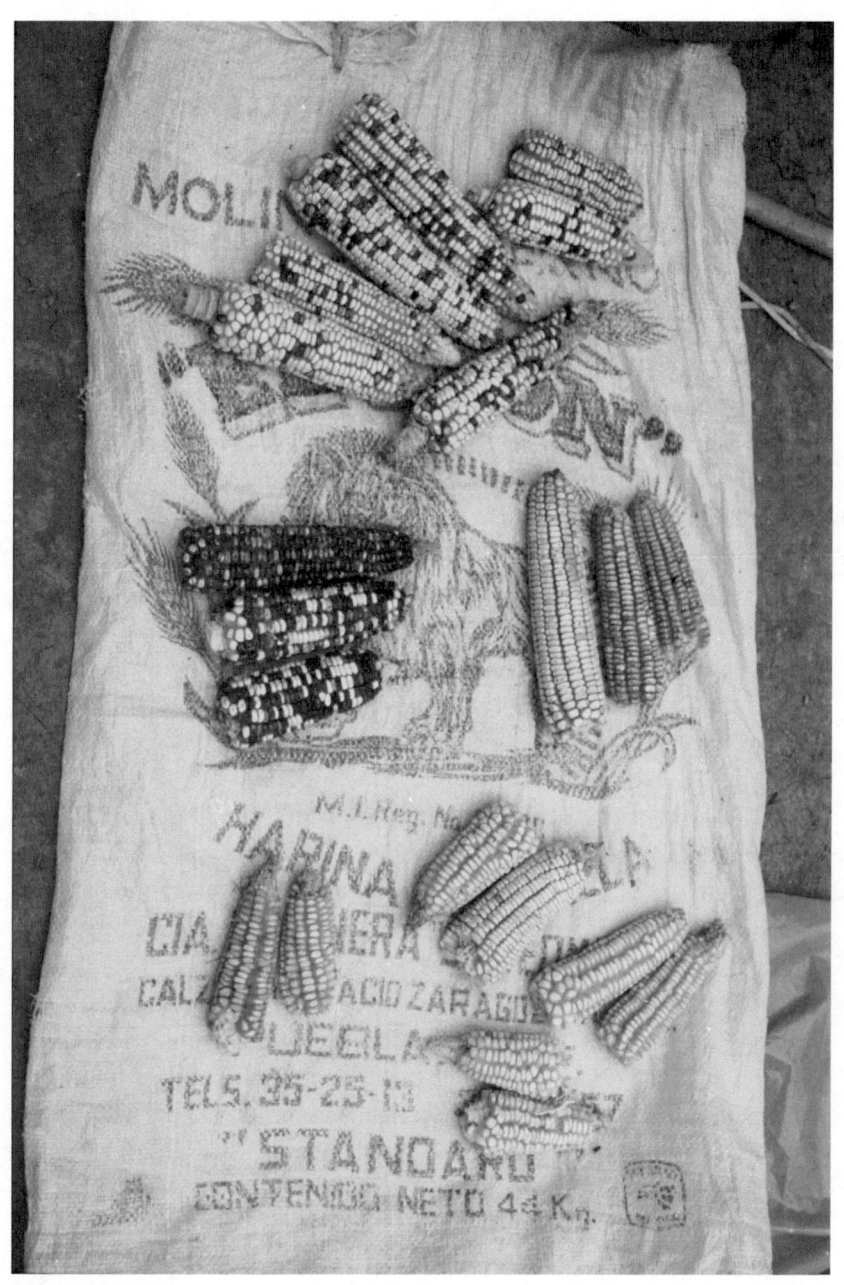

A sample of local maize landraces from Genaro and Sofia's milpa, August 21, 1998.

yellow, and mottled (*pinto*). "Rabbit corn" does not fit neatly into this paradigm, as it is named metaphorically for its rapid growth and may be variously colored. However, even those varieties named for the color of their seeds vary along multiple relevant dimensions (though not always perfectly correlated), such as soil preference, elevation preference (e.g., black and rabbit corn favor higher elevations), tendency to produce abundant foliage, taste, and the size and shape of the cobs and kernels.

The local named varieties show strong fidelity to type, that is, if you plant a black maize seed, you can expect the plant that grows from that seed to produce black maize. The primary exception to this rule is mottled or *pinto* maize (***zhób-pînt***), which shows a mix of black, white, and sometimes red seeds on each cob. Such plants may appear in fields planted to a mix of black and white or yellow corn. San Juan cultivars are thought to be quite similar to those of neighboring towns, but San Juaneros are alert when traveling or visiting neighboring towns to note particularly productive plants and to acquire seed for local experimentation. In this way there is a continuous flow of genetic material between nearby villages, which assures the genetic variability on which continued selection may work. Local farmers may also incorporate seed from greater distances, as in the case of a form of white corn called ***zhób-pòblân***, said to have been brought from Puebla not too long ago.

Wheat (*Triticum aestivum*) is called ***zhób-xtîl*** 'Castillian corn' and is planted occasionally in San Juan, though it is more a specialty of neighboring San Agustín. Wheat flour is preferred for oven-baked bread. A mill to grind wheat flour was built by a San Juan entrepreneur at the river below town about fifty years ago, but it is now a ruin (fig. 5.55).

There is a similar preference for creole bean varieties. Several bean varieties are systematically intercropped with corn. For example, a single family harvested eight varieties of beans from their fields in 1997 (fig. 5.56). A primary distinction is drawn between "green beans" with edible pods (***bziàa-dùuzh*** 'pod bean') and those without. Crosscutting this distinction are distinctions of color, pattern, and size, as in table 5.6. Exotic pulses may be named as if they were varieties of the common bean, though this extension of binomial nomenclature is metaphorical. Fava beans (*Vicia faba*) and peas (*Pisum sativum*) are occasionally planted along with native common beans. Cowpeas, aka black-eyed peas (*Vigna* *unguiculata* ssp. *unguiculata*), may be purchased at the market in Miahuatlán, as they are grown only at lower elevations outside of San Juan.

Planting strategies depend on the growth form of the bean (whether bushy or vining) and, if vining, the length of the bean vines. The "string beans" (**bziàa-dùuzh**, literally, 'pod bean') and a large non-pod bean, **bziàa-guiès**, literally, 'pot bean', are most often planted with maize, as their long vines allow them to reach and then climb up the growing maize stalks.

The classic Mesoamerican triumvirate of corn, beans, and squash still reigns in San Juan Gbëë. Squashes of several species and varieties are cultivated; most but not all are indigenous cultigens. The three species of *Cucurbita* planted in San Juan grow best at different elevations: *Cucurbita pepo* ssp. *pepo* "*calabaza*" (**lbè̱-guìt-wèts**) is planted near town. The introduced Italian squash or zucchini (fig. 5.57) is a variety of this same species distinguished as [**lbè̱-**]**guìt-tàliân**. (The life-form prefix **lbè̱** 'vine', is required only when speaking specifically of the whole plant rather than the edible fruit.) *Cucurbita ficifolia*, the *chilacayote* (**lbè̱-guìt-wĕedz**) grows best above town, while two varieties of *támala*, or pumpkin, *Cucurbita moschata* ([**lbè̱-**]**guìt-gù**, literally, 'tuber squash' and [**lbè̱-**]**guìt-gùbĕ̈ël**, literally, 'meat tuber squash'), thrive at lower elevations. Squashes may be distinguished by seed color, the *chilacayote* having white seeds, the *calabaza* black, while the pumpkins are distinguished by the thickness and color of their rinds (table 5.7). The importance of squashes is further emphasized by the use of special terms for useful parts of the plant other than the fruit. Squash flowers are distinguished from all other flowers as **mzié** (fig. 5.58) and eaten as an herb, while the *guías*, literally 'guides', or tender young twining sprouts of squashes, are **lol-guìt** and are also eaten. An inedible wild relative, *Cucurbita radicans*, is named **lbè̱-guìt-lă**, literally, 'bitter squash' (fig. 5.59).

This classic triumvirate by no means exhausts the list of local cultivars, though these supplementary species are more often planted in home gardens than in the milpa and are predominantly exotic in origin. Several species provide edible tubers. Curiously, these are of South American provenience. Sweet potatoes (*Ipomoea batatas* and/or *Ipomoea orizabensis*) may cover a corner of the home garden, blanketing the ground with deep purplish-green, heart-shaped leaves (fig. 5.60). The occasional potato (*Solanum tuberosum* L., **lbè̱-gù**, literally, 'tuber vine') may be planted in a garden in town (figs. 5.61, 5.62), but mostly they are planted in milpas cut in forest above ca. 2,400 m. The bland, watery tuberous roots of the *jícama* (*Pachyrrhizus erosus*, **gù-guìib**$_1$, literally, 'metal tuber') may be purchased in the Miahuatlán market. A wild morning-glory vine, *Ipomoea* cf. *muricatisepala*, is known by the same term. It bears small tubers that are occasionally dug up and eaten by boys tending goats.

Rancho Agua Fría and Rancho Conejo are pioneering settlements subject to San Pedro Gbëë located side-by-side at 3,100 to 3,300 m on the high divide southeast of San Juan. Perhaps fifty people live in a dozen scattered homesteads here. The settlement lacks electricity, piped water, and a school but is connected by a fair dirt road to the paved highway at San José del Pacifico (about three hours minimum travel time). It is accessible by trail from San Pedro (four hours minimum). It was apparently settled by families who worked in a sawmill here some fifty years ago (ca. 1950). It is too high for maize (which is planted to ca. 3,000 m to the west at La Cieneguilla), so the main crops are potatoes and oregano (*Origanum vulgare*, **guìzh-òrêgànò**), the first for local consumption, the latter sold for cash. Surplus potatoes are traded for corn in San Pedro. During a visit in April 1997, we were offered a bowl of *oca* tubers (*Oxalis tuberosa*) in peach syrup (the peaches also a local product). We inquired after the plant itself, hoping to make a collection, but were informed that it does not flower. We settled for a photograph of the tubers, which grow horizontally and are a deep pink in cross section, rather like a sideways pink carrot (fig. 5.63). Curiously, *oca* is an Andean domesticate not widely known to be cultivated in Mexico. Could it have been a pre-Columbian introduction, maintained in the highest-elevation fields? Alejandro de Ávila thinks so, but the scholarly consensus is that it is an early post-conquest introduction (King and Bastien 1990). The fact that this tuber is known by an indigenous Zapotec term applied generally to the genus *Oxalis*, **gù-bé** '*Oxalis* tuber', contrasts with the situation reported for central Mexico, where Spanish loans are universally applied, and provide some support for de Ávila's view. Tropical tubers such as manioc (*Manihot esculenta*) and yams (*Dioscorea batatas*) are known only by hearsay.

Many fields incorporate scattered fruit trees, magueyes, cacti, or ornamental flowers, typically planted on the field margins in living fences, though sometimes occupying a central portion of the field at an area of seepage or serving as a terrace wall within a field. The century plants and cacti are native cultivars, while the fruit trees and flowers are a mix of native and Old World species.

Agricultural Pests

(Table 5.8. Pests of San Juan Gbëë crops)

An important pest of maize is the notorious *"gallina ciega,"* cutworm larvae of "june beetles," various species of *Phyllophaga* of the Melolonthinae of the Scarabaeidae. (The term *"gallina ciega"* apparently is derived metaphorically from the Spanish term for the game of "blind man's bluff.") These are called **mtsàn** in Gbëë Zapotec. They attack the roots of the corn plant (**lò guiêl**). Chickens (*Gallus gallus*) are brought to the field to help control them, while wild animals, such as skunks (**mèt**), also may help root out this pest. Other *"plagas"* of maize include two Lepidoptera larvae, *"una comején"* (literally, 'moth', **má-zhŏb**$_1$ 'maize bug$_1$') and *"una palomita"* (literally, 'butterfly', **má-zhŏb**$_2$ 'maize bug$_2$').* The larvae of both corn pests are similar, though that of the *comején* is white, while that of the *palomita* is a bit darker, a grayish-white. The larvae infest the maize seeds, then emerge as moths. Weevils (Curculionidae; **ngùxôg**) may infest stored maize and wheat flour as well. Avocado leaves (*Persea americana*) are placed with the corn to repel them.

Gray foxes (*Urocyon cinereoargenteus*, **mèz**), coyotes (*Canis latrans*, **còyôt**), and opossums (*Didelphis marsupialis*, **tlàcuâch**) may eat the green ears of corn. The best defense is vigilance, with the offending animals shot on sight, their bodies hung up in a conspicuous location to discourage their friends. Rats and mice may consume stored ears. Traps and poison may be set against them. Birds such as the common ravens (*Corvus corax*, **ngă**), western scrub-jays (*Aphelocoma occidentalis*, **cuĭl**), great-tailed grackles (*Cassidix mexicanus*, **mguîn-ngăs**), and turkey vultures (*Cathartes aura*, **pĕch**) all may descend upon the milpa to eat the fresh ears of corn. To combat the ravages of these pests the farmers use scarecrows, in Spanish *espanta-pájaros*, in San Juan Zapotec **ngutséb**, literally 'fear

---

* Butterflies and many larger moths are now known in San Juan primarily by the Spanish loan **pàlòmît**, literally, 'moth', in lieu of the original term *méguĭd*, though the small, white cloth-eating moths, *comején* or *polilla*, are set apart as **mxìl**.

causing'. Bean leaves are frequently attacked by tiny metallic beetles (Chrysomelidae) known in Zapotec simply as 'bean bugs' (*má-bziàa*), in Spanish as *catarinas*.

Home Gardens and Orchards

(Table 5.9. San Juan Gbëë cultivated tubers)

San Juan Gbëë town incorporates considerable arable land among the houses. By contrast, neighboring San Pedro has more the appearance of a Nepalese village, with houses pressing against one another and crowding the narrow streets. San Juan's houses are concentrated on ridges, with milpas maintained in the valleys between. Many San Juan houses are set back a bit from the street in a compound with space for extensive garden plantings. Other sites are built up to the point that very little land is left for a garden. In such yards a few herbs and ornamental and medicinal plants may be grown in pots or fenced-off corners of the yard. The time and energy invested in home gardens seems to reflect personal preferences or production strategies. There is a limited development of exchanges among San Juan Gbëë households based on garden specialization, in which families with large gardens may sell flowers and herbs to those without. Curiously, there is apparently no simple Gbëë Zapotec term for "home garden," suggesting that the conceptual separation of fields and gardens may be a recent innovation. I describe San Juan gardens in more detail in chapter 7, with a focus on ornamental flowers.

Riparian Orchards

(Table 5.10. San Juan Gbëë tree species cultivated in the riparian zone orchards)

Stream courses are called **guiùbé** in Gbëë Zapotec. Riparian strips are heavily modified environments, halfway between a "natural riparian woodland" and an orchard/garden. Fruit trees are commonly planted in this zone. Thirty species and ten additional varieties, forty named categories in all, representing twenty-three genera of fifteen families, are listed in table 5.10. Fruits of these trees are regularly consumed within the family, though some people dedicate themselves to growing quantities of apples, quince, haws, peaches, and avocados for sale in Miahuatlán or locally to traveling merchants. Many of the species listed are also planted in town or at springs or seeps. The common feature is the availability of adequate water year-round. San Juaneros are eager to learn techniques to enhance the productivity of their orchards through improved water control, use of fertilizers, and pest control. Thus, they welcomed a visit from Ing. Leonardo León Enrique, agronomist with the Instituto Tecnológico de Valle Oaxaca (ITVO), who, at the request of the community, presented a workshop in orchard management in San Juan in September 1996.

Quelites

Milpa "weeds" are rarely simply discarded. Rather they are gathered either as fodder for domestic animals (see below under "Animal Husbandry") or as potherbs or culinary adjuncts. A key distinction noted in the local Zapotec is that between *"quelites,"* strictly speaking, that is, potherbs, and plants used rather for seasoning. The former are called **ncuàan-yê**, which is also widely used to refer to the *chepiles*, wild edibles of the genus *Crotalaria*. (The "proper" term for chepiles, according to Hermilo, is **pxïizh**.) Plants used primarily for seasoning are collectively **zhlè**. The latter may grow wild or be cultivated, such as onions and garlic. The following species are the most frequently harvested: amaranth (*Amaranthus hybridus*), *pápaloquelite* (*Porophyllum tagetioides*), mustard greens (*Brassica campestris*), berro (*Rorippa nasturtium-aquaticum*), goosefoot (*Chenopodium album*), epazote (*Chenopodium ambrosioides*), chepiles (*Crotalaria* spp.), scarlet runner bean (*Phaseolus coccineus*), verdolaga (*Portulaca oleracea*), and pokeweed (*Phytolacca icosandra*). A complete list of San Juan edible plants is provided in table 5.11 (part 2).

(Table 5.12. Edible weedy greens of local fields and roadsides ["quelites"])

Plants That Contribute Indirectly to Food Production as Fodder, Fuel, and Fertilizer

(Table 5.13. San Juan Gbëë fodder plants [26 families/63 genera/95 species]; Table 5.14. San Juan Gbëë firewood plants [25 families/46 genera/70 species]; Table 5.15. Useful plants by family)

It is clear that San Juaneros have at their disposal a great variety of edible plants that if consumed in adequate quantities and with appropriate complementarity would provide the daily nutritional requirements of the population. In addition, many local plants are harvested not to eat but in order to enhance the abundance and nutritional quality of the diet. Firstly, forage and fodder plants sustain and fatten domestic animals that in turn provide meat and eggs, traction for plowing, transport, and fertilizer to maintain soil fertility. Secondly, firewood and other plant by-products provide the primary fuel source for cooking. Thirdly, plants may be plowed into the soil as *abono* or natural fertilizer, often in conjunction with their use as bedding for goats, sheep, and chickens.

I systematically inquired of each local plant collection whether it could be used as fodder or forage for domestic animals, for firewood, or for composting. Table 5.13: San Juan Gbëë fodder plants (26 families/63 genera/95 species) and table 5.14: San Juan Gbëë firewood plants (25 families/46 genera/70 species) list these uses, while table 5.15 summarizes these reported uses by plant family.

The outstanding importance of the Fabaceae is clear. The value as fuel is a function of the proportion of woody species within the family and of the abundance of such species close to people's homes. The value as forage and fodder seems due to the nutritional value of the plant, with the Fabaceae noteworthy for their ability to bind atmospheric nitrogen, an essential constituent of proteins. That quality is important as well for composting.

Animal Husbandry

Every household in San Juan Gbëë keeps some animals for food. Chickens (*Gallus gallus*) are ubiquitous (fig. 5.64). Turkeys (*Meleagris gallopavo*) are kept less often and in smaller numbers (fig. 5.65), though they are preferred for certain festive *mole* dishes. Turkeys were first domesticated in northern Mexico and spread south to and beyond Oaxaca as a domestic fowl long before the Spanish conquest. The general term for turkeys is **mèr**, apparently related to the term for the wild, native West Mexican Chachalaca (*Ortalis poliocephala*), **mèrzhìg**, literally, 'gourd-turkey', which could have been the original referent of **mèr**, subsequently modified to accommodate the introduction of domestic turkeys. Chickens, of course, are domestic forms of the Southeast Asian red jungle fowl and were introduced by the first Spanish colonists. Curiously, the Gbëë Zapotec term for the chicken is an indigenous expression, **nguĭd**, perhaps derived from the verb root 'to lay (as an egg)'. Chickens provide small numbers of eggs (**dzìt**), which may be eaten on special occasions or sold for cash (at the going retail rate of ca. $1 peso [U.S. $0.09] per egg). Chicken is the most regularly consumed and perhaps the major source of animal protein in the local diet, but it is still reserved for special meals. San Juaneros recognize a considerable variety of creole chicken varieties (table 5.16), which are distinguished by their egg-laying abilities or their ability to endure local conditions. Very occasionally one notices a domestic duck or goose in someone's yard.

(Table 5.16. Varieties of chickens [Gallus gallus] recognized in San Juan Gbëë)

Goats (*Capra hircus*, **chĭv**) are the most prominent animals in terms of total biomass (fig. 5.66). A relatively few families maintain large herds of goats, numbering as many as 100 (fig. 5.67). Young boys, and less often girls or women, herd the family's goats (figs. 5.68, 5.69). Many children study until 3:00 PM in the local primary school, then take their goats out to feed each afternoon. Goats are slaughtered for wedding feasts and other special events, but most are sold. The weekly market at Ejutla between Miahuatlán and Oaxaca City is known throughout Mexico for the quality of its goats, with buyers coming from as far away as Mexico City to shop for local goats. A typical price for an adult goat is $500 pesos (U.S. $45). On several occasions I asked shepherds how many goats and sheep were in their flock, and they invariably knew the number exactly. Goat's milk is not used. Pánfilo Santiago interviewed half of San Juan's households at my request to record certain basic statistics on the types and numbers of domestic animals each family kept. I discuss the results of this census below.

(Table 5.17. Domestic animal statistics for San Juan Gbëë, 2003)

Goats (*Capra hircus*, **chĭv**) outnumber sheep (*Ovis aries*, **mècw-xĭil**) about five to one. Sheep are kept for their meat and wool. Sheep's wool is washed with a local soap-root (*Microsechium helleri*, **bià-tòo**), then carded and spun (on a spinning wheel), then woven on the backstrap loom (figs. 5.70, 5.71) to make the traditional *gabán* or poncho (**càshquêm**).

The most valuable beast of burden is the donkey (*Equus asinus*, **bûrr**). Burros are on occasion ridden and even hitched to the plow (*yunta de burro*, fig. 5.72). Eucario was proud of his *"burro oficial,"* known to breeders as a "hinny," an unusual cross between a female donkey and a male horse (fig. 5.73). Eucario considered it to be superior to both donkeys and mules. Mules (male *E. asinus* x female *E. caballus*, **mûl, mâch**) and horses (*E. caballus*, **càbây**) are rare in San Juan. From the census I estimate a total of thirty-six mules in San Juan and apparently no horses. Despite the lack of horses in San Juan, horse races were revived in 1997 for the patron saint's fiesta (fig. 5.74). Not surprisingly, most competitors—and the winners—were from neighboring towns. Old-timers recount their youthful adventures as muleteers (*arrieros*). They traveled to the Isthmus of Tehuántepec, to the Pacific Coast, and to Miahuatlán and beyond, carrying *petates* from San Cristóbal Amatlán to the Isthmus to exchange for salted fish, or packing the coffee crop from the coffee plantations on the Pacific slope of the Sierra de Miahuatlán to the road heads. So San Juan has never been isolated from regional and national markets and cultural influences. Trucking has now made mule trains obsolete.

We have discussed the essential role played by oxen for plowing. Cattle (*Bos taurus*, **ngŏn** 'ox', **nòví** < Spanish *novillo* 'castrated bull', **tôr** < Spanish *toro* 'bull', **vâc** < Spanish *vaca* 'cow') are rarely kept except for that purpose.

Pigs (*Sus scrofa*, **ngŭts, cŭch**) are conspicuously absent in San Juan. Cándido bought one, which he fattened, then butchered for a birthday meal. One explanation offered is that people do not like to keep pigs because pigs in a town on the south slope of the range once consumed a human cadaver. This motivated a communal ban on pig raising in that town. There is no such ban in San Juan, but the aversion remains.

Domestic rabbits (*Oryctolagus cuniculus*, **cònéf-ró-yù**) are raised by a few families as a source of meat. They are distinguished from the native cottontails (*Sylvilagus mexicanus, S. floridanus*, **cònéf-dân**) as "town rabbits" as opposed to "forest rabbits." Curiously, the Spanish loan derived from "*conejo*" has been extended to the native cottontail species, and the native term has been lost.

Dogs (*Canis familiaris*, **mĕcw**) are common pets, occasionally trained to aid hunters pursue deer, rabbits, and birds (fig. 5.75). Local dogs are predominantly of an indigenous type. Cats (*Felis cattus*, **bĭch**) are uncommon. They are valued primarily as mousers.

Caged birds are few and are mostly local foundlings.

The Ecology of Goats in San Juan Gbëë

Goats have a bad reputation. Goat husbandry has been judged a desperate strategy of peasants forced to eke out a bare subsistence on ravaged soils, caught in a downward spiral of progressive habitat degradation. While there may be instances that fit this stereotype, by no means is it either inevitable or normally the case with goat husbandry (Estabrook 1998). San Juan supports 932 people, plus approximately 1,500 goats, not to mention 330 sheep, 200 donkeys, 36 mules, 69 oxen, and considerably more chickens, turkeys, and ducks. The larger animals (*ganado mayor*, i.e., oxen, mules, and donkeys) are beasts of burden and sources of traction for the plow, carefully tended and fed from winter stockpiles of dried cornstalks brought home by the donkey load, the donkeys piled so high that it's a wonder they can see where they are going. Goats and sheep (*ganado menor*) are far more likely to be taken to pasture each afternoon than to be fed at home. Goats predominate in nearly every flock. Tending goats, in fact, is a central chapter in many a boy's life in rural Oaxaca. Donato recalled those days of his youth fondly, a step toward manhood.

(Table 5.18. Goat statistics for San Juan Gbëë, 2003; fig. 5.76)

Tending goats is a significant responsibility for a boy or girl and a rich opportunity to learn one's country. While I have not completed a systematic investigation of the role of goats in the San Juan economy, it is likely to be similar to that described for Portuguese peasants by Estabrook (1998), that is, goats forage widely on ruderal and shrubby vegetation of disturbed soils and return home each evening to spend the night secure in the household compound, depositing their nutrient-rich dung on a prepared bed of plants gathered for that purpose, which is then collected periodically, carried to the cornfields and spread in horizontal rows to await an early preparatory plowing.

Local farmers certainly appreciate the value of goat dung for restoring soil fertility. They speak of "hot" and "cold" dung. That of goats, sheep, and oxen is "hot," while that of donkeys and mules is "cold." This distinction involves a considerable elaboration upon the familiar hot-cold dichotomy attributed to many foods and medicines, as well as the bodily conditions responsive to these substances (see chap. 6). Yet there is a conceptual link via the local conceptual association of fertility and heat. A woman after the birth of a child becomes cold, and her womb must be infused once more with heat by the administration of hot teas and baths for her to regain the balance of hot and cold required for good health.

Goat dung, as with that of sheep and oxen, does in fact impart greater fertility to the soil than that of donkeys or mules. This is a consequence of the ruminant digestive systems of the "hot-dung" animals (George Estabrook, personal communication). Furthermore, goats in particular more effectively *cycle* nutrients from the margins of San Juan agricultural lands into the soil of the milpas. By contrast, donkeys and mules, and oxen as well, simply recycle stubble grown on the milpa itself, adding nothing new. One might speculate that the primary contribution of goats to the San Juan economy is as producers of high-quality fertilizer, conveniently concentrated at the end of each day in the farmer's *solar*.

However, one should not underestimate the role of goats (and sheep) as sources of animal protein and as monetary investments, which are also critically important. Extrapolating from Pánfilo Santiago's survey of 91 San Juan households (selected opportunistically from the total of 184 and thus not a statistically reliable basis for generalization), 24 San Juan families ate thirty goats (at weddings, funerals, or other special feasts) and sold seventy-one more (for a cash value of approximately $28,000 pesos/$2,800 U.S.) during the previous year.

Thirty-three of 91 families surveyed own neither goats nor sheep; thus there are about 66 such families in all of San Juan. Oxen are less widespread still. Based on our survey we estimate that thirty-two families own oxen; twenty-eight of these own a single team of two, while four families own three oxen. So 150 families must borrow or rent a team when it is time to plow. Or, as one innovative farmer does, plow with a donkey team (*yunta de burro*), cause for widespread amusement in town but reasonably effective and affordable, as a team of oxen may set you back $5,000 pesos ($455 U.S.).

Gathering Wild Plants, Insects, and Fungi

Complementing the agricultural pursuits described above is a range of gathering activities focused on non-domesticated plants and animals. These wild foods add significant variety and nutrient balance to the diet. *Agave salmiana* (**dòb-gú-lò**) and *Agave americana* var. *oaxacana* (**dòb-**

dzìn 'honey maguey', aka ***dòb-mpiè*** '*aguamiel* maguey') are the most important species for the production of *pulque* in San Juan. Individual plants belong to the owner of the land where it grows. Both species grow wild but are also commonly transplanted to establish "living fences" and terrace walls within and between fields near town. *Agave americana* var. *oaxacana* is somewhat larger than *Agave salmiana,* and when the two species grow side by side the longer, straighter, bluish leaves of *Agave americana* var. *oaxacana* are distinctive (fig. 5.78). However, the leaves of older plants of this species tend to fold over, much as is characteristic of the leaves of *Agave salmiana.*

When the floral scape (*yàgùts*) of a mature individual begins to develop, the scape will be cut at the base, and the center of the "piña," or heart, excavated with a large, flat, spoonlike metal scraper. A large individual may give three liters of aguamiel (***mpiè***) per day for a period of fifteen days. This is collected regularly, using a funnel and a plastic bottle. *Pulque* is the result of fermentation of the *aguamiel. Tepache* (***nziù***) is a festive drink made from the fermented juice of a special variety of pineapple grown in certain mountain villages above the valleys of Oaxaca. A certain quantity of *pulque* is added to strengthen the brew, which may be seasoned with cinnamon (***cànêl***) and other spices.

Agave potatorum (***dòb-bé*** '*Oxalis* maguey') is a relatively small, wild species occasionally tapped to make *pulque,* but more often used to make mezcal (***mèzcâl***), the distilled extract of the juice squeezed from maguey hearts or *piñas* baked in an underground oven (fig. 5.78). The modifier refers to several species of *Oxalis* (***guièe-bé***) that grow wild near San Juan. These plants are placed in the earth oven with the *Agave potatorum* hearts to flavor the baked maguey and/or to facilitate the fermentation process. *Agave seemaniana* is not always clearly distinguished from *A. potatorum.* Though similar, it is much larger and has more prominently nipple-shaped spines (fig. 5.79).

San Juaneros do not make mezcal but purchase it from distillers in neighboring communities. Most *mezcaleros* use *Agave karwinskii* or *A. angustifolia.* Neither of these species is native to San Juan, though a few individuals of each have been transplanted near the town. *A. karwinskii* is the characteristic species planted on roadsides below ca. 1,650 m, as between San Cristóbal Amatlán and Miahuatlán. It is a distinctive stalked species endemic to the valleys of Oaxaca (fig. 5.80). A.

angustifolia is seen only in cultivation, typically in geometrically monocropped fields or as linear field dividers (fig. 5.81). It does not grow wild in Oaxaca.

Agave angustiarum (**dòb-guièdz** 'fiber maguey') is another common "living fence" species round about San Juan. It is the only local species of the subgenus *Littaea*, distinguished by its narrow spikelike inflorescence. This species is used primarily as a source of fiber. However, the mature flowering scape may also be eaten.

Guajes

The edible seeds of *Leucaena pallida* and of *Leucaena esculenta* (**yàg-nlíbâd**) are an important dietary adjunct. The tender new leaves are also eaten. The city of Oaxaca was named for the abundance of these trees at the site of the city's founding as an Aztec military outpost. The *guaje* tree is semidomesticated, with three species known in San Juan Gbëë (plus a wild species, the seeds of which are sometimes eaten): **yàg-nlíbâd** (*Leucaena pallida*) is the variety common in and near town, while **yàg-nlíbâd-tsŏ**, literally, 'wide *guaje*' (*Leucaena esculenta*), has wider pods and is found at lower elevations (fig. 5.82). These differ not only in the altitude at which they prosper but also in their season of maturity. *Leucaena leucocephala* ssp. *glabrata*, **yàg-nlábâd-nguiǎ**, literally, 'green *guaje*', is occasionally planted in San Juan but is more commonly cultivated at somewhat lower elevations.

Edible Invertebrates

(Table 4.13. Edible invertebrates harvested in San Juan Gbëë)

A variety of local invertebrates are considered edible, including some that are deemed delicacies and eagerly collected whenever they appear in abundance. Most are available in quantities sufficient to motivate their harvest for brief periods each year. Thus, their quantitative contribution to the local diet is limited. However, they may be rich in protein and fat and may have a significant qualitative impact. Best known is the tasty *chicatana* flying ant (**miób**). These are expected near the date of the fiesta of San Juan, June 24. Leaf-cutter ant colonies are watched for evidence of their imminent emergence, which is indicated by an accumulation of

Verónica Santiago with an edible mushroom, *měy-yùp*, *Amanita cesarea*, July 9, 2002.

material around the nest (figs. 5.83, 5.84). The edible ants are actually the reproductive caste of one or more species of the leaf-cutter ant genus *Atta* (*miâdz*).

Mushrooms

(Table 5.19. Edible fungi harvested in San Juan Gbëë)

Eleven kinds of mushrooms are reported to be eaten: *měy-còlìflôr* 'cauliflower mushroom', *Hydnum repandum*; *měy-dùuzh* 'string-bean mushroom', *Ramaria* sp.; *méy-guièl* 'corn mushroom', *Ustilago maydis*; *měy-guièt-xtîl* 'bread mushroom', *Boletus edulis* (fig. 5.85); *měy-guìin* 'chili pepper mushroom', *Hypomeces lactifluorum* (fig. 5.86); *měy-lân*$_1$ 'wool mushroom', *Agaricus silvaticus* (fig. 5.87) and *Agaricus campestris*; *měy-mdzìn* 'deer mushroom', *Tricholoma* sp.?; *měy-yàg-guièr* 'pinetree mushroom', *Pleurotus* sp. (fig. 5.88); *měy-yù* 'earth mushroom', *Polyporus* cf. *tuberaster* (fig. 5.89); and *měy-yùp* '? mushroom', *Amanita cae-*

sarea (fig. 5.90). Most are harvested during the rainy season, from about June through November. Cuitlacoche (*Ustilago maydis*; **méy-guièl**) infects growing corn ears but is considered a delicacy. *Agaricus* spp., the 'wool mushroom' (**měy-lân**)—the Zapotec name referring to the texture of the cap—may appear as early as May in open areas near town. The rest are sought in pine forests above town between 2,200 and 2,900 m after heavy rains. Mushrooms are cooked by boiling and served in stews.

Hunting

(Table 5.20. Mammal and bird species named as potential prey by San Juan Gbëë hunters)

Hunting is the serious pursuit of perhaps half a dozen men in San Juan. Many more enjoy it more as a diversion (fig. 5.91). A few houses in town sport trophy skulls or skins hung prominently on their front porches. During our stays in San Juan we observed or were shown trapped animals, skins or other parts of one deer (possibly a brocket *Mazama americana*, **mtság**, as opposed to **mdzìn**, the white-tailed deer, *Odocoileus virginianus*), two coatimundis (**mzhìidz**, *Nasua narica*), two gray foxes (**mèz**, *Urocyon cinereoargenteus*), one long-tailed weasel (**mèebè̞**, *Mustela frenata*), one armadillo (**ngùp**, *Dasypus novemcinctus*), one squirrel (**ndzĭz**, *Sciurus aureogaster*), two field mice (**mzîn**, *Peromyscus* sp.), one long-tailed wood-partridge, a fledgling rescued from a forest fire (**mtsòo**, *Dendrortyx macroura*), two horned lizards (**mdzîd**, *Phrynosoma braconnieri*), one salamander, and assorted spiders, snails, and scorpions. We ourselves observed several Mexican cottontails (**cònéf-dân**, *Sylvilagus cuniculus*), an occasional squirrel, and tracks of raccoon (**ngòl-bzhiè**, *Procyon lotor*) near town (fig. 5.92), plus two white-tailed deer near the summit of Cerro Nube Flan at 3,600 m. In short, game is scarce near town, and no great effort is made to hunt at a further remove. Thus, the meat of wild game is of minimal significance in the local diet. This may be due partly to the long-standing conflict with San Juan's neighbor to the south, Santo Domingo Ozolotepec, which has established de facto control of the highest montane forests of San Juan, the areas best for hunting.

Those who hunt favor well-used .22 rifles and may train a dog to help find and flush game. Prey most often targeted are white-tailed deer, cottontails, jackrabbits, squirrels, long-tailed wood-partridge, Montezuma quail, band-tailed pigeons, and white-winged and mourning doves.

Use of Local Materials in Manufacturing

Many San Juan houses use local timbers as structural members, mostly as roof beams. These are cut by hand or with the aid of a chainsaw. Pine trees of several species, but especially the Mexican white pine (*yàg-là*, aka *yàg-grètâd*, *Pinus ayacahuite*), are preferred. With the permission of the Comisariado de Bienes Comunales, timber may be cut from the communal forests above the town. Traditional houses in San Juan and San Pedro Gbëë (and several neighboring towns) show a distinctive local architectural style in which the roof beams project from the top of the wall and are fixed in place by wooden wedges (fig. 5.93). These wedges, or *cuñas*, are made of *Pinus teocote* (*yàg-guièr-quiè*).

In the past, house walls were of local limestone quarried above the town and free for such use with permission of the *comisariado*. In recent years, cement block trucked in from Miahuatlán has become the preferred material for the construction of walls (fig. 5.94). Several local men are accomplished masons (*albañiles*), having learned the trade by apprenticeships while living and working outside San Juan. Kitchens and sheds—as well as the houses of poorer families—are walled by daubed wooden stakes. Most roofs in San Juan today are of corrugated tin or zinc, though a few are of thatch or adobe tile. Neighboring San Pedro has a quite different architectural flavor, due in part to the fact that most roofs there are tile. The tiles are imported from Miahuatlán.

Woods Used in Manufacturing

(Table 5.21. Terms for plowing and parts of the plow in San Juan Gbëë)

San Juaneros are acutely aware of the particular properties of the wood of local trees and carefully select materials appropriate for various technical tasks. For example, the yoke that rests on the neck of the oxen to which the plow shaft is attached should be lightweight but strong. Willow (*yàg-zhguiès*, *Salix bonplandiana*) is thus preferred for this purpose. By contrast, the plough beam (*tomín*, **tòmî**) requires a very hard wood with straight grain. A particular species of oak, common in pine forests above town (*yàg-lbìis*, *Quercus laurina*), is singled out as ideal for this purpose, as it will not warp at extremes of heat and cold. For the plow itself another durable oak (*yàg-zhòg*, *Quercus conzattii* and/or *Quercus crassifolia*) or some other comparable species (e.g., *yàg-yàz*, *Lysiloma acapulcensis*) is chosen. For the *talél* (*tàlêl*), a short crosspiece that links the plow beam to the plow itself, the wood of the mulberry (*zarzamora*, *Morus celtidifolius*; *yàg-bzà*) is preferred. These preferences are similar but not identical to those of the Taleans of Gonzalez's excellent account of plow construction (2001:83–88) (figs. 5.95, 5.96).

Even toys require particular materials. Tops, for example, are carved of the hard wood of such trees as **yàg-lăy** (*Cercocarpus macrophyllus* and/or *Cercocarpus pringlei*) or made of the large seeds of *Jatropha* cf. *cordifolia* (fig. 5.97). Coral bean flowers (*Erythrina americana*, fig. 5.98) make ready-to-hand whistles, which lends this tree one of its local names, **yàg-pĭp**, while seedpods of the weedy cranesbill, **guìzh-gùdz**, literally, 'needle herb' (*Erodium cicutarium*, fig. 5.99) provide toy swords.

CHAPTER 6

Ncuàan / Medicines from Plants

ANCESTORS OF THE present-day citizens of San Juan Gbëë have lived in this same territory for well over a thousand years. They have had ample opportunity to learn to recognize the most effective native plants for curing local diseases. More recently, they have adopted new medicinal plants brought by the Spaniards.

The municipal territory encompasses a great diversity of habitats harboring hundreds of species of plants and animals. I focus in this chapter on plants because plants are the living organisms most useful for traditional medicine. Plants have evolved the capacity to produce powerful chemicals as a defense against the animals that otherwise would eat them. These same active chemicals may be used to kill or eliminate microorganisms that cause many of the most serious human diseases. However, it is most important to apply these remedies carefully, as many medicinal plants may be poisonous if the dosage is excessive.

A hospital is available in Miahuatlán, and a government clinic has operated in neighboring San Pedro Gbëë (with a subsidiary clinic in San Juan, visited by the clinic doctor once or twice a month) since about 1980. San Juaneros, as well as many citizens of San Pedro, were reluctant to make use of these facilities for a variety of reasons, despite the fact that during 1996–1998 the clinic doctor was a dedicated and sympathetic physician, which has not always been the case. As of 2001 San Juan has its own clinic, with two doctors alternating duty there. Nevertheless, herbal remedies remain the first medical recourse for most members of the community.

Are There Traditional Medical Specialists in San Juan Gbëë?

The people of San Juan Gbëë continue to rely first on local plants, wild or cultivated, and on local knowledge of the curative properties of these plants to maintain their physical and psychic well-being from birth to death. Many are nevertheless appreciative of the contributions of modern medical practice in the persons of the rotating doctors and resident nurses who staff local federally funded clinics, and of government public health efforts, such as the antimalaria campaign. These have dramatically reduced infant mortality rates and morbidity generally. Modern medicine provides a safety net, as it were, in the case of life-threatening and otherwise intractable illness. Yet for dealing with common debilitating infections, everyday aches and pains, or the psychic stresses common to the daily routines of village existence, citizens confidently rely on either the ordinary expertise of family members or the more developed experience of a half-dozen local medical specialists.

Such specialization is quite limited. Local specialists are not "professional" in that they do not support themselves and their families from income generated by their medical practice. Rather, the prototypical life story of such specialists highlights a dramatic, often traumatic, personal experience that "called" them to their curative practice. Agripina Hernández Cruz was in her late teens when she was called in a dream to minister to a critically ill relative, who in fact survived with her help. Agripina credits her father for having taught her much of the detailed knowledge she applies in treating sick kin and neighbors. She makes day-long solitary journeys into the surrounding forests and woodlands to maintain her supplies of medicinal plant materials or to collect some urgently needed remedy. She generally will receive a small cash payment for her efforts, but scarcely enough to purchase basic necessities, which are instead provided by the subsistence work of her extended family, work to which she actively contributes. Thus, among those reported to be the most knowledgeable healers, there is some slight degree of specialization, perhaps by interest most of all. I will return to this after a short digression.

The doctors who staff isolated rural clinics of the Instituto Mexicano del Seguro Social (IMSS) are recently matriculated medical students performing their *servicio* as quid pro quo for their subsidized medical education. They may have little interest in or understanding of the village to which they have been posted and may be eager to leave at the end of the year. I arrived in San Juan in July of 1996, just as the clinic doctor in San Pedro was replaced by Miguel Ángel Espinosa S., accompanied by his young wife, Irma, and their children. Dr. Espinosa proved to be unusual in his dedication to and empathy for the local people. In fact, he volunteered to extend his tour of duty for a second year.

We got to know him and his family well, since at that time San Juan had no clinic of its own but was one of three local towns under Dr. Espinosa's care. We made regular trips transporting neighbors to the clinic, and I once drove myself there in our *bocho rojo* with a bandaged and bleeding hand, having suffered a nasty cut in a fall in town. He did an exceptional job patching me up. I learned a great deal from Miguel Ángel about the people's hopes and fears with regard to the modern medical practice he represented. He also freely shared statistical summaries of mortality and children's nutritional status collected by the medical staff over the years since the clinic was founded in San Pedro in 1978.

In part to improve his working relationships with the local *médicos tradicionales* in San Pedro—his local "competition," as he once joked—he organized a half-day workshop, inviting six local practitioners (of whom four participated), his local nursing staff, me, and my assistant Oscar Barrera, who, with the assent of all, videotaped the proceedings (fig. 6.1). I brought a sample of plants to initiate our discussion, but the main goal set by Dr. Espinosa was to invite the local practitioners to express their concerns. Participants included two "herbalists," Alejandro Fabián López and Sofía Fabián Cruz, the latter also a midwife, Graciano Mendoza López, a bone-setter, and Sabina Antonia Méndez, who specialized in the diagnosis—by reading the pulse—and treatment of *chaneque*, a debilitating condition sent by the Earth as punishment for laziness. I learned of the local specializations and of the Mexican government program to license *médicos tradicionales* after successful completion of a short course in Oaxaca City. Sabina, the *chanequera*, proudly displayed her IMSS license and recounted how she was called to her work.

In San Juan Gbëë there seem to be less clearly defined roles among the *médicos tradicionales* or local practitioners. In San Juan there is but one elderly midwife. It is uncertain who might take her place when she dies, other than the staff of the government clinic. In addition there are five elderly persons highly recommended by the municipal authorities as particularly knowledgeable about the curative properties of plants (fig. 6.2). Three are men, two women, and all past sixty years of age.

In San Pedro, one local "expert," Alejandro Fabián of Dr. Espinosa's workshop, has studied with professional herbalists in Oaxaca City, adding remedies to his repertoire selected from a wider transcultural tradition that synthesizes central Mexican, medieval European, New Age, and allopathic curative elements. However, it is not clear how profoundly these "outside" ideas have affected local belief and practice. (My colleague Meinardo Hernández was commissioned by the municipal authorities to decorate the walls on Main Street with admonitions to quit smoking as a public health concern [fig. 6.3], an example of the influence of "modern" medical perspectives.) Twenty-four percent of the medicinal plants I recorded in use locally are nonnative, that is, they were absent from Mesoamerica prior to the European invasion. It is also widely recognized that the pervasive "hot-cold" distinction is likely to have been at least in part inspired by Old World humoral theories (Foster 1953, 1987; but see López Austin 1980; Ortiz de Montellano 1990:220–21). Nevertheless, local people discourse fluently about dozens of diseases and hundreds of plant remedies in their native Zapotec.

The case of Alejandro Fabián illustrates the complexity of local ethnomedical "traditions." He bragged to us that he learned to cure *not* from his parents, but from *books*. This man stood out in his ambition to be recognized as a professional herbalist. He traveled widely (as far as Portland, Oregon, to visit relatives, on one occasion), adopting new remedies from varied sources, and he maintained a house in a *colonia* on the edge of Oaxaca City in addition to his home in San Pedro. We visited him there at his invitation and were proudly shown his medicinal herb garden. We noticed that his son had injured his foot, and we asked how he treated the injury, as the foot was covered with a whitish paste. He announced that the remedy was something new, called *"colgate,"* which, pronounced in Spanish, at first eluded us, until we realized it was a popular brand of toothpaste! Nevertheless, Alejandro's curative practice was solidly rooted in the traditional knowledge of his community, as was apparent in the focus group discussion with San Pedro *médicos tradicionales* organized by the local clinic doctor.

Despite Dr. Espinosa's best efforts to come to terms with his local "competition," he was never quite able to overcome local suspicions and jealousies. He often was at odds with Sofía Fabián Cruz, the herbalist and midwife of our workshop. Some months after that meeting, as I was driving into town, her son flagged me down, pleading for me to come to their house to meet with his mother. Sofía and Miguel Ángel were at an impasse, as he required as a condition of allowing her to deliver infants that she bring the women to the clinic at the appropriate time, so that he might be available if complications should arise. She refused, arguing that the women were afraid to go to the clinic; they feared they or their baby would die there. This fear may well have had a basis in fact, given that it is likely that only the most difficult births were brought to the clinic in the past, and not all were successful. I promised to convey her views to the doctor. However, I suspect the issue was resolved only by the doctor's departure at the end of his tour of duty.

The new clinic in San Juan, which opened in 2000, has not yet generated such public conflicts. However, the doctors who have served here have expressed little understanding of or respect for local curative practice, and the great majority of illness episodes are handled without the benefit of their federally subsidized ministrations.

In the summer of 2000 I presented the San Juan authorities a first draft of a booklet entitled *Las plantas medicinales de San Juan Gbëë* (The medicinal plants of San Juan Gbëë), a summary of what I had learned from my conversations with townspeople, with Spanish text, local Zapotec names, and summaries of local recipes for the medicinal use of some 150 species of plants, a broadly representative but by no means exhaustive sample of local herbal remedies. The municipal president at the time, Florestino Hernández, organized a series of community meetings to review my text, at one point devoting three hours to a paragraph-by-paragraph redaction of the text to a crowd of over a dozen interested townspeople. I was relieved that they were enthusiastic about the project and found little to disagree with in my summaries. The municipal president then encouraged me to review the text in a more leisurely fashion with four designated local experts. I met individually with three of these experts, and one other man not on the official experts list. We reviewed each entry in the book to assess their agreement with the text and to refine my presentation. I found very little disagreement on issues of knowledge and belief among these experts, which supports my impression that knowledge of medicinal plant use in San Juan Gbëë is very widely shared among San Juan adults. I have noted, however, that on certain "sensitive" medical questions, such as the use and abuse of abortifacients and the nature and treatment of certain "supernatural" illnesses, deference may be shown by one expert to another. I suspect this deference is not a question of differential expert knowledge but rather of the willingness of the expert to explicitly discuss these issues.

There is one final element of the complex of local medical practice to be noted. Our neighbor and early confidant, Pedro Miguel Zurita, a devout Catholic deeply involved with local church affairs, fell sick one spring. He was exhausted, lay in bed to conserve his energy, and refused to bathe for fear of the cold, instead swaddling himself in the locally woven woolen *gabanes*. He would not leave his compound, suggesting that to do so would expose him to danger. After some weeks of this, he requested that I drive him to Miahuatlán so that he might participate in a faith healing prayer service at the office of a noted practitioner of that art. I learned later that he had recovered. San Juaneros describe many treatments for diseases of character, spirit, and imagination. I suspect that the unnamed malady that afflicted Pedro had, in his mind, to do with witchcraft, and that as a devout Catholic he trusted more to prayer than to local herbal remedies.

In sum, the citizens of San Juan Gbëë share an extensive and mostly effective body of knowledge about the treatment of disease, primarily focused on herbal applications. Most herbal remedies are "traditional" in the sense that they are learned from family and neighbors rather than from books or training courses such as are offered in Oaxaca City. There is little or no esoteric knowledge and at the present time no shamanistic practice, though one may hear veiled allusions to witchcraft (e.g., ***mzhièe*** 'witch'). The bulk of this traditional medical knowledge is acquired by children of both sexes at an early age informally in the context of helping their parents, grandparents, aunts, uncles, and elder siblings at everyday subsistence work, whether in the kitchen, garden, field, or forest. That there are some striking differences in herbal medical practice between San Juan and San Pedro suggests that there is little direct sharing of such knowledge between these two neighboring communities. Thus, the "traditional" transmission process is strongly community-based with minimal specialization.

Does San Juan Gbëë Traditional Medicine Work?

A key question, whether explicit or implicit, in any analysis of traditional medical practice is, "Does it really work?" "Really" suggests a universal standard by which one may judge the effectiveness of curative treatments. But what is that standard? Does a universal standard exist? Most of us would assume, perhaps without question, that that standard is set by modern or "Western scientific" medical theory and practice. Yet cultural theory in contemporary anthropology is sharply critical of such a view, of attributing anything like omniscience to modern medicine as opposed to other curative theories and practices (Kleinman 1973; Mishler 1981; Haraway 1994). The extreme relativists among these critical theorists—"constructivists" or "poststructuralists"—go so far as to reject altogether the possibility that any theory or practice might claim to represent "the Truth." Science, from this perspective, is but one of many controlling ideological designs that is not powerful because it is true, but is "true" because of its power to define our understanding of "reality." This debate lands us squarely within the bitter "culture wars" of the late twentieth century, a battleground I would as soon avoid.

My view is this: Science—medical or otherwise—is a universal potential of humanity grounded in the obvious adaptive value of empirical validation of the "conceptual worlds" in which we all live. We have seen that Zapotec biological science is highly developed, incorporating a system of classification and nomenclature that compares very favorably with that of modern biosystematics. One may judge the "empirical validity" of the San Juan Zapotec ethnobotanical classification by comparing each Zapotec plant or animal taxon with the Linnaean taxa with which it most closely corresponds. One could then measure the degree of correspondence between the two systems (cf. Hunn 1975b, 1999b). However, it is not so easy to judge the "empirical validity" of local ethnomedical knowledge and practice. Such knowledge systems involve not only the recognition of, for example, the plants selected for use, but also the recognition of categories of "disease" defined by reference to a complex of perceived behavioral and sensory phenomena symptomatic of a particular malady (Maffi 1994), while "successful treatment" is defined by social understandings that the symptoms of the disease have been ameliorated and/or that the disease has been "cured."

It is worth emphasizing that modern "scientific" understanding of disease etiology—which in many cases will define appropriate courses of treatment and the evaluation of their success—is based on microbiological and/or biochemical analyses "visible" only with the aid of a sophisticated sensory technology. For example, should we dismiss Zapotec medicine as unscientific because there is no recognition of viruses as pathogens or of genetic abnormalities as implicated in disease causation? Rather, I prefer the standard defined by Ortiz de Montellano in his analysis of the efficacy of Aztec herbal remedies (1975, 1986). He judged an Aztec treatment "effective" if contemporary scientific research supported the symptomatic relief attributed to that remedy in the context of Aztec theories of disease, whether or not we would judge the Aztec perspective to be correct. For example, Aztec doctors attributed headaches to an excess of blood in the head. They thus might prescribe as an inhalant an herb they called "sneeze plant," known to severely irritate the mucous membrane (Ortiz de Montellano 1990:149–50).

Thus, to evaluate San Juan Gbëë Zapotec herbal medicine requires first that we gain some appreciation of their theories of disease. What "diseases" did they recognize and name, and how did they decide what would be an appropriate course of treatment for those diseases? For starters, it is essential that we not assume that Zapotec disease terms that appear to correspond to some familiar disease category in our own language have the same meaning in other cultural contexts. A case in point is the term "cancer." In Zapotec there is a disease called *cânzr* (and a plant used in its treatment called *guìzh-cânzr*). The term is an obvious borrowing from the local Spanish term *cáncer*. What is cancer? Are we talking about the same thing, whether in English, Spanish, or Zapotec? We understand cancer to be a life-threatening disease caused by "runaway replication" by certain cells in our bodies, induced by DNA damage. We treat it aggressively by surgical removal of tumors—where these rogue cells are concentrated—and/or treatment with chemical poisons or radiation designed to kill the cells responsible without killing the sick person. It is perhaps not surprising that San Juaneros—at least the vast majority of them, barring those who might someday complete postgraduate training in medicine—do not understand *cânzr* in this way. Nor should we expect their treatment protocols to resemble in any way those of our medical specialists, which, of course, are constantly modified on the basis of new evidence.

In San Juan Gbëë *cânzr* refers to a seriously infected wound that resists normal healing. The borrowing from Spanish likely involves conflating two Spanish terms, *cáncer* and *cangrena*, 'gangrene'. This interpretation is supported by a study of local disease categories by a medical doctor in Tlacolula, a market town among valley Zapotec communities (Aguilar Castro 1992:88). Dr. Aguilar Castro notes that his patients equate the two Spanish terms. The appropriate treatment for **cânzr** in San Juan Gbëë involves bathing the wound in an infusion of several local plants, including **guìzh-cânzr,** a category inclusive of several species of the Boraginaceae, such as *Tournefortia densiflora, Tournefortia hartwegiana,* and *Cordia salvadorenesis,* combined with *Bocconia arborescens* (Papaveraceae, named **ârnìcà** locally, though not at all related to plants so-called elsewhere), *Gnaphalium* spp. (**gòrdòlôb**), and *Solanum* cf. *nigrum* (**pchŭux-làs**). I have no way of knowing whether this treatment is effective in curing the infected wound—though the three Borage family species cited have all been reported to have medicinal value, *Tournefortia densiflora* noted in one experimental study as "being the most potent [of eight species tested] against [*Entamoeba histolytica* and *Giardia lamblia*]" (Tapia-Pérez et al. 2003)—but it would certainly be absurd to judge the local treatment ineffective because it does not address what we understand as "cancer."

A second example is the psychosomatic malady known throughout Latin America variously as *susto* or *espanto,* derived from the verbs *asustar* and *espantar* respectively, both meaning 'to frighten'. Scholars debate long and hard such issues as the relationship between these maladies and "soul loss" and the degree to which we should attribute physiological, as opposed to psychological factors as causative (Rubel 1967; O'Nell and Selby 1968; Fabrega and Silver 1973; O'Nell 1975; Klein 1978; Rubel, O'Nell, and Collado-Árdon 1989). Several well-known studies are based on Zapotec material. In the Zapotec communities of these published studies, the disease was named in Spanish or in Zapotec by a Spanish loanword, which might suggest that the syndrome was a colonial imposition. However, in San Juan Gbëë "espanto" is called **dzéb,** clearly an authentic Zapotec term derived from the verb **rtsêb** 'to frighten', and thus presumably naming an indigenous concept. I should also note that San Juaneros have a very elaborate understanding of **dzéb,** recognizing a number of named subtypes and applying an impressive array of plants in their treatment. One might even conclude that San Juaneros are obsessed with **dzéb.** It seems unlikely that **dzéb** would have precisely the same range of meanings as either *susto* or *espanto* in Michoacán or Argentina, for example, though there is a family resemblance. In San Juan the disease is attributed to a frightening experience, and the symptoms include a loss of animation or "spirit" (not "soul loss" per se). One common variety is translated *"espanto de noche"* (***dzéb-guièel***) and is characterized by nightmares and loss of sleep. With the exception of the variety called "great fright" (***dzéb-ròo***), treatments involve drinking teas brewed or steeped from the recommended plants, some of which, but by no means all, are European introductions.

Local Perceptions and Understandings of Disease

My San Juan Gbëë ethnobiological research project was not designed to produce a comprehensive ethnomedical ethnography. Rather, I have tried to record medicinal uses when relevant for every local plant or animal, with notes on the illnesses so treated, the plant or animal part used, the mode of administration (sometimes including the dosage), and whether the treatment is considered "hot" (***ndzëë-w***) or "cold" (***niág-á***), or something in between. A more detailed analysis is reserved for the future (cf. Croom 1983 for methodological standards).

We have recorded local medicinal uses for 266 species of plants (of 174 genera of 76 families), both native and introduced, and a few additional animal and mineral product treatments. This does not entirely exhaust the medical resources available to San Juaneros, but the local herbal remedies constitute a very significant fraction of such resources. Predominant plant families include Asteraceae (43+ species of 22 genera), Fabaceae (20+ species of 10 genera), Lamiaceae (11+ species of 8 genera), Solanaceae (12+ species of 5 genera), and Rosaceae (9 species of 6 genera). Very few local herbal remedies are truly exotic: 97 percent of medicinal herb species used in San Juan Gbëë grow in the *municipio*. Thirty-seven percent of medicinal herb species are cultivated (11 percent of these also grow wild); 68 percent grow wild. However, 41 percent of these may be classified as ruderal species, that is, weedy species that are typical of disturbed soils on the margins of towns, roads and trails, and cultivated fields. Seventy-six percent of local herbal remedies are native species. As one might expect, most introduced herbal remedies (88 percent) are cultivated, and the noncultivated introduced species are weeds.

(Table 6.1. Medicinal plant species by origin [native to Mexico or introduced from elsewhere] and management status [cultivated, wild, both, or market herbs]; Table 6.2. Noncultivated medicinal plant species [including those that occur both cultivated and noncultivated] by association with human disturbance; Table 6.3. Summary of types of medicinal plant treatments in San Juan Gbëë)

How to Talk about Disease in San Juan Gbëë Zapotec

'Disease' in general is **guièl-guîdz**, compounded of the prefix **guièl-**, which sets apart names for an extensive set of moral abstractions of both positive and negative valence (table 6.4), plus a suffix **-guîdz**, which serves as the head element of a number of terms for specific diseases, typically of a psychosomatic character (table 6.5). 'Health' is **guièl-ndâan**. Allied verbs include **rzàcnè** or **rlân-guîdz** 'to get sick' and **rùn-guiàc** 'to heal' (**rùn-** 'to do, make').

(Table 6.4. Examples of terms with the prefix guièl-; Table 6.5. Examples of diseases with the suffix guîdz)

There is no explicit distinction between symptoms, syndromes, and diseases, as each may be treated in its own right. For example, "fever" (**xlěë**) as a symptom may be treated with baths or teas of "cold" plants, but the presence of fever with other symptoms may require special treatment, as in the case of the distinction between "hot" and "cold" diarrheas. Some diseases are named by reference to a symptom with a modifier. Terms we might translate as 'pain' are commonly employed in such compounds, much as in English: e.g., **yòob-zdòo** 'stomachache' < **yòob** '[severe] pain, ache' + **zdòo** 'stomach', but **zdòo** may also refer to the heart, lungs (**zdòo-pùlmôn**), and/or liver, which introduces a certain ambiguity. Additional examples include **yòob-guìc** 'headache', **yòob-lây** 'toothache', **yòob-yàn** 'tonsillitis' (literally, 'sore throat'), **yòob-zhìts** 'backache', and **yòob-dzìt** 'rheumatism (literally, 'bone ache'). In Gbëë Zapotec one is "hit/stuck with pain" (e.g., **rquià yòob guìc nàa**, 'I have a headache' ('to hit/stick' + '[severe] pain' + 'head' + 'I'). However, if the pain is minor, it is better to say **nè guìc nàa** < 'I have a headache' ('[minor] pain' + 'head' + 'I'). The two terms for pain contrast not only in intensity, but also conceptually, as **nè** is treated as a physical sensation, while **yòob** is treated as an external force affecting the person.

San Juan Gbëë Zapotec has altered the meaning of the widespread Zapotec term **ncuàan**. In Mitla Zapotec, for example, it refers to any edible green (Messer 1978), but in San Juan it serves as a general term for 'medicine', roughly equivalent to the Spanish loan **rmêd** (*remedio*). However, **ncuàan** also means 'poison'. This near equation of medicine and poison is a quite accurate perception, as many medicines are derived from plant chemicals that have evolved as defenses against herbivores (Johns 1996), discouraging predation by poisoning the predator. The challenge—whether for modern allopathic medicine or traditional Zapotec ethnomedical practice—is to determine a dosage that "poisons" the disease without killing the patient.

Several plants used medicinally are named by expressions of the form 'medicine [for] X': **ncuàan-bzhiân** 'rage medicine', **ncuàan-yâas** 'black [meat] medicine', and **ncuàan-zân** 'childbirth medicine'. Most notable is **ncuàan-dzéb** 'fright medicine', several varieties of which are used to treat *espanto*. In each of these cases, the disease is somehow extraordinary, perhaps suggesting a certain antiquity to this usage. One further instance supports this impression: **zhì-ncuàan-ná-zhnâzh** 'the Virgin Mother's medicine', by which the notorious Aztec hallucinogenic morning glory, *Turbina corymbosa*, is known. By contrast, one does not refer to ***ncuàan-yòob-guìc** 'headache medicine', perhaps because a headache is a more routine malady.*

In additional cases the medicinal plant name refers explicitly to the targeted disease but assigns the plant not to the general category 'medicine' but to a life-form based on plant morphology (cf. Berlin 1992; Brown 1984): **yàg-bdìin** '*mal aire* tree', **yàg-guídz-zân** 'childbirth tree', **yàg-ngùd-lèn** 'hernia tree', **yàg-ngùd-guèy-pcàal** 'nightmare white zapote', **guìzh-cânzr** 'cancer herb', **guìzh-biè** 'cataract herb', **guìzh-zân** 'childbirth herb', **guìzh-rquià-yàn** 'herb for the throat', **guìzh-zhì-wìin** 'herb of his/her weeping', and **blàg-pâsm** '*pasmo* leaf'. The sixteen examples just cited of plant names that explicitly refer to the disease treated make up just 7 percent of the total inventory of Gbëë Zapotec medicinal plant

---

* The term **ncuàan-yè** '*chepíl*' (*Crotalaria* spp.), which might appear to refer to 'green/unripe medicine', in fact names a plant best known as an edible green, though it has medicinal applications. It is likely that this usage reflects the more widespread, and thus presumably prior, Zapotec usage of **ncuàan** to refer to edible greens.

names. In the great majority of cases, the plant is named for some other characteristic or bears a name that cannot be analyzed.

Ethnonosology

I regret that I failed to investigate systematically how San Juaneros conceptualize the relationship among the diseases they recognize, that is, their *ethnonosology* or taxonomy of diseases. Such an account would be an *emic* perspective on the phenomenon of disease. This might be approximated by a pile-sorting task in which several individuals representing varied perspectives (e.g., male vs. female, young vs. old, expert vs. layperson) are asked to sort cards on which are written a sample of disease names, in Zapotec whenever possible, or in both Zapotec and Spanish. Lacking that, I have invented an *etic* classification, which, I trust, does not do too serious violence to local understandings or those of modern allopathic medicine. Altogether I have recorded some 390 remedies involving 215 distinct plant taxa named in the local Zapotec.

Briefly, I have grouped locally recognized disease entities as follows:

1. Gastrointestinal diseases, for example, such complaints as stomachache, diarrhea, and dysentery. In several analyses of Mexican traditional medicine, this category encompasses the greatest number of remedies. In fact, Elois Ann and Brent Berlin devoted an entire 557-page volume entitled *Medical Ethnobiology of the Highland Maya of Chiapas, Mexico* (1996) to "the gastrointestinal diseases." This category also ranks first in San Juan Gbëë, with eighty treatments cited, over 20 percent of the total. These remedies involve seventy generic folk plant taxa.
2. Diseases of the eyes, ears, nose, and throat, that is, the traditional anatomical territory of the otolaryngologist. This category includes respiratory complaints such as colds, coughs, and sore throats (including the mumps), but also includes nosebleeds, cataracts, and dental caries. I have recorded forty-one remedies utilizing thirty-nine plant taxa under this heading.
3. Skin diseases, ranging from diaper rash to "cancer," that is, the seriously infected wounds so-called in Oaxaca. This is a large category of fifty-four remedies that employ forty-six named plant taxa. I have

included measles here and a strange local malady called in Zapotec, literally, "black meat" (*bĕël-yâas*), characterized by black blotches on the skin and "sore bones." This may be due to a buildup of toxins due to liver or kidney failure.

4. "Bodily aches and pains" is the second-most "popular" disease category (though I must emphasize that it is a rather arbitrary collection of maladies), with seventy-four recorded remedies that employ fifty-seven plant taxa. These are defined broadly to include bone, joint, and muscular pains due to systemic and/or physical traumas, plus headaches and fevers.

5 & 6. My fifth and sixth categories are closely related in my mind, at least, and might be united. The fifth category includes eleven remedies for urino-genital complaints, while the sixth includes thirty related to childbirth. Together the forty-one remedies for these complaints involve thirty-six named plant taxa.

7 & 8. Diseases of character, mind, and soul. By labeling them psychosomatic and supernatural I do not wish to underestimate the reality and severity of these conditions, as several can kill and all can be severely debilitating. More than any other illnesses, these reflect the critical moral balance that San Juaneros seek to maintain among the individual, the family, the community, and the land on which their lives depend (cf. Ortiz de Montellano 1990 for Aztec parallels). Together these two categories account for eighty-eight remedies, employing seventy-two distinct plant taxa. Thus, if combined they would outrank even the gastrointestinal diseases in local estimation. The most prominent subcategory of these diseases is known in the local Zapotec as *dzéb,* which may be glossed in Spanish as either *susto* or *espanto* and in English as 'fright'.

Finally, there is a handful of complaints that defy ready categorization or are still imperfectly understood. In this miscellaneous category I include three veterinary remedies, three plants used to discourage insect pests, six diseases of uncertain nature, and another seven cited only as "medicinal."

I make no claim that this scheme reflects how the people of San Juan Gbëë conceptualize the domain of "illness." However, I have reviewed a draft of this analysis with a number of San Juaneros, and they seem to find it reasonable. I cite local Zapotec terms for each condition when I am reasonably certain that the Zapotec term corresponds closely to the English gloss. Otherwise, English glosses are translations of Spanish terms provided by bilingual consultants. An interesting comparison is provided by the more extensive glossary of Tlacolula Zapotec illness categories of Salvador Aguilar Castro (1992), whose analysis is based on his twenty years of experience as a private medical practitioner in Tlacolula, a town near Mitla and some fifty kilometers north of San Juan. The 102 illness categories he describes are named in Spanish, however, so their semantic comparability with the Zapotec systems of neighboring Zapotec-speaking communities is uncertain. I list below eighty-nine distinct medical problems treated with herbal remedies in San Juan Gbëë. A more intensive analysis would no doubt expand this list.

Gastro-intestinal complaints (13): diarrhea (**guídz-dán**); dysentery (**yòob-chèn**), whether "bloody" (*de sangre*) or "of white mucus" (*de moco blanco*); stomachache (**yòob-zdòo**) and "*ataque del estómago*"; vomiting (**guídz-rdzìb**); nausea (**rdzié guìc**); intestinal blockage, aka "*empacho*" (**èmpâch**); constipation (**guídz-ràgw**); bile, aka "*bilis*"; intestinal worms (**lòmbrîz**); and hangovers (*la cruda*).

Eye, ear, nose, mouth, and throat complaints (17): coughs (**rò**); whooping cough (**rò-dòo**); colds (**guìdz-guià**) and flu, and stuffy nose; nosebleed; tonsillitis (**yòob-yàn**) and sore throat; mumps (**bĕdz**); canker sores, aka "*fuegos, granos en la boca*"; toothache (**yòob-lây**); cavities (**mêy**); rampant caries in children (**mdzoc**); gingivitis (**baa**); cataracts (**biè**); bloodshot and/or infected eyes (**nĕ lô mé**, not to be confused with the "evil eye," **rquín-lô**, which is attributed to witchcraft); and earache.

Skin complaints (16): pimples, boils, and sores, aka "*granos*," "*ronchas*" (**guièdz, guièdz-bâb**); diaper rash, aka "*granitos*," "*salpullidos del bebé*" (**mchèel**); blisters (**merguieg**); vitiligo, aka "*manchas blancas*" (**bĕy**); eczema or shingles, aka "*cuero de res*" or "*cuerdas*"; mange (**guièdz-mĕed**); burns; cuts; wounds; gangrenous or badly infected wounds with blood poisoning (**cânzr**); insect bites and stings; swelling and itching due to contact with poisonous plants; stings and bites of insects; and dandruff (**ctòo**).

Aches, pains, and fever (11): fever (**xlĕë**); headache (**yòob-guìc**); rheumatism (**yòob-dzìt**); sore back (**nĕ zhìts**); sore hands (**nĕ niă**); sore feet (**nĕ** *nì*); *chaneque* (*chànêcw*); hemorrhaging; heart palpitations; *běël-yâaz* 'black meat', a condition characterized by black spots on the skin and sore bones and tendons; and *pasmo* (*pâsm*), characterized by chills and fever, sore joints, and swelling with skin eruptions (cf. Artschwager Kay 1996:53).

Urinary tract and blood problems (4): urinary difficulty, aka "*mal de orina*"; back pain (due to kidney problems); kidney and gallstones (*cálculos*, *guìdz-riân*); and diabetes.

Reproductive problems and treatments related to childbirth (*guídz-zân*) (9): to facilitate birth; to abort a fetus (*rdèd zhìn*); to relieve the pain of childbirth; to regain strength ("heat") after childbirth; to draw out "air" from the mother's body following birth; to stanch hemorrhages; to treat retained placenta; to maintain menstrual regularity; and to augment potency.

Psychological, characterological, and spiritual complaints (12): epilepsy (*guídz-gùtiè, guídz-rcòw, guídz-rzhìdz*); nerves, aka "*nervios*"; fright, aka "*espanto*" (*dzéb*), including "night fright" (*dzéb-guièel*) and "great fright" (*dzéb-dòo* or *dzéb-nrôob*); jealousy, aka "*muina*"; rage, aka "*berrinche*," "*coraje*" (*bzhiàn*); separation anxiety, aka "*llanto*" or "*trizteza*" (*wìin*); nightmares; insanity; "evil airs" (*guídz-bdìin*), (*guídz-mê*), (*mé yôzh*); and "evil eye" (*rquín-lô*).

Miscellaneous (5): repel flies; trap fleas, combat chigger and noxious insect infestations; veterinary medicines; poisoning of animals.

"Hot" and "Cold"

As is the case throughout greater Mexico, medicines, foods, and diseases are characterized with respect to a pervasive qualitative dimension labeled metaphorically in terms of contrasting poles: "hot" and "cold," in Spanish *caliente* or *fresca* (or *templada* if intermediate), in Mixtepec Zapotec *ndzěë-w* or *niág-à*. Scholars endlessly debate the origins of this system, the dominant view being that it represents a stripped-down version of the Old World classification of bodily humors as variously hot, cold, wet, or dry, a system perhaps first devised in India some 3,000 years ago, subsequently pervading human understanding of health and disease from China (Anderson 1984) to the Mediterranean, to be finally introduced to New World native communities by Spanish priests (Foster 1953, 1987).

However, I find the minority view convincing (e.g., López Austin 1980), that a similar but distinct dichotomous classificatory system had been independently developed in Mesoamerica. Ortiz de Montellano (1990:213–21) notes that sixteenth-century European accounts of Aztec medicinal practice (Hernández 1959 [1577]; Sahagún 1950–69 [1560–65]) criticize Aztec doctors for *misclassifying* diseases as hot or cold, suggesting that the Aztec doctors had not learned the system from their overlords but rather were analyzing disease by reference to a distinctly different indigenous system.

Scholars also continue to debate the issue of whether the Mesoamerican hot-cold classificatory scheme is a "logical" system with some as yet imperfectly understood empirical basis or rather a mishmash of disconnected attributions. One thing is certain: "hot" and "cold" in this context do not refer in any simple way to temperature. Of course, in English we describe chili peppers as "hot" regardless of their temperature, not to mention "hot" licks and "cool" jazz. The English semantic equation of "spicy" and "hot" is not found in Spanish: chilies are *picante*, literally, 'biting', not *caliente*, literally 'hot'. Nor are chilies "hot" in Zapotec, but rather **niǎn**. Be that as it may, the underlying logic of the Mesoamerican metaphor of "hot" and "cold" continues to challenge analysis.

In response to those who have argued that there is no "system" to the designation of plants as of "hot" or "cold" natures throughout Latin America, I offer this comparison of the attributions current in San Juan Gbëë with those attributed to the same or closely related species according to Linares, Bye, and Flores in their *Plantas medicinales de México: Usos y remedios tradicionales* (1999). Of forty-six medicinal herbs treated in their popular summary of common Mexican curative plants, nineteen closely match herbal remedies in my inventory from San Juan. Of these seventeen are characterized as "hot," "cold," or "temperate" in both (two are characterized by Linares, Bye, and Flores but not specified as to "heat" in my data). Of those, six of seven considered "cold" by Linares, Bye, and Flores are likewise characterized in San Juan, while all ten characterized as "hot" by Linares, Bye, and Flores are similarly treated in San Juan. The single exception is partial. The *rosa de castilla* is considered to be "cordial," that is, neither particularly "hot" nor "cold," by Linares, Bye, and Flores, while it is considered to be "cold" in San Juan. Finally, fennel (*Foeniculum vulgare*), though "cold" in both inventories, may be used to treat "cold" illnesses if mixed with chamomile (*Matricaria recutita*), a "hot" plant. This strategy of "tempering" the quality of an herb to avoid a conflict between the quality of the plant and of the disease to be treated is specifically noted by both Linares, Bye, and Flores (1999:58, 90) and my San Juan consultants.

(Table 6.6. Medicinal herbs characterized as to "hot" or "cold" by Linares, Bye, and Flores [1999], with San Juan Gbëë correspondences)

Katz (1992:101–2) develops an intriguing analysis of the hot-cold system of a community in the Mixteca Alta. The distinction is labeled in the local Mixtec language as *ihni* 'hot' and *viji* 'cold'. Foods are variously classified as hot or cold: tortillas are "hot," while beans are "cold"; chicken is "hot," while pork is "cold." Katz enumerates a range of criteria that may be applied. The classification of foods may reflect habitat, whether grown in "hot [and humid] country" or "cold [and dry] country," and/or season, that is, whether gathered in the rainy ["cold"] or dry ["hot"] season. (Note that there is no consistent equation of "hot" and "cold" with "wet" and "dry"; this "four-celled" classification more closely approximates the Old World humoral system than does the more widely reported twofold contrast of "hot" and "cold.") In this context, the distinction accurately reflects typical ambient temperatures, since the first rains in late May or early June mark the transition from the hot and dry months of spring to the warm but wet months of the summer monsoon.

Foods may also be classified with regard to the plant part consumed. Aboveground parts such as leaves and stems are more likely to be considered "hot" than underground parts, such as roots, tubers, or bulbs, which are typically considered to be "cold." In addition, plants and animals gain "heat" as they mature, then lose it as they wither or age. Foods are also classified by taste. Those that are spicy or sweet tend to be considered "hot," while those that are sour or bitter are likely to be "cold" (n.b., in San Juan bitter plants are "hot"). Hot foods aid digestion (in moderation), while greasy, heavy, or raw or poorly cooked foods (or simply those cooked "wet," that is, maintaining their humidity by boiling, frying, or baking) are "cold," and thus more difficult to digest. Ideally, a meal is composed of an artful balance of these qualities.

Katz notes further (1992:103–4) that the relevance of the hot-cold and wet-dry dimensions extend beyond diet to climate, agriculture, and procreation. Katz's Mixteco consultants considered the conjunction of heat and humidity to promote fertility, as when the rains begin, saturating the hot earth, spurring the rapid growth of maize, or when the humid womb of a sexually mature woman is impregnated. A pregnant woman is "hot." After she has given birth, her womb is "cold" (as is her infant child, which has drawn off the heat of her womb but who nevertheless remains "cold" and delicate) and must be heated by appropriate treatments, such as bathing in the steam bath, or *temazcal* (symbolically equated with the womb, caves, and pots for cooking).

The Mixtec classification of a number of illnesses as "hot" or "cold" makes sense in the context of the Mixtec worldview outlined above. Indigestion, stomachache, and *"empacho"* are considered to be "cold" conditions that should be treated with "hot" remedies. Diarrhea is considered to result from poorly digested food and is thus a "cold" condition. Likewise, *empacho* (Zolla et al. 1988) is caused by eating too much "cold" food, which "sticks" in one's intestines. However, constipation is a "hot" condition, as it is seen as the opposite of diarrhea.

It is also worth noting that the "hot-cold" dimension is interpreted quite literally in certain contexts. For example, San Juaneros, in agreement with Katz's Mixtec consultants, are firmly convinced that it is harmful to one's health to drink cold liquids when one is overheated by work in the hot sun. They consistently prefer their beer, soft drinks, or water at ambient temperature, particularly when they feel "hot." They explain that the radical conjunction of extreme heat and cold in the body is physically damaging. One's health depends upon a judicious balance of the opposed qualities of "heat" and "cold."

The people of San Juan Gbëë rarely disagree among themselves as to the proper placement of a disease or remedy on the "hot-cold" continuum. A few of the more obvious examples (that is, even a naive outsider can appreciate the logic in play) include treating fevers (*xlëë*), which are "hot" in more than a metaphorical sense, with plants or other curative substances considered to have a "cold" nature. Thus "yellow chamizo" (*yàg-yàaz-nguĕts, Barkleyanthus salicifolium*), which is "cold," is appropriate for treating a fever (fig. 6.4), while "white chamizo" (*yàg-yàaz-nquĩts, Baccharis salicifolia*), which by contrast is "hot," is employed to treat a stomachache, a "cold" condition (fig. 6.5). After giving birth, a woman's womb is "cold," and she is bathed with infusions of "hot" plants, such as *yàg-guídz-zân*, Solanum lanceolatum (fig. 6.6).

In certain cases a "hot" plant may be of value in treating a "hot" condition, or conversely a "cold" plant used to treat a "cold" illness. However, in such cases elaborate mixtures (*compuestos*) are brewed that cool the hot plant or warm the cold to produce a cure that is neither notably hot nor cold, and thus does not exacerbate the quality of the condition treated.

From Plant to Herbal Remedy

The first step in documenting a system of herbal medicine is to list the particular plants used in the treatment of particular diseases, matching local emic categories of plants with local emic categories of illness. So, for example, we may note that *yàg-blàg-bnù* (*Ipomoea intrapilosa*, a tree morning-glory) is used to treat *yòob-guìc*, literally, 'headache'. This counts as one remedy. The example just cited is one of approximately 400 I have so far recorded in San Juan Gbëë. Of course, many plants are used to treat multiple ailments, while a variety of plants may be used to treat some particular disease. So, *Ipomoea intrapilosa* is also recommended for toothaches (*yòob-lây*), among other problems, while *guièe-ló-yàg-guièts* ('flower on [the] spine-tree', *Psittacanthus auriculatus*, a species of mistletoe that parasitizes certain thorny acacias) and a range of other species may also be used to treat a headache (though which remedy is chosen may depend on precisely what sort of headache). In short, the relationship of plants to illnesses is rarely one-to-one, but more often a many-to-many relationship. So in San Juan 266 types of plants are used to treat approximately 100 kinds of illness by means of nearly 400 remedies.

Yet these linkages of plants to illnesses but scratch the surface of what one must know to effectively (i.e., in a culturally appropriate manner that at the same time achieves the expected result in fact) cure with local plants. One must also know *how* to collect, prepare, and administer each remedy (cf. Croom 1983).

Collection requires knowing where and when to harvest the plant and which plant parts are to be used. Parts used range from the entire plant to the root, bark, foliage, flowers, fruits, and/or sap. Some parts, such as flowers and fruits, are available only at the appropriate season. Other parts, such as the bark, may vary in potency through the year, or even from place to place. I cite several illlustrative examples below.

(Table 6.7. Some examples of plant parts used in San Juan remedies)

X-pàan-ngùtsiĕts, literally, 'iguana's tail' (*Equisetum myriochaetum, cola de caballo*, horsetail fern), is an important medicine for kidney problems, including kidney stones (*guìdz-riân*) (fig. 6.7). It grows in the millrace at an abandoned mill on the river some two hours below town. Cándido Cruz Hernández took advantage of his role as our guide on an exploratory hike down into the canyon of the Río Grande to harvest this species in quantity. He planned to dry some for sale.

Yàg-lgâzh (*Abies guatemalensis, abieto*, balsam fir) is a tree of humid pine forests above 2,700 m (fig. 6.8). There is a grove at the town's main water intake. My first voucher specimen was of a branch that had fallen from a donkey load onto the road descending to San Juan from La Cieneguilla on the high southern ridge, apparently dropped by someone who had collected the plant while traveling through the forest. The aromatic foliage is used to treat 'frights' and 'bad airs'.

Yàg-bèch-mbăr (*Rhus oaxacana* and allied species, *zumaque*, sumac) is a dominant element of the *matorral* habitat that merges with the *selva baja caducifolia*, or 'low deciduous forest', below and north of town. The leaves are dried over the fire, pulverized, then applied as a powder for diaper rash. The sour seeds are chewed to ease the pain of canker sores (fig. 6.9).

Several varieties of *yàg-yàaz* 'chamizo' (including under their respective specific names *Baccharis salicifolius, Barkleyanthus salicifolium, Montanoa tomentosa*) are common shrubs in fencerows in and near town, possibly planted there. It is a simple matter if such plants are needed to send a child to fetch a sample, and even a child of five will know how to tell one from the other, though I often was confused.

The majority of introduced medicinal herbs are cultivated in the *solares* or yards behind or adjacent to the houses in town. This is true of **guìzh-mîrt** (*Salvia microphylla, mirto*) used in concert with a variety of other mostly introduced herbs to treat "cold" conditions, particularly postpartum hemorrhaging (fig. 6.10).

(Table 6.8. Some examples of San Juan medicinal plants restricted by habitat)

Preparation

Once one has located the plant and harvested the appropriate parts, it must then be properly prepared. At this point it is important to distinguish *simple* remedies, which involve a single plant, from compound remedies, or *compuestos*, which involve often complex mixtures of parts from several different plants.

The value of compound cures is explicitly noted by local herbalists. In some cases this appears to be intended to balance the "hot" or "cold" properties of a primary ingredient to overcome the contrary quality of that ingredient for treating a particular condition. Such herbal cocktails may work on the principle that it is likely that at least one of the ingredients will be effective, even though some are not. Berlin and Berlin (1996:448–49) suggest that compound cures may serve a practical function in that the curative effects of the several plants may be *additive* so that the likelihood that one or more of the several plants employed will be materially effective is increased. This is particularly true if the illness has multiple causes. It is also possible that the combined effect may be *multiplicative*, that is, ingredients in one plant may enhance the effects of ingredients in another. One may also note that in a disproportionate number of compound cures, the "secondary" or "complementary" ingredients are of nonnative plants, mostly of European origin. Thus, perhaps the use of compound cures is attributable to colonial influences.

A well-known example involves the use of **guièe-sàntàmàrî** (*Tanacetum parthenium, flor de Santa María,* feverfew) to bathe a woman who has just given birth (fig. 6.11). To prepare her bath, foliage of feverfew, rosemary, laurel, and avocado and fruits of white zapote are ground together, then steeped in water. A tea may be prepared for the same purpose, using feverfew, rosemary, *alusema*, and mint. In these cases, all the ingredients are "hot," as is the compound remedy, as the condition to be treated is "cold." In other cases, plants of contrasting "heat" will be mixed to temper the remedy, avoiding extremes of "hot" or "cold." For example, borage, which is "hot," is boiled with *Loeselia mexicana* and *Crataegus pubescens* to produce a remedy that is *templada*, that is, neither "hot" nor "cold" (cf. Linares, Bye, and Flores 1999:58, 90). It may then be used to treat a "hot cough" (i.e., cough with fever).

Modes of Application: Topical

Yet even "simple" remedies are hardly simple. Note, for example, the diversity of methods of preparation of such "simples." Topical applications may involve leaves, sap, or the whole plant. Leaves may be applied as a poultice whole, often with distilled alcohol, such as with locally distilled mezcal or *catalán*. Presumably, the alcohol acts as a solvent to facilitate the transport of bioactive chemicals from the leaves, through the skin, into the bloodstream. Popular remedies applied in this fashion include the leaves of **yàg-yàaz-nquïts** (*Baccharis salicifolia*, chamiso blanco, mulefat) to the abdomen for stomachaches, leaves of **blàg-wì** (*Buddleia sessiliflora*, butterfly bush) to the soles of the feet to treat *chaneque*, and leaves of **yàg-yàaz-làs** (*Baccharis mexicana*) rolled up and inserted in the ear with mezcal to cure an earache. Leaves may also be stuck on with the help of sticky sap from the stem of the plant. One of my first encounters with San Juan herbal medicine was while visiting Roselía Hernández Cruz's family one evening. As I was served dinner I noticed a leaf sticking out from under a bandanna tied around Roselía's head. She explained— her daughters translating—that she had a headache and that the girls had run out to fetch leaves from a **yàg-blàg-bnù** tree growing along the road at the edge of town. I later was able to attach the Zapotec name to the plant, which proved to be better known among Spanish speakers as *pájaro bobo*, literally, 'booby' (*Ipomoea intrapilosa*, a tree morning-glory) (fig. 6.12). How the plant got this name remains a mystery, as the "booby" is a seabird of tropical coastlines, hardly the habitat of the plant, which is common and seasonally blankets the arid hillsides of the valleys of Oaxaca (the closely related *Ipomoea murucoides*) with its showy white flowers.

Leaves may also be dried and pulverized to produce a powder that is applied to rashes, boils, or burns (e.g., *Rhus* spp., *zumaque*, sumac) or the leaf peeled so that the soothing viscous sap might be applied directly to the injured skin, as with **dòb-xtîl** 'aloe vera' (*Aloe barbadense, sávila*). This last remedy is known worldwide, and its curative powers demonstrated beyond a doubt (fig. 6.13).

A number of plants with caustic sap are used to treat *nubes en los ojos*, literally, 'clouds in the eyes', presumably cataracts. One to three drops of sap are put in the affected eye, which is then either washed with water or left for the tears to wash the eye. Plants reportedly used in this way include *Argemone mexicana* and *Bocconia arborescens* of the Papaveraceae and *Euphorbia hyssopifolia* (fig. 6.14) and *E. heterophylla* of the Euphorbiaceae. This treatment would seem rather dangerous, but perhaps at a time when there were no alternatives, the risk was worth taking.

A few plants provide either spores or fibers that are applied to wounds to stanch bleeding and/or to provide a sterile dressing. Puffball fungi (e.g., *Lycoperdon perlatum*, fig. 6.15) and the fern *Cheilanthes beitelii*, the root of which provides absorbent fibers, are examples.

A final topical application is the *limpia*, in which the body of the sick person is "swept" (***rlioòb mé***, literally, 'to sweep the person') with the branches of certain curative plants to remove evil influences, or *mal aires* 'bad air', thought to have caused the illness. This mode of treatment is closely allied with the use of the plant as a fumigant by burning it in the house, which is also described as "cleaning" the house. Nearly all *limpias* (I have recorded eleven such remedies) are intended to "lift" a 'bad air' (*mal aire*) or to protect against nightmares, frights, or the effects of the evil eye. Most plants so used are considered "cool," perhaps because *mal aire* is typically a "hot" condition.

(Table 6.9. Examples of limpias employed in San Juan Gbëë)

Modes of Application: Teas and Baths

The most common method of treatment involves boiling the plant or the appropriate part of the plant in water, then drinking this as a tea, most often after it has cooled to room temperature (to avoid ingesting liquids that are either very hot or very cold, which is thought to be harmful). Each remedy is typically precisely defined; for example, using ***lùdz-mdzìn*** 'deer's-tongue' (*Elaphoglossum* spp., fig. 6.16) for bloody dysentery (***yòob-chèn***, literally, 'blood pain') requires that one "boil leaf in water for 10 minutes, drink a tablespoon or a cup, mornings before eating." Or, to "heat" a woman who has just given birth, prepare a tea of feverfew (*Tanacetum parthenium, flor de Santa María*), drink twelve to twenty-four hours after giving birth, three times, but every second day, "to clean the heart, the stomach." "It is very strong, very bitter" (hence 'hot' and warming). To facilitate a delayed birth, grind the leaves of *zoapatli*, literally, from Nahuatl 'woman's medicine' (*Montanoa tomentosa*, fig. 6.17), strain it, drink a small cup to induce labor. For a cough, take three leaflets of *tronadora* (*Tecoma stans*), boil, drink the decoction with three drops of sap from a leaf of aloe vera (*Aloe barbadensis, sávila*).

The same decoctions or infusions may be applied by bathing the patient instead of or in addition to their consumption as teas.

Treating Gastrointestinal Maladies

(Table 6.10. Gastrointestinal remedies)

As noted above, GI illnesses are among the most common maladies. Prominent GI complaints include diarrheas, of which three types are recognized. The unmarked category is known in Zapotec as **guídz-dán** ['sickness' + 'mountain/forest'] and may be equivalent to the "watery diarrhea" of Berlin and Berlin's Highland Maya consultants (1996:69–71). More severe is **yòob-chèn** ['pain' + 'blood'], which presumably refers to "bloody diarrhea," widely recognized as the most severe type. Of intermediate severity is "mucoid diarrhea," referred to in San Juan Spanish as "white diarrhea" (cf. Berlin and Berlin 1996:91). Although imprecise, we use the term *dysentery* here for the two more serious types of diarrhea, the mucoid and the bloody. As the parasites that cause dysentery, such as amoebas, are microscopic, it would be surprising if local people were cognizant of them. However, one consultant credited *Coreopsis mutica* var. *carnosifolia* (**ncuàan-bzhiân** 'rage medicine') as effective against "amoebas" as well as for stomachache attributed to *bilis* 'bile', that is, 'repressed anger'.

Diarrheas are also distinguished as "cold" or "hot," requiring contrasting treatments with respectively "hot" or "cold" remedies. For example, **lùdz-mdzìn,** the "deer's tongue" fern, *Elaphoglossum* spp., is considered "medium hot" and thus is prescribed for "cold" diarrheas (the watery and mucoid varieties).By contrast, another fern, **bàz,** known in local markets as *canaguala* (*Phlebodium aureolatum*), is "cold" and thus appropriate for treating "hot" or bloody diarrheas (fig. 6.18). Fennel (*Foeniculum vulgare*) is a well-known "cold" remedy, but when combined with chamomile (*Matricaria recutita*), which is "hot," is used to treat a "cold" diarrhea. In the cases noted above, the entire plant is boiled in water and drunk as tea.

Several remedies are specified as appropriate for diarrhea in children, presumably for their mildness. A delicate wild relative of the famed

Mexican marigold (*Tagetes erecta*) is one such (fig. 6.19). It is known as **guìzh-nìzh,** literally, 'anise herb' (*Tagetes filifolia*, possibly including *Tagetes micrantha*), as it smells sweetly of anise.

A very frequent problem is stomachache (*yòob-zdòo*). Though the Zapotec term *zdòo* may refer to the heart, stomach, and even the liver and lungs, *yòob-zdòo* is understood to refer to gastric distress. Stomachaches may be simple or combined with a "bilious" or nauseous sensation, with "*cólico,*" or with inflammation, diarrhea, or fever. Treatments are selected as needed. Simple gastric distress is treated with no fewer than thirteen distinct plant remedies. A common remedy for *yòob-zdòo* is white chamizo (*Baccharis salicifolia*). Leaves are tied to the abdomen with mezcal at the site of the pain. It is possible that the alcohol acts as a solvent, facilitating absorption through the skin of some effective ingredient in the leaf. The remedy is "hot" for this "cold" ailment. Also recommended is the bush sunflower (*Tithonia tubaeformis*), known locally as **bâr-dòo-lă,** literally, 'very bitter stalk' (fig. 6.20). Bitterness and "heat" are conceptually linked. Thus, bitter plants are often used to treat "cold" stomach disorders. Likewise, the bitter European herb horehound (**guìzh-màrrûb,** *Marrubium vulgare*) is drunk for a "bilious stomach" (cf. Linares, Bye, and Flores 1999:76) (fig. 6.21).

An illness peculiar to Latin America is *empacho* (**èmpâch**), which is understood as due to poorly digested "cold" food blocking the intestines and causing an infection. It is far more than what we understand as "indigestion." A tea of the diminutive, powerfully lemon-scented trailing weed *Dalea foliolosa* (**nlìt-quiè**) is a favorite local cure. Also recommended is a *compuesto* brewed of *Chenopodium ambrosioides* and *Chenopodium graveolens* with bits of bark from three local trees, *cuatle* (*Eysenhardtia polystachea*), *guaje* (*Leucaena pallida*), and frangipani (*Plumeria rubra*), which acts as a powerful laxative.

Chenopodium ambrosioides (**ptiè**) is widely known—and has been since Aztec times—for its utility as a vermifuge, particularly to rid the patient of parasitic roundworms (**lòmbrîz,** e.g., *Ascaris lumbricoides*), one common cause of gastric distress and a range of related symptoms, particularly in children (fig. 6.22). In San Juan it is recommended that one boil the root of *Chenopodium ambrosioides* for 15 to 20 minutes, then drink the decoction to deworm the intestines. The powerful effects of *Chenopodium ambrosioides* in particular are thought to be due to the oil ascaridole, which may be dangerous at excessive dosages (Artschwager Kay 1996:132–34; Berlin and Berlin 1996:408–17).

The harmful effects of excessive alcohol consumption are widely recognized, if not always carefully avoided. For a hangover (*la cruda*; there appears to be no Zapotec term for this condition), one should drink a tea of *poleo* (*yàg-wăas*, *Satureja macrostemma*), a shrub of the mint family found in pine forests above town, or of one of the common weedy *Bidens* species (beggar-ticks, or *aceitilla*, *guièe-tĭ*). Curiously, *yàg-wăas* is said to be "hot," while *guièe-tĭ* is "cold."

There is an uncertain link between gastric ailments and certain psychological or spiritual disturbances, known as *bilis*, literally 'bile', a condition due to repressed anger, and the intrusion of *aires malos*. These psychosomatic involvements are not surprising but may require special treatments. A well-known example is *jarilla* (*yàg-blàg-bîdz*, *Dodonaea viscosa*, fig. 6.23), which is applied the same way as *chamizo blanco* (*yàg-yàaz-nquĭts*, *Baccharis salicifolia*), the leaves tied over the painful area and moistened with mezcal. *Dodonaea*, however, is considered effective against a variety of pains, all attributed to invasive *aires*, such as in the back, arms, ears, or bones (for which tie the leaves on the soles of the feet), and for *clavillo*, a piercing abdominal pain.

Eyes, Ears, Nose, Mouth, and Throat

(Table 6.11. Remedies for complaints of the eyes, ears, nose, mouth, and throat)

Of some 40 remedies for conditions of the eyes, ears, nose, mouth, and throat, nearly half are for treating coughs. Given that San Juan Gbëë is located at an elevation of 2,050 m, and that for much of the year the town is subject to cloud, mist, rain, and even the rare snowfall, and that overnight temperatures are typically chilly (5° to 10°C), it is not surprising that respiratory complaints are prominent. In the local Zapotec a cough is *rò*. Whooping cough is distinguished as *rò-dŏx* 'fierce cough'. Whooping cough is no longer a concern, but "smoker's cough" (*tos fumador*) is now recognized as a special problem. Coughs are typically treated by teas of decoctions of single plants or of complex compounds involving a half-dozen or more species. One plant is named for its value in treating coughs: *guìzh-guièe-rò* 'cough flowering herb' (Mexican wormwood, *Artemisia ludoviciana* ssp. *mexicana*, fig. 6.24). It is bitter and "hot." Combined with eucalyptus (*Eucalyptus globulus*), it is recommended for *tos pasmado* 'spasmatic cough'. *Artemisia ludoviciana* is known as *estafiate* in Mexican Spanish, a name borrowed from Nahuatl *iztauhyatl* 'sal amargo' (Linares, Bye, and Flores 1999:52). Its use in San Juan for coughs contrasts with patterns of use in other parts of Mexico.

Treatments for coughs may be "hot," "cold," or "temperate." "Cold" treatments may be prescribed in particular for coughs with fever, as is the case for *espinosilla* (*Loeselia mexicana*). For coughs one should use the whole plant, including the root. *Espinosilla* may be included in one of the most complex compound remedies I have so far recorded for San Juan, a treatment prescribed for both whooping cough and smoker's cough. *Loeselia mexicana* is mixed with a bit of the root of hawthorn (*Crataegus pubescens*) and borage (*Borago officinalis*), slices of green apple (*Malus domestica*), leaves of **blàg-chôg**, aka **guìzh-cânzr** 'cancer herb' (in particular *Tournefortia* spp.) and *gordolobo* (*Gnaphalium* spp.), flowers of the *manita de león* tree (*Cheiranthrodendron pentadactylon*) and rose of Castille (*Rosa x centifolia*), topped off with "black corn," a local variety of *Zea mays* cultivated at relatively high elevations. Cook this up, then drink the decoction at room temperature to avoid heating the patient. As it incorporates a variety of both "hot" and "cold" plants, the tea itself is "temperate."

Sore throats and tonsillitis (known in local Spanish as *angina*, not to be confused with "angina pectoris," a symptom of heart disease) are treated by the topical application to the neck of certain leaves. Again, one local species is named for this role, **guìzh-rquià-yàn** 'herb for the throat/neck' (*Eupatorium petiolare*, fig. 6.25). The other remedies utilize introduced plants, *dormilón* (*Calendula officinalis*) and *mastuerzo* (*Tropaeolum majus*). In each case the leaves are heated in water, then applied wet.

For the ubiquitous "stuffy nose" of cold sufferers, San Juaneros recommend a form of "aroma therapy." Inhale the scent of **guièe-sàntàmàrî-mòntês** 'Saint Mary's flower of the mountains' (*Helenium mexicanum*), which is in fact a common weed about town (fig. 6.26). A bloody nose might receive similar treatment, or, more likely, one should insert the leaf of **guièe-zhàn-biǎa** 'flower beneath the prickly pear' (*Oenothera rosea*) in the nostril to stanch the flow of blood (fig. 6.27).

Earaches may be attributed to *aires* or the influence of "cold," such as in the condition referred to as *oído de frío* 'cold inner ear'. Treatments rely on "hot" plants, for example, *jarilla* (*Dodonaea viscosa*) and feverfew (*flor de Santa María, Tanacetum parthenium*). The most often noted remedy for earache (and to "open" a "plugged-up" ear) is a variety of *chamizo*, **yàg-yàaz-làs** (*Baccharis mexicana, B. serraefolia*). Chop the leaves or shoots and insert these in the outer ear. It may be used for adults or children (fig. 6.28).

Eye complaints are not uncommon, with clouded vision (*nubes en el ojo*, likely due to cataracts, **biè**) or bloodshot eyes (*sangre en el ojo*) particularly troublesome. Painful conjunctivitis is also implicated. The normal treatment is to drip into the eye a few drops of the milky sap, often quite caustic, of the following plants: prickly poppy (*chicalote*, *Argemone mexicana*), *Euphorbia hyssopifolia*, and/or *E. heterophylla, Pinaropappus roseus*, and frangipani (*cacalosúchitl*, *Plumeria rubra*). The *Euphorbia* species are tiny, prostrate weeds of roadsides in town. In Zapotec they are known as **guìzh-biè**, literally, 'cataract herb'.

The oral health of San Juaneros has deteriorated dramatically with the introduction of candy and bottled soda pop, now widely available from a half-dozen homefront stores in town. Yet this may not be an entirely novel phenomenon, as there is a Zapotec term for 'rampant caries in children' (**mdzoc**) (Hernández Pérez 2002:11). The pain of a toothache is treated topically by inserting either the sap or the crushed leaf of the curative plant in the cavity. Two such plants are named for their curative role. The showy, weedy milkweed, *Asclepias curassavica*, is called **guìzh-lây** 'tooth herb' or **guìzh-měy** 'fungus herb' (fig. 6.29). It is thought that the infection in the tooth is due to a "worm," but which is referred to as a "fungus" (**měy**). *Brickellia veronicaefolia* is known as **guìzh-yòob-lây** 'toothache herb'. The gummy sap is chewed for pain relief. Finally, a loquat (*níspero*, *Eriobotrya japonica*) leaf is applied to inflamed gums (**yòob-bàa**).

Skin Problems, Including Wounds and Burns

(Table 6.12. Remedies for skin problems, wounds, etc.)

As I have noted, the fact that there is a plant called **guìzh-cânzr** (also known as **blàg-chôg** 'rough leaf') in San Juan Gbëe Zapotec does not mean that San Juaneros have discovered that long-sought cure for cancer. Rather, we must make allowance for the vagaries of translation, whereby the English word *cancer* has been redefined via local Mexican Spanish into the Zapotec loanword **cânzr**, with the quite different meaning of a badly infected wound. The term apparently refers indifferently to three local species of the Boraginaceae, *Tournefortia densiflora*, *Tournefortia hartwegiana*, and *Cordia salvadorensis*, all of which have confirmed antimicrobial effects. To enhance the power of the remedy, **guìzh-cânzr** is commonly cooked with some or all of the following: **ârnìcà** (*Bocconia arborescens*), **guìzh-bòrrâj** (*Borago officinalis*), **gòrdòlôb** (*Gnaphalium* spp.), **yàg-bèch-mbăr** (*Rhus* spp.), and **yàg-guièdz-zân-zhĭil** (*Solanum lanceolatum* in part) to prepare a decoction for bathing the wound. Bleeding wounds may be stanched by applying the absorbent spores of puffball fungi (**měy-diè**, e.g., *Lycoperdon* cf. *perlatum*) or the nonsticking fibers of the roots of **guìzh-zhĭil-wlâgw** (*Cheilanthes beitelii*) or **guìzh-zhĭil-dán** (*Acourtia* sp.), varieties of **guìzh-zhĭil** 'cotton herb'.

Two specific treatments for burns are mentioned. The first is the well-known aloe vera (*sávila*, *Aloe barbadensis*). Peel a segment of the leaf and apply the viscid sap directly to the burn. The second is also an introduced plant, the garden geranium, **guièe-jèrân** (*Pelargonium zonale*), particularly the magenta-flowered variety **guièe-jèrân-sùlfèrîn**. Grind the leaves, then apply to the burn.

A wide range of plants are prescribed for conditions variously named in Spanish *ronchas* ("welts," "wales") or *granos* ("boils," "pimples"), *granitos* or *salpullidos* ("rash") if small, and *fuegos* ("itchy rash," "skin eruption") *en la boca* if on the mucous membranes inside the mouth. These terms appear to encompass what we would call variously "boils," "pimples," "cold sores," "diaper rash," and "canker sores." Treatments are topical, either by applying a powder of the dried leaf, bathing with a decoction of the plant, or, if the condition is inside the mouth, sucking or chewing the seeds. In Zapotec one refers to **guièdz** for *granos*, **mchèel** for diaper rash. One of the most often mentioned remedies is **yàg-bèch-mbăr**, literally, 'sour knot tree', sumac (*Rhus oaxacana* and allied species). The leaves are dried on the *comal*, pulverized, then applied to the affected skin. For canker sores one is advised to suck on the sour orange seeds of this same plant to relieve the pain. For cold sores in particular, the remedy of choice is **yàg-guièts-zhìg** (*ocotillo*, *Fouquieria formosa*); one should chew the buds or flowers (fig. 6.30). For diaper rash one may use in lieu of sumac the ground leaves of **guièe-mòrâd** (*Pinaropappus roseus*) or the flowers of **blàg-guiùu** (*Piper auritum*), or bathe with a decoction of **bëël-dŏ** (*Piqueria trinervia*) or **gbày-té** (*Helianthemum glomeratum*).

Measles produces a rash, of course, but has a distinctive etiology, in particular as it is associated with high fever. Three species are cited as remedies for measles. One may drink a tea of borage (*Borago officinalis*) with *gordolobo* (*Gnaphalium* spp.). A tea or bath of a decoction of mallow (**blàg-mêd**, *Malva parviflora*) with rose of Castille (*Rosa* x *centifolia*) is recommended, as is washing with an infusion of **màlbàrîscw** (*Sida rhombifolia*). The last two treatments are "cold," as one would expect in dealing with a disease characterized by fever. However, borage and *gordolobo* are "hot."

A malady quite distinct from *granos* is *manchas* 'spots', which may be white or black and appear on various parts of the body, including the face and hands. The Zapotec term is **bĕy**. One treatment, particularly for *manchas blancas* 'white spots', involves washing with an infusion of the leaves of **bëël-dŏ** (*Piqueria trinervia*) mixed with tree sunflower (**bâr-dòo-lă**, *Tithonia tubaeformis*). It is perhaps worth noting that *Piqueria* is also prescribed for *debilitad de las niñas* 'weakness in children'. This condition may be symptomatic of malnutrition. *Manchas blancas* sounds very much like vitiligo, a poorly understood condition thought to be associated with pernicious anemia, a vitamin B-12 deficiency, as well as emotional trauma (http://www.vegsoc.org/info/b12.html).

Quite differrent is the illness called **bëël-yâas** 'black meat', characterized by *manchas negras* 'black spots' and sore bones. The preferred treatment in this case is **ncuàan-yâas** 'black medicine' (*Heimia salicifolia*) (fig. 6.31). These black spots often appear on women's faces when they are pregnant. This may be the relatively benign disease known as *paño*, thought to be caused by a spirochete (Mata Pinzón et al. 1994:654–55).

Contact dermatitis from such poisonous local plants as "*hinchahuevos*" (**yàg-lăadz**, *Pseudosmodingium multifolium*), poison ivy (**lăadz-guiùu**, *Toxicodendron radicans*), and "*mala mujer*" (**yàg-làg**, *Cnidoscolus multilobus*) is typically treated by rubbing the affected skin with the leaves and flowers of *chepíl* (**ncuàan-yè** and **pxĭizh**, *Crotalaria* spp.). The pain of insect bites is relieved by an application of *Crotalaria* spp. or *Senna* spp. (**guièe-mzhòodz** 'bee flower'). The latter is a specific remedy for the powerful sting of the ant **mrè-ndŭn**. *Agave marmorata* leaves may relieve snakebite. *Schkuhria anthemoides* kills chiggers (*aradores*, **mèx**). The root of **bià-tòo** (*Microsechium helleri*) produces a harsh soap effective as a shampoo against dandruff or lice.

Bodily Aches and Pains and Fevers

(Table 6.13. Remedies for bodily pains and fevers)

These maladies may result from trauma, systemic disturbances due to infection, or, in the local theory, intrusive *aires* or spiritual afflictions. As fever is a frequent concomitant of trauma and systemic infections, treatments for fever seem most readily discussed here. The last named are more logically discussed below under the general heading of "supernatural" illnesses.

Traumatic injuries (*golpes*) may be treated by a topical application to the part affected. Two plants of the Euphorbiaceae, both named **còrdèvân**, are prescribed, *Euphorbia rossiana* and/or *Pedilanthus* cf. *tomentellus* (fig. 6.32). Both are odd plants, nearly leafless at maturity but with green, photosynthetic stems. The latter is sometimes planted in home gardens. Both produce a caustic milky sap, which is smeared on a piece of paper, then applied to the injury as a plaster. This is the remedy of choice also for broken bones. The pain of traumatic injuries may also be treated by bathing with an infusion of the following plants: avocado leaf (*Persea americana*), laurel leaf (*Litsea glaucesens*), *mezon zapote* (*Licania platypus*), feverfew (*Tanacetum parthenium*), and rosemary (*Rosmarinus officinalis*). Pain and swelling from sprains may be treated by applying the "cooked" leaf of *Agave marmorata* (**dòb-pcuêl**), a wild maguey species with distinctive rough-textured leaves found below town in the *selva baja caducifolia*. This treatment is also believed effective against snakebite. Of particular interest is a remedy said to have been learned by observing how injured rabbits favor a special plant, known as **guìzh-cònêf** 'rabbit herb' (*Asclepias fournieri*). One should eat the raw root of this milkweed to remedy the injury.

Headaches (*yòob-guìc*) are treated by the topical application of leaves of the tree morning-glory (**yàg-blàg-bnù**, *Ipomoea intrapilosa*), tree tobacco (**yàg-brètâyn**, *Nicotiana glauca*), or nasturtium (**màl-tuêrs**, *Tropaeolum majus*). Those afflicted tie the leaves to their temples with a bandanna. The tree morning-glory leaf is stuck on with a drop of the milky sap, while the leaves of tree tobacco are first peeled, then applied. A species of mistletoe parasitic on acacias (particularly *Acacia pennatula*; *guièe-ló-yàg-guièts*, *Cladocolea* cf. *andrieuxii* and/or *Psittacanthus auriculatus*) is also recommended for headaches (fig. 6.33), but in this case the remedy involves bathing with an infusion of the plant. The tree morning-glory and the mistletoe are considered "hot," while the tree tobacco and nasturtium are "cold," thus applied particularly when the headache is accompanied by fever.

The pain of arthritis or rheumatism is called "sore bones" or *reúma* (which term has a rather wider application in local Spanish than in English, as one may suffer *reúma del estómago* 'rheumatism of the stomach'). The Brazilian pepper tree or *pirúl* (*Schinus molle*), widely introduced as an ornamental cultivar, is prescribed for sore feet or sore bones. Apply the leaves with mezcal to the site of the pain.

Backaches are often treated by applying the pitch from one or another species of *copalero* (*yàg-yâl*, *Bursera* spp.), trees that are the source of copal incense. Copal trees of several species (e.g., *Bursera glabrifolia*, *B. bipinnata*) are commonly planted as "living fences" in and near town, while several additional species (e.g., *Bursera* cf. *fagaroides*, *B. galeottiana*) are characteristic features of the *selva baja caducifolia* below town. The bark is scraped, the pitch collected on a piece of papery bark or paper, then applied at the site of the pain. The castor bean, or *higuerilla* (*yàg-blàp*, *Ricinus communis*), is also used for back pain. One pastes two leaves to the affected area with mezcal, leaving them in place overnight. By morning the pain should be gone. One may also drink an infusion of the leaf.

Back pain may be due to kidney problems, in which case remedies for *mal de orina* such as *Arctostaphylos pungens* or *Valeriana* cf. *densiflora* may be more appropriate. These are discussed in more detail in the following section. San Juaneros distinguish *dolor de costado* 'pain in the side, ribs' from *dolor de espalda* 'back pain'. One remedy for the former is **guìzh-mèt** (*Chenopodium graveolens*), primarily employed to treat *empacho* or intestinal worms, which suggests that this pain may be a side effect of gastric distress. Alternatively, "side aches" may be attributed to *aires*. A related manifestation of particular concern is known in Spanish as *clavillo* 'nail', and in the local Zapotec as **wdzìdz**. It is described as a stabbing pain that feels as if one has been run through from one side to the other and attributed to *un aire que se pega* 'an air that hits you'. Leaves of the *jarilla* bush (*yàg-blàg-bîdz*, *Dodonaea viscosa*) are applied topically with mezcal or alcohol. A bitter tea of horehound (*guìzh-màrrûb*, *Marrubium vulgare*) is also recommended for this malady.

Fevers are invariably treated by "cold" remedies, mostly drunk as teas or applied as soothing baths. An impressive demonstration of the ability of San Juaneros to distinguish otherwise very similar plants is the distinction between two varieties of *chamizo*, the "white" and the "yellow." Both are slender shrubs of the aster family with willowlike leaves, common in fencerows about town. In flower they are readily distinguished, one with white flowers, the other with yellow, but most of the year they bear no flowers and must be distinguished by subtle differences of leaf and stem (fig. 6.34). White *chamizo* (*yàg-yàaz-nquĭts*, *Baccharis salicifolia*) is "hot" and used to treat stomachaches, while yellow *chamizo* (*yàg-yàaz-nguĕts*, *Barkleyanthus salicifolius*) is "cold" and used to treat fevers. In each case one applies the leaves topically with mezcal or alcohol, but in the first instance to the abdomen, in the second instance tied to the bottoms of the feet and left overnight, to "draw down" the fever.

For fevers one may also bathe with an infusion of *malva* (*guìzh-mêd*, *Malva parviflora*) boiled with *espinosilla* (*Loeselia mexicana*), rose (*Rosa* spp.), and *malvavisco* (*Sida rhombifolia*). All these plants are "cool," as is the mixture. "Hot pains" (stomachache with fever) likewise require "cold" remedies, such as dock (*blàg-dòoz*, *Rumex* cf. *mexicana*), considered to be exceptionally "cold," or rue (*Ruta chalepensis*) mixed with the root of the lime (*yàg-lîm*, *Citrus aurantiifolia*) and a market remedy of uncertain identity known as *guaco*. Dock is administered either as a poultice or by grinding the leaf in cold water and drinking the extract. The *compuesto* with rue is drunk as a tea.

One treats swelling or inflammation (*guì*) due to *aire* by one or the other of two plants of the Solanaceae family noted for their hallucinogenic properties, jimsonweed, or *toloache* (*blàg-rzûdz*, *Datura stramonium*) (fig. 6.35), and angel's-trumpet, or *floripondio* (*guièe-pûnt*, *Brugmansia* x *candida*) (fig. 6.36). This condition is known more precisely as *nzëëb* (*se hincha su pie, su cara* . . . "your face, feet . . . swell up") and seems related etiologically and symptomatically with *chaneque* (see below). One massages the affected area with the leaves of the plant. Inflammation of the abdomen is treated by heating and then applying the leaves of aloe vera (**dòb-xtîl**, *Aloe barbadensis*) and/or the pads of prickly pear cactus (**biăa**).

A somewhat mysterious malady is that called *pasmo* (**pâsm**) in local Spanish. This has nothing to do with "spasms" but rather is characterized by chills and fever, sore joints, and swelling with skin eruptions (or, in contradiction, has to do with wounds that resist healing; but cf. *cáncer*) (cr. Artschwager Kay 1996:53). (This could be malaria, in which case *pasmo* may involve a contraction of *paludismo* 'malaria', but the symptoms don't correspond well with that interpretation.) One plant species is particularly associated with this illness, **lbè̯-blàg-pâsm** '*pasmo* leaf vine' (*Cissus sicyoides*), a native weedy vine that sprawls across fences in and near town (fig. 6.37). It may be planted to assure a ready supply. The leaf is boiled and the infusion used to bathe the patient, and/or leaves are applied as a poultice to the swollen limb. Two varieties of *pasmo* are recognized, **pâsm-nìs** 'of water' and **pâsm-ngùbìdz** 'of the sun' [one is cold/wet, the other hot/dry], suggestive of a "supernatural" cause. The plant is neither "hot" nor "cold," but *templada* (*medio* **niág-á**).

Urogenital System Conditions

(Table 6.14. Remedies for urinary tract problems)

Kidney malfunction is known in local Spanish as *mal de orina*. This general term includes the inability to urinate (*tapación*) and the excruciating pain of kidney stones (*cálculos*, **guìdz-riân**), as well as other causes of painful or burning urination (perhaps venereal disease). San Juaneros apply two plants for these conditions that are very widely known (Linares, Bye, and Flores 1999:42–43), *pingüica* (**yàg-bḭ̈ë**, *Arctostaphylos pungens* [fig. 6.38]) and *cola de caballo* (**x-pàan ngùtsiĕts**, *Equisetum myriochaetum*), as well as several less widely recognized remedies. All are considered "cold." The fruits, leaves, and stems of *pingüica* mixed with *cola de caballo* and the root of the hawthorn (**yàg-mànzànít**, *Crataegus pubescens*), are boiled or simply steeped in water, the infusion drunk as tea twice a day for two days, by which time the condition should have "calmed." Other plants used to treat *mal de orina* include **guièts-mél-lò** (*Eryngium* cf. *cymosum*), **guiéer-ngüèets** (*Rhodosciadium* cf. *tolucensis*), a wild Apiaceae of pine forests above town, and *espinosilla* (*Loeselia* spp.), taken as a tea. Aloe vera is specifically recommended for burning urination, likewise taken as a tea.

Finally, for want of a better place to treat of hernias, I will mention here a plant called **guìzh-ngùd-lèn** 'hernia [literally, 'belly lump'] plant' (*Valeriana* cf. *densiflora*), a tall herb of the pine-oak forest understory. The root of this plant is said to be elongate in "male" and round in "female" plants. The root is boiled and the infusion drunk not only for hernias but also for diabetes, for back and stomach pain, and to regulate the menstrual cycle. There may be an element of "sympathetic magic" or the "Doctrine of Signatures" in its use for hernias, as the root resembles the form of the hernia.

Reproduction and Childbirth

Well over 80 percent of births in rural Oaxaca are attended only by traditional *parteras/parteros*, that is, "midwives" (though this role is not exclusive to women). The actual figure for San Juan Gbëë is likely to be closer to 100 percent, at least until very recently, as San Juaneros have been quite reluctant to take advantage of the government clinic in San Pedro Gbëë and have had their own clinic for just two years. A recent study of traditional childbirth practice in Oaxaca indicates a chasm of misappreciation between the "hegemonic" biomedical model and the traditional community-based model of birthing. In general, government-sponsored efforts to promote "modern, scientific" biomedical practices with regard to birthing—including government-sponsored training and certification programs for midwives—have failed by virtue of the fact that the promoters of the biomedical practice are deeply ignorant of and generally dismissive of the knowledge, experience, and theoretical understanding that is the foundation for traditional practice. While traditional practice may be judged inadequate in some respects—in particular, the lack of recognition of certain danger signals during pregnancy—it nevertheless is the only practical recourse for pregnant women in rural Oaxaca for the foreseeable future, given financial constraints that limit the expansion of available biomedical services and the cultural barriers to the ready acceptance of such services even when available (Sesia 1992).

Sesia describes the common practice of local midwives, in particular the use of external massage to evaluate the progress of a pregnancy and to orient the fetus if improperly positioned prior to birth. Her interviews with midwives and their clients show dramatically how the intrusive and authoritarian biomedical approach embarrasses and alienates rural women, while marginalizing traditional healers. While it is clear that biomedicine may take credit for a significant reduction in maternal mortality in childbirth—cf. 120 per 100,000 births in Oaxaca compared to just 54 per 100,000 for Mexico as a whole—the mortality rates even without the benefit of modern medical practice are sufficiently low that it is likely that most rural communities will not have experienced a single maternal death during the lives of villagers. By that measure traditional midwifery must be judged highly effective.

Sesia has little to say, however, with respect to the effectiveness of local herbal medicines in facilitating birth and reducing morbidity and mortality of both mothers and infants. While I cannot systematically assess the effectiveness of San Juan Gbëë herbal medicine with respect to childbirth, I will describe some twenty remedies widely known in the village to treat such conditions as irregular or delayed menstruation or to induce abortion, to facilitate childbirth, to expel the placenta, to stop hemorrhaging, and to promote postpartum healing. We may compare these remedies with those reported elsewhere in Oaxaca by Browner (1985a, 1986) and her colleagues (Browner, Ortiz de Montellano, and Rubel 1992) and elsewhere in Mexico by other authors (McClain 1975; Castañeda et al. 1992). Certain plants are widely and consistently applied and have been so since before the Spanish conquest. These are likely to be effective, at least with respect to local understanding of the birth process. One, the well-known Aztec *zihuapatli* 'woman's medicine' (*Montanoa tomentosa*), has been shown effective in laboratory experiments (Levine et al. 1979; Smith et al. 1981). As we shall see, its power to stimulate uterine contractions—whether to induce abortion or to induce a delayed labor—is also recognized in San Juan.

(Table 6.15. Remedies of childbearing)

Black chamiso (*yàg-yàaz-yâas*, *Montanoa tomentosa*) is used to facilitate birth. If the baby is three days overdue, grind the leaf, strain it, and drink a small cup to induce labor pains. It is also used "for women when they don't want to give birth." The use of herbs to induce abortion is recognized but generally condemned. In addition to *Montanoa tomentosa*, the power to abort a fetus is likewise attributed to *sosa*, aka *berenjena* (**yàg-guièdz-zân**, *Solanum lanceolatum*). This may be used to facilitate a birth or to induce an abortion. In either case, the treatment involves drinking a tea made of the leaf, three tablespoons each time, repeated three times (*se friega* 'it scours'); the smooth variety (without spines) is best. Two additional abortifacients are *pericón* (**guièe-dzùu**, *Tagetes lucida*, fig. 6.39) and the "cabbage rose" (**guièe-rôsà-côl**, *Rosa* cf. *chinensis*) (fig. 6.40) as a consequence of their being excessively "hot." Note that the humoral quality of the "cabbage rose" is diametrically opposed to that of the other varieties of rose. These "excessively hot" plants are described as *prohibida* "prohibited" and dangerous, though who "prohibits" these plants is left unsaid. Nevertheless, the *pericón* may be used with appropriate caution for women in childbirth; an infusion is drunk as a tea.

As one might expect, an irritant such as *Chenopodium graveolens*, used to expel intestinal worms, might likewise be effective, and it is prescribed "to bring down the menstrual period" when it is late, which, of course, might be accomplished by aborting an early-term fetus. The use of plants with similar purgative properties might be advised to expel the placenta after childbirth in order to avoid a potentially dangerous postpartum complication. San Juan healers recommend coriander (**sìlândr**, *Coriandrum sativum*) and corn husks (*totomostle*, **pcuêl**) in that eventuality.

To control postpartum hemorrhaging one uses **yàg-lĕ** (*Acacia angustissima* [fig. 6.41]) (cook, then drink the infusion three times daily) or **guìzh-pĕch** (*Tripogandra* cf. *serrulata*) (drink an infusion of the leaf). Turkey vultures (*Cathartes aura*, **pĕch**) are said to eat this plant, hence the name. One might alternatively apply **guìzh-nàad** (*Mentzelia hispida* [fig. 6.42]): boil the root, then drink the infusion as a tea. *Acacia angustissima* was the most often cited herbal remedy in a study of Mexican traditional childbirth practices (Browner 1985b).

The most cited category of childbirth remedy is for "heating" the mother's womb, to give her strength and to facilitate her recovery from the stress of the birth. The birth process is believed to drain heat from the mother, disturbing the balance required for her recovery. These treatments involve bathing in infusions of a variety of herbs, vapor baths (formerly in the *temascal* or traditional sweat bath, now rarely used), and vaginal douches, as well as teas. The remedies are "hot" to counteract the "cold" postpartum condition, though you will note that several "cold" plants may be used in combination with "hot" species for this purpose.

Two species are named specifically for their medicinal value in childbirth. One widely recognized for such purposes is the aforementioned **yàg-guièdz-zân,** literally 'childbirth tree' (*Solanum lanceolatum*). Note that a pregnant woman is referred to as **mèn-zân,** while childbirth is *zân*. The woman is bathed in an infusion of the leaves, beginning fifteen days after the birth. *Calea hypoleuca* is similarly named, **ncuàan-zân** 'childbirth medicine', and is used for a postpartum bath. A wild mint, *Salvia breviflora,* **ncuàan-zân-làs** 'slender childbirth medicine', is used likewise.

Among the many additional options are the leaves of the maguey (**dòb-pcuêl,** *Agave marmorata*), burned as a fumigant. Teas of various combinations of the herbs cited in table 6.15 are said "to clean the heart, the stomach." Also recommended for a woman who has just given birth is **guìzh-cànêl** 'cinnamon herb' (*Pluchea odorata*), to draw out the "airs" from the woman's body ("*que se saca todo el aire del cuerpo*"). One may combine for this purpose the leaves of **guìzh-cànêl** with those of **yàg-guièdz-zân** (*Solanum lanceolatum*). The woman must bathe with an infusion of the leaves at least three times a day for the first several weeks following the birth.

Note that a number of these herbs are of a "cold" nature. However, in combination that quality is balanced by the "hot" nature of other ingredients. Grind these together, mix in water, then drink a glass: rosemary (*Rosmarinus officinalis*), flor de Santa María [hot] (*Tanacetum parthenium*), laurel leaf [hot] (*Litsea glaucescens*), avocado leaf (**yàg-ngùd-guièx,** *Persea americana*), sour orange leaf (*Citrus aurantium*), mezon zapote fruit (*Licania platypus*), mostranz (*Mentha rotundifolia*), alucema [cold] (*Salvia lavanduloides, Salvia muscuroides*), mirto [probably hot] (*Salvia microphylla*), and malvavisco [cool] (*Sida rhombifolia*). Rosemary (*Rosmarinus officinalis*), mostranz (*Mentha rotundifolia*), and *flor de Santa María* (*Tanacetum parthenium*) are used for a vaginal douche postpartum.

Mix *malva* [cold] (**blàg-mêd,** *Malva parviflora*) and rose of Castille [cool/temperate] (*Rosa x centifolia*) for a vaginal douche or enema. Since both components of this remedy are "cold," it is not likely recommended postpartum. The circumstances of the application of this remedy are unclear.

Illnesses Due to Emotional Distress

A variety of emotional disturbances are classified as "diseases" in San Juan Gbëë and treated with herbal remedies. The most frequent complaint is of 'fright', which in the local Zapotec is called ***dzéb***, testifying to its indigeneity. In the local Spanish the malady may be called either *espanto* or *susto*, in San Juan without distinction, despite the fact that elsewhere in Latin America the first is considered a more severe form of the second (Rubel et al. 1989). Frights are distinguished by proximate cause and by the symptoms expressed. For example, there are frights attributable to aggressive dogs, frights caused by anger (i.e., directed at the sufferer), and frights caused by near drowning. A student may even suffer 'teacher fright' (***dzéb-maêstr***). All are characterized by a "loss of spirit" or animation (not necessarily "soul loss," as reported elsewhere). The most common subcategory by symptom is 'night fright', associated with disturbed sleep and nightmares. 'Great fright' (***dzéb-dòx*** or ***dzéb-nrôob***) requires a complex ritual cure.

Fright remedies (***ncuàan-dzéb***) are more often named with respect to some distinguishing feature of the plant used. Examples include ***ncuàan-dzéb-zhòmbrêl***, literally, 'sombrero fright medicine' (*Aristolochia* cf. *pentandra* [fig. 6.43]), so named for the odd shape of the flower, ***ncuàan-dzéb-cônch***, literally, 'conch fright medicine' (*Glandularia* spp., *Verbena* spp. [fig. 6.44]), so named for the purple color of the flower of these plants, which recalls the famed "royal purple" dye extracted from a local species of sea snail, and ***ncuàan-dzéb-strêy***, literally, 'star fright medicine' (*Pellaea ternifolia*), so named for this fern's star-shaped leaflets. An ambiguous case is ***ncuàan-dzéb-mècw***, literally, 'dog fright medicine' (*Cheilanthes sinuata*), which may be named for the leaf shape, said to resemble a dog's track, or because it is used specifically to treat frights caused by aggressive dogs. Alternatively, the medicinal application may be motivated by the resemblance of the form of the plant to the presumed cause, a case of the "doctrine of signatures." In addition, a number of other plant species are prescribed for fright that are not explicitly named for that use, such as **yàg-guièe-zhǐn** (*Cestrum dumetorum* [fig. 6.45]), named for the strong, unpleasant odor of its flowers.

(Table 6.16. Remedies for fright)

The plant species prescribed for fright are a varied lot. Especially prominent are several species of ferns of the Adiantaceae. *Pellaea ovata* (fig. 6.46) is particularly widely recognized, in particular as a treatment for 'night fright', for which it is named (**ncuàan-dzéb-guièel** 'night-fright medicine'). Of the twenty-seven vascular plant species cited as remedies for fright, six (22.2 percent) are nonnative, roughly the percent of nonnative species in the total recorded flora.

It is noteworthy that the weedy European "scarlet pimpernel" (*Anagallis arvensis*) is singled out for 'night fright' (figs. 6.47, 6.48). In fact, two subspecies of this plant are distinguished as 'male' and 'female', the former with blue flowers (ssp. *caerulea*), the latter with salmon-pink flowers (ssp. *arvensis*). Local specialists prescribe the 'male' plant for male patients, the 'female' for female patients. The scarlet pimpernel was once used in Europe "to dispel sadness" (Hyam and Pankhurst 1995:22). The *King's American Dispensatory* notes that, "Its internal use has been advised in *mania, epileptic attacks, dropsical affections,* and other derangements of the nervous system, but it should be employed with caution" (http://www.ibiblio.org/herbmed/eclectic/kings/anagallis.html, December 31, 2003). It is possible that on further examination many of these remedies may be found to have a calming effect, or alternatively, a stimulating effect to counteract the malaise so often associated with 'fright'.

Extreme cases of fright, called **dzéb-dòo** or **dzéb-nrôob** 'great fright', require elaborate ritual in addition to special herbal recipes. 'Great fright' may be due to an encounter with an animal in the forest or some other exceptionally traumatic experience with the forces of "nature." It involves "soul loss." The ritual cure must be performed at midnight on Cerro San Isidro over a period of several days. Those who know how to effect such a cure burn copal incense and call out the person's name on the mountain, while the afflicted person waits in his or her house. Sofía Hernández Díaz, now past ninety, described the treatment for a 'great fright' that may afflict a child who narrowly escapes drowning while trying to cross a swollen river, for example. This is a fright of water. The recipe requires seven pieces of pitch pine wood (*ocote*), seven cotton seeds, seven reeds from the small reed **guìzh-gòob** (*Lasiacis cf. nigra*), seven leaves of the "sacred palm," *Brahea dulcis* (which they may buy in San Cristóbal Amatlán), plus copal incense. The emphasis on the number seven suggests some European influence.

(Table 6.17. Remedies for emotional distress)

Other emotional maladies include a form of depression to which children who have been lost or have been left by their parents are particularly subject. It is called *tristeza* 'sadness' or *llanto* 'weeping' in Spanish, **wìin** 'weeping' in Zapotec, though we might call it "separation anxiety." The remedy is to bathe the child in an infusion of **guìzh-zhì-wìin** (*Stachys coccinea*) (fig. 6.49) or **bâr-dòo-lă** (*Tithonia tubaeformis*). Perhaps related are such conditions as *nervios*, heart palpitations, and/or the sadness of a woman "dying of love." Treatments include the odd fern-relative *siempre-viva* (*Selaginella lepidophylla* [fig. 6.50]) that "never dies," needing only to be immersed in water to revive, or the weedy stick-tight, or *aceitilla* (**guièe-tĭ**, *Bidens* spp.), of which any of several named varieties may be used. A tea of these "cold" plants is prescribed.

"Rage"—in Spanish *coraje* or *berrinche*, and in Zapotec **bzhiàn**—is likewise treated with an herb named for the target condition, **guìzh-ncuàan-bzhiàn** (*Coreopsis mutica* var. *carnosifolia* and/or *Galphimia glauca*). This condition may be a side effect of excessive drinking. One should grind the leaf, then drink the infusion as a tea. It is very bitter. Two other bitter plants are likewise recommended, **bâr-dòo-lă** (*Tithonia tubaeformis*) and **bëël-dŏ** (*Piqueria trinervia*). Children should be bathed with the infusion, while adults drink it as a tea.

Epilepsy has three names in San Juan Zapotec, **guídz-gùtiè, guídz-rcòw**, and **guídz-rzhìdz**. I do not know if these three terms are synonyms or whether they may distinguish varieties of an affliction so-named in Spanish. It is considered a kind of "nervous attack" in which the "nerves" ascend to the brain. The treatment is harsh, requiring that the patient be purged by drinking an infusion of the root of **bià-tòo** (*Microsechium helleri* of the Cucurbitaceae), the taste of which is nauseating (*puro ascos*). Insanity (**mén ràctônt**) is treated the same way. **Bià-tòo** is a slender vine of mountain forests that grows from a large underground tuber noted also as the source of a harsh soap used to rid the scalp of lice (**mĕets**) and dandruff (**ctòo**).

Illnesses of Spiritual or Supernatural Origin

(Table 6.18. Remedies for spiritual maladies)

A number of conditions may be attributed to what we might call "supernatural" causes, particularly the intrusion of *aires* or *aires malos* 'bad airs' (**bdìin, mê**). These are clearly distinguished from *aire en la barriga* 'air in the stomach', what we would call "gas." One is said to "have" air in the stomach. By contrast, the spiritual "airs" are said to 'hit' or 'nail' the person ("*se le pega, se le clava a la persona el aire*"; **riàaz mé**). In certain cases, the causal agent is more clearly personalized, such as the "evil eye," the Earth (for *chaneque*), and witchcraft (**mzhiè**).

Chaneque appears not to be named in Zapotec, as it is known only by a Spanish (originally Nahuatl) loanword, **chànêcw**. Yet it is the focus of considerable concern, judging by the frequency and detail with which it is discussed in San Juan and the fact that a traditional healer in San Pedro specializes in the diagnosis and treatment of *chaneque*. The most prominent symptoms are sore feet and extreme fatigue, to the point that the sufferer is unable to work. It is said to be a punishment from the Earth for laziness, though it may seem curious to punish laziness with a debilitating fatigue. *Chaneque* is also considered an *aire* (**mê**), which would appear to be a general characterization of invisible spiritual forces inhabiting the local environment.

It is necessary to divine the cause of the symptoms, as they may be due simply to the hard work required of the cultivator. Diagnosis may be accomplished by tying the leaf of a butterfly bush (**blàg-wì**, *Buddleia* spp.) with mezcal, *catalán*, or some other form of distilled alcohol to the sole of the foot, leaving this overnight. If blood is drawn out, it is *chaneque*. This treatment is prescribed as well to cure the malady. There are two varieties of **blàg-wì**, **blàg-wì-nzhên** 'broad[-leaved] butterfly bush' (*Buddleia sessiliflora*, fig. 6.51) and **blàg-wì-làs** 'slender[-leaved] butterfly bush' (*Buddleia lanceolata, B. microphylla, B. parviflora*). The slender-leaved variety is specific to *chaneque*, while the broad-leaved species is used to treat stomachache (**yòob-zdòo**). Alternatively, diagnosis may involve massaging the patient's knee with a *floripondio* flower (**guìèe-pûnt**, *Brugmansia* x *candida*) or a *toloache* leaf (**guìzh-rzûdz**, *Datura stramonium*). Both are dangerously hallucinogenic and both are personified as *la señorita*, likely an allusion to the Holy Virgin, a source of spiritual power in a number of local plants. Lilia Miguel, my eleven-year-old plant-trail guide, first taught me that one should "pay" *la señorita* seven pebbles in exchange for the leaves of *Datura* harvested as medicine. While some grown-ups dismiss this as childish fantasy, others confirm the belief. The same quid pro quo is said to be due for *Brugmansia* flowers.

One may "lift" *aires* bedeviling one's house—which inflict nightmares (*mcàal*) and insomnia induced by a 'fright'—with *limpias* 'cleanings' or 'sweepings', either by burning specific curative plants—as, for example, balsam fir (*yàg-lgâzh*, *Abies guatemalensis*)—in the house or literally sweeping (*rlioob*) the room (or the patient) with the plant. One such plant is *yàg-ngùd-guèy-pcàal* 'nightmare white zapote' (*Bysonima crassifolia*). Another is *yàg-bdìin* 'bad airs tree', aka *guìzh-zhwèe* 'injury herb' (*Eupatorium mairetianum*). Leaves of these specially designated herbal remedies are mixed with leaves of rue (*Ruta graveolens*) and white zapote (*yàg-ngùd-guèy*, *Casimiroa edulis*) to prepare an infusion for bathing or to be taken as a tea. The leaves soaked in mezcal, *catalán*, or alcohol may also be used to sweep the body as a *limpia* or tied to the head with a cloth. Rosemary (*guìzh-ròmêr*, *Rosmarinus officinalis*) may be combined with balsam fir, *alusema* (*Salvia lavanduloides*, *S. muscuroides*), and *mirto* (*Salvia microphylla*) for another powerful protective compound cure, while an *aire caliente* 'hot air' may be treated with rue combined with horehound (*Marrubium vulgare*), basil (*àlbâc*, *Ocimum basilicum*), and such exotic ingredients as *ánis estrella* (*Illicium verum*, Illiciaceae), *cancerina* (unidentified), and *guaco* (unidentified), the last three purchased dried in local markets.

Aires may cause pain in various parts of the body, which may require specific treatments. One such manifestation produces a pain in the ribcage (*dolor de costado*), for which *pájaro bobo* (*yàg-blàg-bnù*, *Ipomoea intrapilosa*) is prescribed, the leaf pasted on at the site of the pain using the milky latex that oozes from the broken stem, just as is done for headaches. *Jarilla* (*yàg-blàg-bîdz*, *Dodonaea viscosa*) is judged effective against *aires* of various types, including those causing earaches, stomachaches, and the stabbing pain of *clavillo*. In each case the leaves, soaked in mezcal, are tied on at the site of the pain.

The effects of "evil eye" (*rquín-lô*) may be counteracted by ***blàg-zhnâzh*** 'Virgin leaf' (*Croton ciliato-glandulifer*, fig. 6.52). This odd shrub of the *selva baja caducifolia* is treated with respect, whether for its power to protect against sorcery or as a poisonous plant. In some Zapotec towns it is believed that touching the plant causes blindness. In San Juan Gbëë it is used as a *limpia* or to prepare a special bath for those afflicted by "evil eye."

Another local plant directly associated with the Virgin is the famed hallucinogenic morning-glory of the Aztecs, *ololiuqui* or *piule* (*zhìncuàan-ná-zhnâzh* 'Virgin Mother's medicine', *Ipomoea* cf. *bicolor*, fig. 6.53). The seeds are eaten to divine the cause of a "fright" suffered while far from home, likely attributable to the anger of a stranger. This plant covers roadside walls in towns along the road into San Juan but does not grow so high as the town.

Two plants are known to protect children from the ill will of witches (*mzhiè*). One elderly woman in San Juan was pointed out to me as a witch, so it seems such beliefs survive. Scatter a handful of wild mustard seeds (**guìzh-mòxtâz**, *Brassica campestris*, *Brassica nigra*) or place a thorny branch of huisache (**yàg-guièts-clâv-nquîts**, *Acacia farnesiana*) beneath the child's bed for protection from witches and, more generally, from *aires malos*. Why mustard seeds should be ascribed such power is not clear, though it may relate to their pungency. Since mustards are Old World imports, this application may relate to the biblical parable of the mustard seed (e.g., Matthew 17:19-20) and the related Christian practice of using a mustard seed as an amulet or a charm (Lisa Williams, pers. comm.). However, thorny plants are very often believed to offer protection from spiritual harm among Native American peoples (cf. Hunn 1990:198), likely an instance of sympathetic magic.

Miscellaneous Remedies

(Table 6.19. Remedies for conditions afflicting animals)

This last category includes veterinary remedies and what might be called "environmental" preventive measures, that is, the use of plants to repel or defend against noxious pests, such as mosquitoes, flies, and fleas. A number of plants are known to be deadly to livestock or to dogs. One is considered so deadly that it is rooted out and placed out of the reach of stock whenever it is found. I have thus not been able to collect a specimen with flowers or fruits and can only surmise that it is *Roldana* cf. *ehrenbergiana* (= *Senecio canecida*, fig. 6.54). As one Latin name indicates, it is a well-known dog-poison, that is, "*canecida.*" The Zapotec name is rather uninformative: *guìzh-yêrb* 'herb herb'. Another poisonous plant is the wild iris, *Rigidelia orthantha*, known simply as *guìzh-ncuàan* 'poison herb' (fig. 6.55). If your donkeys, mules, or oxen eat this plant, they should be fed salt, garlic (*lchâzh*, *Allium sativum*), and chilies (*guìin*, *Capsicum annuum*).

Cuatle flowers (*yàg-guièe-guiâ*, *Eysenhardtia platycarpa* [fig. 6.56], *Eysenhardtia* cf. *polystachea*) are almost overpoweringly sweet-scented. Some people hang the flowering branches in their doorways to repel flies. *Solanum erianthum* (*yàg-guièdz-zân-mběe*) is burned to make smoke to keep mosquitoes (*mlènts*) away. The huge, coarsely haired leaves of *hoja de San Pablo* (*blàg-wê*, *Wigandia urens* [fig. 6.57]) are placed beneath the bed as a flea trap. Fleas are attracted to the leaves, which may then be collected and burned. Eucario cracked that such a remedy is used only by those too poor to own a proper bed!

A Brief Survey of San Juan Gbëë Medicinal Plant Species

I have recorded the medicinal use in San Juan Gbëë of 267 vascular plant taxa of 266 distinct species of 174 genera representing 76 families. These are classified in 214 terminal folk taxa named in Zapotec. Of the families utilized for herbal remedies, the following are best represented, in terms of the total number of species used medicinally and/or the total number of Zapotec categories used:

- the Asteraceae, with at least 43 Linnaean taxa grouped in 34 Zapotec categories;
- the Fabaceae, with at least 20 Linnaean taxa grouped in 16 Zapotec categories;
- the Lamiaceae, with at least 11 Linnaean taxa grouped in 11 Zapotec categories;
- the Solanaceae, with at least 12 Linnaean taxa grouped in 10 Zapotec categories;
- the Rosaceae, with at least 9 Linnaean taxa grouped in 9 Zapotec categories;
- the Rutaceae, with at least 9 Linnaean taxa grouped in 8 Zapotec categories;

the Euphorbiaceae, with at least 9 Linnaean taxa grouped in 8 Zapotec categories; and

the Anacardiaceae, with at least 11 Linnaean taxa grouped in 5 Zapotec categories.

(Table 6.20. Comparison of plant families by medicinal salience)

We may compare these leading families with those reported as of greatest significance in several floras analyzed by Moerman et al. (1999). The families best represented in our data are very similar to those ranked highest in their comparative analysis. For example, among the Highland Maya of central Chiapas, Mexico, the Asteraceae are ranked first, as they are in San Juan Gbëë; the Lamiaceae, second (third in San Juan Gbëë); the Solanaceae, third (fourth in San Juan Gbëë); and the Rosaceae, fourth (fifth in San Juan Gbëë), among the top five families in the highland Maya medicinal flora. However, the Fabaceae, which ranks second in San Juan Gbëë, ranks 131st in Chiapas (but second in the Ecuadorean medicinal flora).

(Table 6.21. Statistical comparison of several regional floras [cf. Moerman et al. 1999])

However, their statistical analysis ranked families in terms of their departure from the number of species expected on the basis of the size of each family, expressed as a z-score. This statistical manipulation controls for family size. Thus, if medicinal plants were selected at random, one would expect a relatively large number of medicinal plants from families with many local species, for example, the Asteraceae in North America and Mexico. It is thus curious that our data are most closely comparable with those of Moerman et al. only when we do not make allowance for family size, but rather rank families in terms of the total number of medicinal plant species. If we ranked our San Juan Zapotec plant families by the *proportion* of the total species of the family that have reported medicinal values, our medicinal flora appears strikingly different from those of native North American and Highland Chiapas as reported by Moerman et al. Thus, the medicinal species of the Asteraceae in our medicinal flora represent just 23.6 percent of the total of Asteraceae species reported for the locality, while 25.9 percent of all local angiosperm species have reported medicinal value. I am at present unable to account for this odd result.

CHAPTER 7

Guièe / Flowers

In Xóchitl in Cuícatl (Nahuatl)

> Flower and song, that is, poetry, the only earthly truth.
> Eagerly does my heart yearn for flowers . . .
> —quoted from MSS *Cantares Mexicanos* (León-Portilla 1963:77, 103)

THIS FASCINATION WITH flowers is deeply rooted in the Mesoamerican aesthetic sensibility. I believe this sensitivity to the beauty and symbolic power of flowers is as pervasive today in San Juan Gbëë as it was for the Aztec philosophers. One prosaic manifestation of this fact is the rich detail of the San Juan Zapotec vocabulary for flowers of all sorts, wild and cultivated, showy or of subtle delicacy. Consider these images: San Juan women climbing Cerro San Isidro with bouquets of *flor de mayo* to offer at the summit shrine to **ngùzì**, god of thunder, to bring the rain (fig. 7.1); San Juan women parading up the street toward the cemetery, arms laden with garden flowers; a young girl returning from weeding a milpa, an immense bouquet of wildflowers strapped to her shoulders (fig. 7.2); the profusion of marigolds (**guièe-cŏb**) on home altars for Todos Santos (fig. 7.3); the church full of poinsettias (**guièe-chên**, literally, 'blood flower') at Christmas, the church entry framed by pine-needle garlands and **mèl ptsìis**, *Dasylirion* "stars" (fig. 7.4) set in a bed of *Tillandsia usneioides*; the wedding corsages (**guièe-niè**, literally, 'hand flower') of frangipani blossoms (**guièe-yăl**) wrapped in citrus leaves offered to each guest (fig. 7.5); the floral sculptures crafted for the grave after a year of mourning (fig. 7.6).

Utilitarian versus Intellectual Motivations

Ethnobiologists have long argued whether the cultural recognition of a plant or an animal is motivated by "utilitarian" or "intellectual" concerns. The debate was framed broadly first by Malinowski, who argued that the native developed expertise in the interest of filling his stomach. "The road from the wilderness to the savage's belly and consequently to his mind is very short. For him the world is an indiscriminate background against which there stand out the useful, primarily the edible, species, whether of plants or animals" (Malinowski 1974:44). Lévi-Strauss countered with an opening salvo in *The Savage Mind* (1966), at pains to disabuse us of any such straightforward reductionist explanation for the elaborate and by and large empirically accurate folk classifications of plants and animals. Berlin made the case for a classificatory motivation nearly free of utilitarian considerations, a position qualified by Hunn (1982). The debate continues (cf. Diamond 1966; Hays 1982; Randall and Hunn 1984; Berlin 1992).

I believe this debate suffers from a less than clear exposition of what is meant by "useful." For Malinowski, the "savage" was first of all concerned with the edible. However, it should be abundantly clear from a perusal of the ethnobiological knowledge of the people of San Juan Gbëë that plants and animals are of interest and are put to use for much more than dinner. In chapter 5 I detailed the multifarious practical applications for subsistence of the local knowledge of plants, from cultivating key staples and a wide range of supplementary foods and condiments to the harvest of weeds and wild plants for food and the collection of plants for fodder, fuel, and fertilizer, all indirectly contributing to basic subsistence requirements for food and shelter. In chapter 6 I described the use of nearly 300 species of medicinal plants, cultivated and wild, and the complex modes of their preparation and administration. In this chapter I further extend the notion of what plants are deemed *useful* (the root meaning of "utilitarian") in San Juan Gbëë, examining the role of plants as "decoration," an English term that does not adequately capture the Spanish term *adorno* used by bilingual consultants to categorize the use values of many local flowers.

Is a flower "useful" if it serves only to decorate the graves of a departed ancestor? I believe it is, and the people of San Juan would agree. Witness the elaborate nomenclature in use there for such ornamental plants. The local Zapotec verbal noun **ngál-guièe** 'decorated' indicates the essential semantic link between **guièe** 'flower' and the activity of adorning crosses, altars, and graves. **Guièe** 'flower, flowery' may also be used as an adjective suggesting particular beauty: a showy weedy grass (*Melinus repens*) that

Memorial floral cross prepared for the Acabo del Año ceremony a year following the death, August 1, 1997.

sports a feathery panicle of reddish flowers may be distinguished as **guìzh-dĭp-guièe** 'flowery grass' (fig. 7.7). This fascination with flowers is of long standing in Mesoamerican culture. Classical Nahuatl poetry equates flowers with poetry and poetry with sacrificial offerings to the gods, living things of great worth, and a medium of communication with the spirit world. San Juaneros do not articulate these connections, though they seem clearly implicit in their regard for flowers.

A Floral Sampler

Guièe-cŏb: Marigolds.

Consider the composites (Asteraceae), the despair of many field botanists due to their confounding variety and the difficulty of sorting one species and genus from another. Some are familiar to everyone, such as the dandelion (*Taraxacum officinalis*) and the marigolds of the genus *Tagetes*, the *flor de muerto* 'death flower' that graces offerings to the spirits of the dead on Todos Santos at the onset of November, peak flowering season throughout the mountains of Mexico. In the course of global commerce these marigolds—native to Mexico and domesticated here long before Cortés arrived—have been appropriated as "African marigolds."

You will find two cultivated varieties of *Tagetes erecta* in San Juan gardens, always growing side by side, as it is said the one is female, the other male, and they must be planted together if they are to thrive. The "male," **guièe-cŏb-yâg** 'tree marigold', is tall and lanky, the "female," **guièe-cŏb-mzhĭg** 'pine-cone marigold', is shorter but with a denser "doubled" floral head, the multiple rays of which resemble the overlapping scales of a pine-cone (fig. 7.8). As with all *Tagetes*, translucent glands in the bracts enclosing the flower head give off a strong sweet scent, perhaps like copal incense, sending a spiritual message. A third domesticated variety, *Tagetes patula*, has broad rays, orange with a decorative red center for which it is named in Zapotec **guièe-cŏb-guìin** 'chili pepper marigold' (fig. 7.9).

A weedy flower characteristic of fallow fields is **guièe-cŏb-gŏn** 'plowed field marigold', an allusion to this ecological association. Though at first glance this is just another *Tagetes*, close inspection reveals an intriguing fact: this "flower" is not only not a simple flower or just a composite inflorescence (as is characteristic of virtually all the Asteraceae), but is doubly composite, the floral head constructed of *six* composite inflorescences, five asymmetrical heads each bearing two showy rays on one side framing the floral disc so that in tandem they appear to be a normal marigold but with ten rather than the usual five orange rays (fig. 7.10). The center of this "flower" is formed of a single discoid head with the discs of the five surrounding floral heads. The Latin name is *Dyssodia tagetifolia*, *Dyssodia* a genus closely related to *Tagetes*, with the specific epithet *tagetifolia* noting how well it mimics a true *Tagetes*.

The wild ancestors of the domesticated *Tagetes erecta* may have closely resembled the diminutive *Tagetes lunulata* or *Tagetes jaliscensis*, common weedy species known in San Juan Zapotec as **guièe-cŏb-làs** 'slender/small marigold' (fig. 7.11) or as **guièe-cŏb-dán** 'forest/mountain marigold'. I believe these two terms are synonyms applicable with equal force to either of these two wild species, which to my eye appear much the same.

Finally, in some San Juan gardens one may find planted a diminutive marigold, like the wild species just mentioned but with a "double" flower, clearly the result of artificial selection of wild variants. These may be called **guièe-cŏb-làs-chîn** 'China slender/small marigold', the "China" of the name a metaphor for a certain aesthetic exuberance. We can appreciate the role of household gardens as sites for continuing domestication.

Guièe-tĭ: Beggar-Ticks.

You may have encountered "beggar-ticks" (*Bidens*) in your wanderings through weedy pastures. Their many seeds sport two to four spines that cling to clothing, an effective means of seed dispersal. There are several species in San Juan. They have toothed or cut leaves in various configurations, and most are trailside weeds, likely a consequence of their seed dispersal strategy, though at least one species grows beside mountain streams in pine forests. Some have white rays. These are known as **guièe-tĭ-nquĭts** 'white beggar-ticks' (*Bidens pilosa*, fig. 7.12). Others have yellow rays: **guièe-tĭ-nguĕts** 'yellow beggar-ticks' (*Bidens aurea*, *Bidens* cf. *ferulaefolia*, fig. 7.13). The pine forest species may be distinguished as **guièe-tĭ-dán** 'forest/mountain beggar-ticks' (*Bidens ostruthioides*, fig. 7.14). The attributive *tĭ* has no clear meaning apart from its use in these names.

These are multipurpose flowers, serving not only for decoration but also for animal fodder, for composting, and as medicine, drunk as a tea for hangovers or for lovesickness. The mountain variety is considered the more powerful medicine.

Guièe-bnîil: Simsia and Tithonia.

Like **cŏb** and **tĭ, bnîil** has no explicit meaning in isolation, though it connotes a rough (*ruñosa*) leaf texture. This Zapotec category seems oddly polymorphic, including two rather different (to my eye) types of flowers. Best known and seemingly prototypical are two species of *Simsia*, one with yellow rays, *Simsia amplexicaulis*, named, as you might have guessed, **guièe-bnîil-nguĕts** 'yellow *Simsia*'. A purple or lilac rayed species, *Simsia sanguinea*, is distinguished as **guièe-bnîil-mòrâd** 'purple *Simsia*'. Both are weedy annuals, coarsely hairy (figs. 7.15, 7.16). This features justifies calling both **guièe-bnîil-guièts** 'spiny *Simsia*'. Though not commonly named in full, they may be called **guièe-bnîil-guièts-nguĕts** 'yellow spiny *Simsia*' and **guièe-bnîil-guièts-mòrâd** 'purple spiny *Simsia*'.

These "spiny" **guièe-bnîil** contrast with a "silky" species, **guièe-bnîil-zhŭil** 'cotton *Simsia*,' which is not a *Simsia* at all but a species of *Tithonia*, a bush sunflower (fig. 7.17). There are at least two species of *Tithonia* in San Juan. Both are like *Simsia* in being conspicuous weeds with conspicuous rays (yellow in this case), but there the resemblance would appear to end. Our *Tithonias* are substantially larger plants and with a very different leaf and stem texture, as the names note. Perhaps the relationship is attributable to the similarity in leaf shape, both genera having clasping, somewhat spade-shaped leaves, and the weedy habits they share.

Complicating the picture is the fact that the larger *Tithonia*, *Tithonia tubaeformis*, is often set apart as a distinct folk genus, **bâr-dòo-lă** 'bitter large stem', which is an important medicinal plant. By contrast, *Tithonia diversifolia* and *Simsia* lack medicinal applications.

Finally, somewhat similar composites, such as the delicate *Galinsoga parviflora* or *Melampodium divaricatum*, may be included in the extended range as **guièe-bnîil-làs** 'slender/small *Simsia*', **guièe-bnîil-nquĭts** 'white *Simsia*', or **guièe-bnîil-dán** 'forest/mountain *Simsia*', though other names are just as likely to apply in such cases.

Guièe-dâl: Dahlia and Cosmos.

More widely renowned even than the marigolds are the dahlias (*Dahlia* spp.) and their kin of the genus *Cosmos*. Both genera are characteristically Mexican, achieving their greatest diversity in Mexico's pine-and-oak-forested mountains (35 species of *Dahlia* are recognized, all Mesoamerican). Early colonial illustrated documents prove that the Aztecs, at least, had begun the domestication process, producing double-flowered forms and other cultivated hybrids (Bye 1993). Flower lovers in Europe and Asia since the eighteenth century have recognized the incredible plasticity of dahlias and have developed to date thousands of distinct varieties, some of which returned to Mexico and are now grown in San Juan gardens. Curiously, despite their indigeneity, the local Zapotec name for both cultivated and wild species of these two genera is *guièe-dâl*, the attributive borrowed from Spanish *dalia*, which is ultimately attributable to the eighteenth-century Swedish botanist Anders Dahl.

I have so far recorded six species of *Dahlia* and three of *Cosmos* in San Juan. Of these, two *Dahlia* species and one *Cosmos* are cultivated; the rest grow wild. *Dahlia* is distinguished from *Cosmos* in that the former are perennials with tuberous roots, the latter annuals or biennials with simple roots. One may also note that the involucral bracts differ, those of *Dahlia* forming a cylindrical cup, those of *Cosmos* a flat plate. In any case, the people of San Juan do not explicitly recognize this distinction. Instead, they distinguish wild from cultivated forms, that is, those with simple, eight-rayed floral heads from those with dense, "double" heads. The former are **guièe-dâl-mrùux,** literally, 'june bug dahlias'; the latter are **guièe-dâl-mzhĭg** 'pine-cone dahlias' (*Dahlia* x *hortensis* Guillaumin and *Dahlia pinnata* Cav.) "Pine-cone" is a metaphoric descriptor also applied to the double-flowered marigolds. However, this dichotomy fails to account for the domestic *Cosmos bipinnatus* (fig. 7.18), which is neither wild nor double-flowered and is further set apart by its finely divided fernlike leaves. It is generally distinguished as **guièe-dâl-làs** 'slender/small dahlia'.

All three of these folk specific categories may be further differentiated by ray color: for example, **guièe-dâl-mrùux** includes several species. The scarlet-rayed *Dahlia coccinea* may be named **guièe-dâl-mrùux-nìzhniê** 'red June-bug dahlia' (fig. 7.19); *Dahlia australis* var. *australis* (fig. 7.20), and *Cosmos crithmifolius* may be called **guièe-dâl-mrùux-mòrâd** 'purple June-bug dahlia' (fig. 7.21), while *Dahlia merkii* and *Cosmos diversifolius* may be termed **guièe-dâl-mrùux-nquĭts** 'white June-bug dahlia' (fig. 7.22). Moreover, the domestic *Dahlia pinnata* of the Decorative Flower Group and *Cosmos bipinnatus* exhibit a range of color varieties, including magenta, white, and peach (fig. 7.23). So one may hear **guièe-dâl-mzhĭg** and **guièe-dâl-làs** similarly modified. However, it is more common to abbreviate these varietal names, thus speaking simply of **guièe-dâl-mòrâd** 'purple dahlia' or **guièe-dâl-nquĭts** 'white dahlia', whether the species is wild or cultivated.

The giant *Dahlia excelsa* is not specifically distinguished, at least not by the great majority of San Juaneros. It is called **guièe-dâl-mrùux** or **guièe-dâl-mòrâd**, as it has simple, eight-rayed, magenta flowers (fig. 7.24), though I measured one individual growing wild in a *barranca* in town at six meters tall with a trunk eight centimeters in diameter and leaves to match (fig. 7.25), joined to the stalk by what looked like some sort of truck camshaft.

Guièe-bgùs: Zinnia.

The zinnias are another well-known cultivated ornamental with deep roots in Mexico. The Zapotec name means literally 'spindle flower', aptly descriptive of the spindle-shaped involucre (fig. 7.26).

Guièe-nziù: Stevia.

At least twelve species of *Stevia* grow wild in San Juan. Most are recognized as **xín-guièe-nziù** 'relative of the *tepache* flower'. The "true" **guièe-nziù** '*tepache* flower' is *Stevia salicifolia* (fig. 7.27), a particularly sweet-smelling, white-flowered species of pine forests above town. No wedding party is complete without the festive, slightly alcoholic drink **nziù** (*tepache*)—made of the fermented juice of a special mountain pineapple strengthened with a *pulque* accelerant. *Stevia* species are known to produce a natural sweetener a hundred times more potent than cane sugar. However, my consultants deny that the flower was used in any way other than as decoration.

***Guièe-chên* 'Blood Flower':** Poinsettia or *flor de Noche Buena* (*Euphorbia pulcherrima*).

This well-known "flower" is another Mexican native that has since colonized the world (fig. 7.28). The "flower" is in fact formed of modified leaves, scarlet to pink bracts that surround the rather inconspicuous yellow flowers. It represents the winter season much as marigolds represent fall, and frangipanis spring. The name 'blood flower' is apt. Poinsettias are found in cultivation in San Juan, though they grow wild elsewhere in Mexico. A wildflower of the Amaryllis family, the Jacobean lily, *Sprekelia formosissima*, which bears a similarly showy blood-red flower, is known as **guièe-chên-dán** 'forest/mountain poinsettia' and is likewise valued as an ornamental.

***Guièe-dzîl*:** Orchids.

The Orchidaceae is one of the most diverse of all plant families, with more than 25,000 species worldwide. The family is also well represented in Mexico with 1,300 species so far described, of which 692 have been reported in Oaxaca (Soto Arenas and Salazar 2004:271–72). Though San Juan Gbëë is not your stereotypical humid, tropical, orchid-infested jungle, it nevertheless hosts at least twenty-one species of fifteen genera of orchids, and likely considerably more. One species is a recent find, newly described (or perhaps rediscovered) based on one of my specimens. If it should prove to be a new species, we intend to give it a Zapotec name, *Platanthera guieedzil* (Salazar and Hunn n.d.).

The less showy species tend to be dismissed with descriptive nonce forms in lieu of true names or simply not recognized. However, the more showy species are each considered a particular species of the Zapotec folk generic **guièe-dzîl**. These are gathered when encountered, most often while hunting or gathering wild plants in the higher-elevation forests above town. They are carried home, where they may keep for long periods, drawing sustenance through aerial roots and stored nutrients in a swollen bulb. This is due to the epiphytic habits of many species:

> **guièe-dzîl-nzhíxtò** 'hanging orchid flower' (*Euchile citrina*), with waxy yellow blossoms that hang from the branch to which the bulbs cling (fig. 7.29);

guièe-dzîl-ndzĭz 'squirrel orchid flower' (*Rhynchostele cervantesii*) (fig. 7.30);

guièe-dzîl-cònêf 'rabbit orchid flower' (*Laelia furfuracea*), epiphytic, often on oaks in pine-oak forest above town; so named for the basal leaves, which resemble a rabbit's ears; showy in pink (fig. 7.31);

guièe-dzîl-mòrâd 'purple orchid flower' (*Laelia anceps*), like *Laelia furfuracea* but flowers larger and bi-colored, white and pink;

guièe-dzîl-ló-liù 'orchid flower in the earth' (*Bletia reflexa, Bletia jucunda, Oncidium graminifolium*), a terrestrial species, distinguished as inedible or poisonous (*ncuàan*);

guièe-dzîl-dán 'forest/mountain orchid flower' (*Govenia capitata*), a tall, showy terrestrial species of pine forests above town (fig. 7.32);

dzîl-dán 'forest/mountain orchid' (*Encyclia michoacana*), valued for its succulent, edible bulb; perhaps that explains the contrast with *guièe-dzîl-dán*.

A showy yellow lady's-slipper (*Cypripedium molle*) occurs sparingly in and near San Juan. One name offered was *guièe-dòoz* 'young-milpa flower' (fig. 7.33), though this may be a nonce form.

Guièe-dzĭng 'Hummingbird Flower'.

The common feature of the diverse assortment of species so named are showy spikes of tubular flowers of some shade of red, all of which are attractive to hummingbirds. The form and color is likely a coevolutionary adaptation to pollination by these tiny avian dynamos. The category encompasses at least twenty species of six genera of five families: Campanulaceae, *Lobelia* (2 spp., fig. 7.34); Lamiaceae: *Salvia* (4 spp., fig. 7.35); Lythraceae: *Cuphea* (2 spp., fig. 7.36); Orobanchaceae: *Castilleja* (6 spp., fig. 7.37); Scrophulariaceae: *Lamourouxia* (4 spp., fig. 7.38) and *Penstemon* (2 spp., fig. 7.39).

Two distinct generic categories may be "pulled out" from this diverse background. For example, *Castilleja arvensis* may be distinguished as *x-côl-mĕcw-zhĭil* 'sheep's tail' (fig. 7.40), descriptive of the shape and texture of this particular species. Likewise, the two *Penstemon* species may be called instead *guièe-mĕets* 'louse plant', a name suggested by the yellow anthers exerted from the floral tube, which resemble nits.

Fuchsias are also attractive to hummingbirds and may be included as ***guièe-dzı̄ng*** but are more often called ***guièe-sènyòrît*** 'the young lady flower' (*Fuchsia cylindracea*, *Fuchsia microphylla*, *Fuchsia parviflora*). "The young lady" is likely an allusion to the Virgin Mary, the subject of propitiatory offerings as owner of such magical medicinal plants as *Datura stramonium* (see chap. 6), and perhaps as a more recent equivalent of the Zapotec term ***zhnâzh*** 'virgin', as in ***zhì-ncuàan-ná-zhnâzh*** 'Virgin Mother's medicine' (*Turbina corymbosa*) and ***blàg-zhnâzh*** 'virgin leaf' (*Croton ciliato-glandulifer*), also magical plants.

Guièe-xtsèe 'Dinner/Evening Flower' (*Milla biflora*,
Oenothera laciniata ssp. *pubescens*).

The 'dinner/evening flower' includes two quite dissimilar types and may best be interpreted as two identically named folk generics. First is the famed *azucena* or 'lily' of Oaxaca (*Milla biflora*) featured on the state seal, as according to legend this lily grew from the corpse of Donají, Zapotec princess married to a Mixtec king to forge an alliance designed to halt an Aztec conquest (fig. 7.41). The Zapotec name refers to the fact that the flower opens in the evening, remaining closed in full daylight. It may involve a bilingual pun, as ***xtsèe*** means *cena* 'supper', which is called to mind by the term *azu<u>cena</u>*.

Sharing the name is a weedy evening primrose (*Oenothera laciniata* ssp. *pubescens*), which like the *azucena* opens at dusk and closes at dawn (fig. 7.42). Not all *Oenothera* species are called ***guièe-xtsèe***, however. The diminutive *Oenothera rosea* is distinguished as ***guièe-zhàn̄-biǎa*** 'under prickly pear cactus flower', noted for its medicinal value in treating nosebleeds.

Guièe-rrè 'Vase Flower' (*Ipomoea* in part,
of the Convolvulaceae).

At least a half-dozen morning-glory species are so named (fig. 7.43), as is a superficially similar flowering vine of the Scrophulariaceae, *Maurandya scandens*. As all are vines, they are sometimes called ***lbḕ-guièe-rrè*** 'vase flower-vine', descriptive of the shape of the flower. These delicate flowers, however, are better appreciated on the vine than on an altar, as they wilt in a matter of minutes. The psychedelic morning-glory of Mesoamerican fame, *Turbina corymbosa*, is known as **zhì-ncuàan-ná-zhnâzh** 'Virgin Mother's medicine', a medicine for fright suffered far from home and a tool for divining in dreams supernatural causes of disease.

Guièe-yùzh 'Sand Flower' (*Echeverria, Sedum*, of the Crassulaceae).

These decorative succulents grow on poor sandy or gravelly soils, adding a splash of bright yellow or carmine red to a barren stretch of trail or to an exposed cliff face. They will hold their form and color well on an altar or grave. All grow wild except the shrubby *Sedum prealtum* (fig. 7.44), which may be set apart as **sièmprvîv**, borrowed from the Spanish term *siempre-viva* 'live forever'. The cemetery above San Pedro Gbëë is a veritable woodland of this stonecrop. The name **sièmprvîv** applies also to certain club mosses, for example, *Selaginella lepidophylla*, noted for their resistance to drought. Red-flowered species include several species of *Echeverria* (fig. 7.45).

Guièe-ló-yâg 'On-Tree Flower' (Loranthaceae).

These are the mistletoes, including all fourteen species of five genera of the family so far recorded in San Juan. A few species produce showy red flowers, but most are valued as decoration for their durable foliage. If pressed for a more specific name, certain species may be distinguished by their host tree, for example, **guìzh-ló-yâg-dùr** 'pine-tree mistletoe' (NB, **guìzh**, not **guièe**, as its flowers are inconspicuous) for *Arceuthobium globosum* or **guièe-ló-yâg-guièts** 'thorn-tree mistletoe' for *Cladocolea* cf. *andrieuxii* and *Psittacanthus auriculatus*, which frequently parasitize *Acacia pennatula*, **yàg-guièts-ngǎs**, and other related species. Certain species of one mistletoe genus, *Struthanthus*, with sticky seeds that are used to make birdlime, may be distinguished as **lbề-dzǐ** 'birdlime vine'.

Wildflowers Named for Odd Patterns or in Terms of Similar or Related Domesticates

The following are a representative sampling of wildflowers singled out for some distinctive quality.

nlĕch-bĕz 'fox onion', *Nothoscordum striatum*, of the Alliaceae (onion family) (fig. 7.46); a slender wildflower of swampy ground, only faintly onion-scented;

guièe-còrôn-côp 'cup crown flower', *Bomarella hirtella*, of the Alstroemeriaceae (fig. 7.47); a showy flowering vine of streamsides in pine forests; likened to the belladonna lily (*Amaryllis belladonna*), a favorite in gardens (see below);

x-tòoz-pĕch 'turkey vulture's milpa', *Echeandia* cf. *reflexa*, of the Anthericaceae (fig. 7.48); a tall, slender, lilylike wildflower with scattered yellow blooms; the reference to turkey vultures is obscure to me;

x-tòoz-ngă 'raven's milpa', several species of the Commelinaceae (fig. 7.49); like the previous example, a delicate, erect monocot, equally semantically obscure;

guièe-nìt 'sugarcane flower', *Commelina erecta, Tinantia erecta, Tradescantia crassifolia*, all of the Commelinaceae (fig. 7.50); so-called for their jointed stems and sheathing leaves; the term for sugarcane ultimately is derivative of the term for green maize stalks, which were chewed in pre-contact times for their sweet juice;

guièe-guìib 'metal flower', *Eryngium gracile*, of the Apiaceae (fig. 7.51); named for the seemingly metallic silvery bracts that cup the tightly compact umbel;

guìzh-quês 'cheese plant' and ***guìzh-mèl*** 'star plant', *Anoda* cf. *cristata*, of the Malvaceae (fig. 7.52); this attractive weed is quite variable in the leaf pattern; the most common type with a plain but shapely hastate leaf is named for the oddly shaped fruits, which resemble cylindrical cheeses; another variety has the leaf decorated with a very pale green starburst pattern, hence the second name;

diàg-cûch 'pig's ear', the Mexican butterwort, *Pinguicula moranensis*, of the Lentibulariaceae (fig. 7.53); named for the round fleshy basal leaves, which are covered with sticky hairs to catch insects on which it feeds.

Flowers by Color

Prominent in the foregoing discussion are ornamental or otherwise culturally conspicuous plants of the Asteraceae, that is, the "composites," our most diverse and taxonomically difficult family. I have recorded at least 183 species of seventy-eight genera of this single family. The majority of these species are grouped in seventy-six named terminal taxa within forty-three well-defined folk generics. However, a substantial residual group of composites remains to be dealt with. In San Juan Zapotec much of this residual diversity is treated by applying what appear to be descriptive phrases but which, in certain instances at least, qualify as true names. Three such "names" are ***guièe-mòrâd*** 'purple flower', ***guièe-nguĕts*** 'yellow flower', and ***guièe-nquĭts*** 'white flower'. Each of these terms refers to one or more prototypical species, then is extended to a range of variously 'purple', 'yellow', or 'white' rayed composites not otherwise distinguished, and often to any flowers of the appropriate hue not named in their own right. I believe it best to recognize as so-*named* only the prototypical referents, as judged by the degree of consensus in naming and/or descriptive detail clearly associated with the referent (see the discussion of this issue in chap. 4).

One prototypical referent of ***guièe-mòrâd*** is *Pinaropappus roseus* (fig. 7.54), a weedy lilac-rayed dandelion relative. Crush the stems and apply the milky sap to skin sores or drip a few drops into the eye to treat "blood in the eye" (see chap. 6). ***Guièe-nguĕts*** (or alternatively ***guièe-gùts*** 'yellowish flower') may be applied to a range of Asteraceae species of such genera as *Acmella, Aldama, Hieracium, Jaegeria, Melampodium, Rumfordia, Tridax,* and *Trixis*. A prototypical 'yellow flower' is the *dormilón*, a European garden cultivar *Calendula officinalis* (fig. 7.55), valued as a medicine. ***Guièe-nquĭts*** includes various species of *Aster, Actinomeris, Chrysanthemum, Conyza, Erigeron, Eupatorium,* and *Kuhnia*. A prototype is *Aster moranensis* (fig. 7.56), perhaps by virtue of the fact that it is such a characteristic weed of fallow fields and trail margins near town.

Tree-Flowers

A nomenclatural peculiarity of the local Zapotec is the use of "double life-form" prefixes, typically in a specific order. For example, the 'hummingbird flower' may be known also as ***guìzh-guièe-dzĭng*** 'hummingbird flower-herb'. Many trees and shrubs, that is, *yâg*, bear flowers, of course, but only in certain instances are the flowers so prominent that the plant is given a double life-form name ***yàg-guièe-X*** 'X flower-tree'. I describe below a few prominent examples, then give a more comprehensive listing.

The rose, *yàg-guièe-rôs* 'rose bush', *Rosa* spp., is perhaps the best known garden flower in San Juan. There are no native roses in Oaxaca and but a single species, *Rosa montezumae* (Humb. & Bonpl. ex Thory), ranges as far south as the pine-forested mountains that ring Mexico City. Nevertheless, roses have held a special place in the Mexican imagination since shortly following the Spanish conquest. The most Mexican of saints, the Virgin of Guadalupe, is linked to the rose. According to the story, Juan Diego's vision of the Virgin on Tepeyac Hill just ten years after the fall of the Aztec capital city to Cortés, was authenticated by the roses she bade Juan deliver in his peasant cape to a skeptical Bishop Zumárraga. Juan Diego's cape, bearing the Virgin's image, now hangs as the centerpiece in the basilica dedicated to her worship in Mexico City. According to the legend, these roses grew miraculously in mid-winter on barren Tepeyac Hill. Why roses? Clearly not for their indigenous ethnobotanical significance, given the limited distribution of the one native rose species, but more likely for their symbolic power within the European tradition transplanted to the New World with Christianity by missionary friars. Be that as it may, roses are now well established in the San Juan ethnoflora. Most are cultivated in gardens, though they have escaped cultivation in a few instances and have been accommodated in riparian thickets near town. Several varieties of roses are consistently recognized and named:

> *guièe-rôs-càstî* 'Castillian rose', most likely the cabbage rose (*Rosa centifolia*), bears fully double, rose-pink, richly scented flowers; these are of medicinal value to lower fevers as the plant is considered to be "cool" (see chap. 6);
> *guièe-rôs-nquĭts* 'white rose' may be a variety of tea rose (*Rosa* x *odorata*); despite the Latin name, the flowers are less heavily scented than the Castillian variety, though this form shares the same medicinal applications;
> *guièe-rósà-côl* 'cabbage rose' may be a variety of China rose (*Rosa chinensis*); there appears to be a nomenclatural inversion here, as it is *Rosa centifolia* that is known in English as the "cabbage rose"; the Zapotec 'cabbage rose' also bears double rose-pink flowers but lacks the Castillian rose's aroma; it is also opposite in humoral value, as it is considered to be extremely "hot," to the point of being

a special danger to pregnant women. It is recognized as an abortifacient. This belief may be derivative of European medicinal practice, as *Rosa chinensis* is noted as an emmenagogue and is widely used "for women's complaints" (www.scs.leeds.ac.uk/cgibin/pfaf/arr—html?Rosa+chinensis&CAN=LATIND).

As a bewildering variety of roses have been cultivated from China to Europe since the Middle Ages, it is not surprising that the distinctions recognized in San Juan do not map neatly to some few rose species. In fact, specimens identified at the Mexican National Herbarium as *Rosa* x *odorata* were named variously as 'white', 'Castillian', and 'cabbage' roses by one or another San Juan consultant. I believe a more comprehensive analysis would show that the San Juan rose classification is systematic. The present analysis is a provisional approximation only.

The frangipani, or *flor de mayo*, is **yàg-guièe-yăl** (*Plumeria rubra* f. *acutifolia*, Apocynaceae). This tree presents a stark, spreading, angular outline as the spring dry season progresses. Then in May the bare branches explode in fragrant bloom, followed, with the onset of the rains, by thick elliptic leaves. Some are planted in town; others grow wild, often spared when fields are cleared near town, leaving them standing alone in midfield (fig. 7.57). I have seen white- and yellow-flowered varieties in San Juan, but never the magenta bloom sometimes seen in Oaxaca City. Thus, just two specifics are noted, **yàg-guièe-yăl-nquĭts** 'white frangipani' and **yàg-guièe-yăl-nguĕts** 'yellow frangipani'. The 'white frangipani' is said to grow wild and be the stronger medicine with a more durable flower, while the 'yellow frangipani' is known only in cultivation. As briefly noted above, frangipani flowers are sewed into a ring of citrus leaves (**blàg-lîm**, *Citrus aurantiifolia*) to make an aromatic wedding corsage called **guièe-niá** 'hand flower', which is presented to each guest as they arrive at the wedding *fandango*. The flowers are also strung to make a floral necklace and quantities are sold—by the basket—in local markets.

Some Children's Plants

While most local plants may be classified unambiguously as valued for food (including condiments), medicine, construction material, firewood, forage, compost, adornment, or some combination of those uses, a few still "useful" plants remain to the side. Yet they are noticed, named, and not infrequently commented on. These plants of miscellaneous utility include, for example, plants used as toys (**wguìt**):

> **guièe-gùzh** 'needle flower', our crane's-bill (*Erodium cicutarium*, of the Geraniaceae), provides San Juan children the equivalent of our toy gun, a floral sword for mock jousts;
>
> **guièe-nàad** 'sticky flower' or **guìzh-nàad** 'sticky herb' includes an assortment of plants that attach themselves to clothing by a naturally Velcro-like surface or gummy exudate, such as the leaves of *Mentzelia pallida*, of the Loasaceae, or the frail trailing branches of bedstraw, *Galium mexicanum*, of the Rubiaceae. Another is an obscure clambering weed, highly glandular, with tiny purple flowers. This is *Plumbago pulchella*, of the Plumbaginaceae. I included as a particular challenge one of these among the fifty species of plants on a plant trail I laid out through the center of San Juan to test what children of various ages knew of local plants (see chap. 8), as it seemed beneath notice. I was surprised that it proved the only plant that children knew better than adults. The explanation seems to be that its sole "use" is as a child's toy, for a game of "stick-on."

Two other plants are of special note for children, though not "toys" exactly. Parents warn children that if they touch **guièe-rzìòob** '[teeth-]fallout flower' their teeth will fall out! The bright red or red and yellow flowers of *Bouvardia cordifolia* and *Bouvardia ternifolia* do fall at the slightest touch. The same name is applied to *Lantana camara*, which is the most prominent species of this genus of the Verbenaceae. Three other *Lantana* species are known instead as **guièe-xòob-mèz** 'fox's-maize flower' (*Lantana frutilla*, *Lantana involucrata*, *Lantana velutina*), an imaginative description of the clusters of black fruits typical of *Lantana*, which are a favorite of foxes. Why *Lantana camara* should be set apart in this way is not clear to me, though the flowers share the contrasting red, orange, and yellow color pattern of *Bouvardia ternifolia*. This color pattern has also inspired a new name for *Bouvardia ternifolia*, **guièe-cèrî** 'match flower', as the local brand of matches (*cerillo* in Spanish) has a red and yellow head.

Decorative Foliage

Not only flowers are decorative. A variety of mosses, lichens, and leaves are appreciated as adornment. Noted for its decorative value is *bzhăazh* 'moss' in its several varieties, which include a range of mosslike lichens called *bzhăazh-zhlôzh* 'beard moss'; a trailing club moss that favors rocks, *Selaginella wrightii*, classed as *bzhăazh-nquiă* 'green moss'; and even a bromeliad, *Tillandsia usneoides*, *bzhăazh-nquĭts* 'white moss', tellingly known in English as "Spanish moss," though it is, in fact, a flowering plant (fig. 7.58). Other species of *Tillandsia* are named *bliòo*. These resemble miniature arboreal agaves. They are brought home to grace altar and church, particularly when in bloom, brandishing floral spikes of pink, blue-violet, red, yellow, or white (fig. 7.59). One delicate species with reddish leaves is further differentiated as *bliòo-nìzhniê* 'red *Tillandsia*'.

Pine needles (*dùr*) are strung on a cord to make a garland to drape over the frame of the church door or twine about the arch formed of giant African reeds, *Arundo donax*, *gòob-guì*, that frames the home altar. Pinecones (*mzhĭg*) are hung from the cross shrine on the summit of Cerro San Isidro (fig. 7.60), not so much as decoration but as a symbolic request to the god of thunder (*ngùzì*) for the benefits of oxen and goats in the case of the larger cones of the Oaxaca pine (*Pinus pseudostrobus* var. *apulcensis*); the small cones of *Pinus teocote* represent fowl. Fir boughs of *Abies guatemalensis* (*yàg-lgâzh*) add the scent of balsam to the altar as may branches of juniper, *Juniperus flaccida*, included with the Montezuma bald cypress (*Taxodium mucronatum*) as *yàg-guìzdòo* 'Miahuatlán tree'.

Ferns, *guìzh-crûz* 'cross plant', may owe their ornamental value in part to their symbolic association with the Christian cross, given the "cruciform" pinnate fronds of most ferns. Most ferns are included as *guìzh-crûz* (twenty-eight species of fourteen genera of six families), excepting only those of medicinal value or with particularly distinctive morphologies, which are set apart under separate generic headings. The prototype may be the ubiquitous bracken fern (*Pteridium aquilinum*, fig. 7.61). All *guìzh-crûz* are decorative, as are certain sedges (Cyperaceae) with distichous florets, such as *Cyperus* cf. *flavus* and *Rhynchospora* sp., singled out as *guìzh-dĭp-crûz* 'cross grass' (fig. 7.62), and accorded similar ornamental and symbolic value.

Pedro Miguel inspecting a decorative "star" under construction, made of the leaves of *sotol, Dasylirion serratifolium,* June 10, 1997.

I witnessed a memorial *acabo del año* 'completion of the year' ceremony one damp August in San Juan. This ceremony closed a year of mourning for the deceased and involved a night-long wake at which an elaborate floral cross was constructed in the house of the family by forming a mosaic of flowers, leaves, and moss on a bed of sand spread on a board. A *rezador* 'one who prays' from the Catholic church led the vigil, organized the burning of copal incense, the lighting of five candles to represent the "five wounds" suffered by Jesus before his crucifixion, and the recitation of prayers. The room, smoky with incense, packed with quiet relatives and neighbors, was decorated with 'stars', a decorative art, **mèl ptsìis** '*sotol* star' formed by weaving together the leaves of the *sotol*, a yucca-like plant, *Dasylirion serratifolium*.

In the early morning the floral cross on its bed of sand was raised, lifted, and carried intact to the church, where it was blessed again before the altar, then carried in procession through the streets of the town—tracing the route of the funeral procession of the previous year—to the cemetery, where it was placed on the grave amid additional floral offerings. By this point I was exhausted and ready to go home to bed. I thought I might slip out of the cemetery gate unnoticed but found the route blocked by a young man and several older women who seemed disinclined to let me pass. I later learned that this was indeed intended, to assure that every mourner return to the family home at the conclusion of the cemetery ritual to share a special feast provided by the family.

Meanwhile, I took the opportunity to closely inspect the floral cross (fig. 7.63). The background was a field of bright green formed of interlaced fern fronds. A white cross on a white pedestal was formed on the green background by feverfew flowers (*Tanacetum parthenium*). Flames flanking the cross were of a red-orange marigold, **guièe-cŏb-guìin** (*Tagetes patula*). Orange floral candles were set on the pedestal beside the cross, formed of yellow-orange marigold flowers, **guièe-cŏb-mzhĭg** (*Tagetes erecta*), as were the letters "D E P," "descanso en paz," 'rest in peace'. Marguerites, **guièe-crùsàntêm** (*Chrysanthemum frutescens*), shone like stars scattered across the green field, while purple asters, **guièe-mòrâd** 'purple flower' (*Aster novi-belgii*), bordered the field. The floral image was now set in a bed of green moss (**bzhăazh-nguiă**) of an unidentified species and ringed about by bouquets of belladonna (**guièe-còrôn-rêy** 'king's crown flower', *Amaryllis belladonna*), calla (**guièe-càrtûch** < Spanish *cartucho*, *Zantedeschia aethiopica*, fig. 7.64), Peruvian lilies (*Alstroemeria aurantiaca*), and lilies of the Nile (**guièe-pânt** 'agapanthus flower', *Agapanthus africanus*).

A Survey of San Juan Gbëë Houseyard Gardens

Gardens are mostly the responsibility of the women of the household. They often seem a chaotic mix of plants placed wherever there is space, but gardeners know the location and identity of each plant. Gardens provide ready access to a variety of culinary herbs, salad greens, and fruits that complement the milpa staples. Gardens are experimental plots also, for commercial seeds, transplants of species encountered traveling outside the community, and even of wild native species that might ultimately become domesticates (as has happened with such ornamental and medicinal plants as *Dahlia coccinea*, *Cosmos bipinnatus*, and *Tagetes erecta*). They are also important venues—schools might be an appropriate term—

for the cultural transmission of ethnobotanical knowledge, as children from a very early age learn about a great variety of plants and their uses playing in their home gardens.

Garden Flowers

All but the mosses and ferns in the memorial cemetery floral cross were products of local houseyard gardens, and all but the marigolds among these were exotics. This illustrates two important ethnobotanical facts: the value of houseyard gardens in the local subsistence economy (broadly construed) and the role of such gardens as experimental plots for incorporating new plants into the local botanical repertoire. It is worth noting also in this regard that since women own and operate these gardens, they are key forces in shaping the dynamic culture of the town.

Several garden flowers are represented by multiple varieties, distinguished nomenclaturally most often by flower color but sometimes by other morphological characteristics. I list a number of illustrative examples below:

> *guièe-blàg-bdiò* 'banana-leaf flower', aka *guièe-còtêcw*, the canna lilies, *Canna indica*, of the Cannaceae (fig. 7.65), are garden favorites, with four color varieties named, yellow, red, white, and rose;
> *guièe-jèrân* 'geranium flower', the common cultivated geranium, *Pelargonium zonale*, of the Geraniaceae, may be dark, rose, cherry, purple, orange, white, red, or cherry; two folk specifics differ more fundamentally in form, *guièe-jèrân-lbẽ̀* 'vine geranium' (*Pelargonium peltatum*) and *guièe-jèrân-strànjêr* 'stranger/foreign geranium' (*Pelargonium sp.*);
> *guièe-glàdiôl* 'gladiolus flower', *Gladiolus* x *hortulanus*, of the Iridaceae, comes in six colors: orange, cantaloupe, yellow, red, white, and rose;
> *guièe-màrpôl*, literally, 'poppy flower', the hollyhock, *Alcea rosea*, of the Malvaceae, may be white, rose, or cherry;
> *yàg-bùgàmbîl* 'bougainvillea tree/shrub', *Bougainvillea* x *buttiana*, of the Nyctaginaceae, and the related weedy *guièe-màràvî* 'miracle flower', *Mirabilis jalapa* (fig. 7.66), may both be purple, white, or yellow;

guièe-dâl: domestic *Cosmos bipinnatus* comes in white, cherry, and rose-purple, while domestic *Dahlia pinnata* may be white, peach, and various shades of purple.

Of the plants noted above, only the last named are native to Mexico. Popular showy garden flowers with less varietal exuberance include:

guièe-pânt < Spanish *agapanthus*, the lily-of-the-Nile, *Agapanthus africanus*, of the Alliaceae, from South Africa, a favorite in the cemetery;

guièe-còròn-rêy 'king's crown flower', the belladonna lily, *Amaryllis belladonna*, of the Amaryllidaceae, from South Africa; there are white and rose varieties;

guièe-ncâj 'lace flower', Queen Anne's lace, *Amni majus* (fig. 7.67), of the Apiaceae, from Europe;

rlăal-x-pëëd-á 'scatters its children', the spider plant, *Bryophyllum (Kalanchoe) pinnatum*, of the Crassulaceae, from South Africa; aptly, if awkwardly named, as it may reproduce by buds that form along the stems and then drop to the ground;

yàg-guièe-rôs-làurêl 'laurel-rose-tree', the oleander, *Nerium oleander* (fig. 7.68), of the Apocynaceae, from the Mediterranean region; not considered to be a true rose; white and rose flowers may be seen on adjacent bushes; the poisonous sap contains deadly glycosides; however, this was not noted in San Juan;

guièe-càrtûch < Spanish *cartucho*, the calla lily, *Zantedeschia aethiopica*, of the Araceae, from South Africa; though cultivated commercially in many Oaxacan communities, it is grown in San Juan only for local use;

guièe-sàntàmàrî 'Saint Mary flower', feverfew, *Tanacetum parthenium*, of the Asteraceae, from southeastern Europe; an important medicinal plant (see chap. 6); a native weed, *Helenium mexicanum*, is allied with feverfew, as it is named *guièe-sàntàmàrî-mòntês* 'montane feverfew'; I treat this as a distinct folk generic, as it is not thought of as a kind of feverfew, despite the name;

guièe-ròs-chîn 'China-rose flower', perennial morning-glory, *Ipomoea indica*, of the Convolvulaceae, from South America; not considered to be a kind of rose, despite the name;

guièe-guièts 'spine flower', lion's ear, *Leonotis nepetaefolia* (fig. 7.69), of the Lamiaceae, pantropical; cultivated and naturalized in San Juan;

yàg-guièe-tùlìpân 'tulip flower-tree', hibiscus, *Hibiscus rosa-sinensis*, of the Malvaceae, from tropical Asia; two color varieties are recognized, white and rose;

ârnìcà, *Bocconia arborea*, of the Papaveraceae, native to Mexico, cultivated in and occasionally wild near San Juan; medicinal, used to wash wounds (see chap. 6); the term "arnica" may have widely varying referents; in Europe it refers to flowers of the genus *Arnica* of the Asteraceae; in central Mexico the term is most often applied to *Heterotheca inuloides* Cass., also of the Asteraceae (Linares, Bye, and Flores 1999:32–33); I do not know how widespread the San Juan application of the term may be;

guièe-pèrrît 'puppy flower', snapdragon, *Antirrhinum majus*, of the Scrophulariaceae, from Europe; two varieties are recognized, white and purple;

guièe-pûnt < Spanish *floripondio*, angel's trumpet; **guièe-pûnt-nquîts** 'white angel's trumpet' is *Brugmansia x candida*, and **guièe-pûnt-ròsâd** 'rosy angel's trumpet' is *Brugmansia* cf. *versicolor*, of the Solanaceae, from the Andes of South America; violently hallucinogenic, but not taken internally in San Juan; *Brugmansia x candida* is applied externally to treat a condition known as **nzëëb**, characterized by swelling of the feet and face; also to diagnose *chaneque*, a type of *aire* (see chap. 6); the plant is spiritually powerful and thus must be "bought" with an offering of seven pebbles, as is the case with the related *Datura stramonium*;

guièe-àsâr 'wedding flower', the potato vine, *Solanum jasminoides*, of the Solanaceae, from Brazil; favored as a wedding decoration;

guièe-màltuêrs < Spanish *mal-tuerzo* 'badly twisted', the nasturtium, *Tropaeolum majus*, of the Tropaeolaceae, from Peru, domesticated in Europe (fig. 7.70); medicinal as well as ornamental, for tonsillitis, headache, and fever.

Home Gardens as Larder, Lab, and School

Traditional Mesoamerican subsistence agriculture involves many variations on the in-field/out-field system. The "out-field" component is the well-known milpa or cornfield, typically intercropped with beans and squashes, the triumvirate of the Mesoamerican diet. However, it is important to recognize the key role of the "in-field," or home garden (*huerto familiar*), typically planted in the *solar* or patio adjacent to the houses and kitchen structures of each family. The milpa in San Juan is cultivated by ox-drawn plows, planted at the onset of the summer rains, and harvested in late fall, to produce an annual stockpile of the three key staples. By contrast, the home garden yields year-round, as it is both irrigated (mostly by hand) and fertilized with kitchen scraps and animal dung. The great biological and structural diversity of the home garden contrasts sharply with the structural simplicity and regularity of the milpa. As we have seen, home gardens may contain from 20 to over 200 cultivars at any one time, with the species planted often changing substantially over the course of the year. These gardens provide ready-to-hand culinary supplements, in particular, chilies, husk tomatoes, and avocados, to name just a few of the condiments and fruits available. In addition, a few species primarily cultivated for their medicinal value, such as rue and feverfew, share space with a decorative variety of ornamentals, native and introduced. One might also say that the milpa is the primary responsibility of men, the home garden of women, though this division of labor by sex should not be exaggerated, as all family members help with milpa cultivation, throughout the agricultural cycle, as we have seen in chapter 5. The gardens are rather more exclusively the domain of women, but men certainly take pride in their home gardens and are knowledgeable of what grows there.

During the summer of 1998, a University of Washington undergraduate student, a knowledgeable gardener with a fascination for ethnobotany, Lisa Schneider, investigated a sample of eight San Juan gardens. Her report is published in part 2 of this book. She spent many hours visiting the women in their gardens and recorded each plant found in each garden along with notes on their origins (e.g., seeds bought in the Miahuatlán market; cuttings from the gardens of neighbors or kin; transplants from the forests; even gifts from the anthropologists). She also noted their Zapotec and Spanish names whenever possible and their use values. I added data from an inventory of Roselía Hernández Cruz's garden, which I had visited many times in search of new and interesting plants (see figs. 5.13, 8.2). These data are summarized in table 7.1. The nine gardens surveyed represent 5 percent of San Juan families and are representative of the village gardens, with the caveat that our sample is no doubt biased toward the larger and more diverse gardens maintained by the more enthusiastic gardeners.

The nine gardens included a collective total of 284 distinct plant varieties representing 200 species in 140 genera of 67 families. Floriana's was the largest and most diverse of the gardens in our sample, incorporating 128 varieties. Sofía's and Roselía's each included 92 varieties at the time of our surveys. The two smallest gardens held 40 and 47 cultivars respectively. The average diversity for the nine gardens was 74 varieties. The distribution of cultivars across gardens demonstrates a remarkable individuality (see chart 7.1), as 132 (47 percent) of the total varieties were planted in just a single garden; 190 (67 percent) were planted in just one or two of the gardens. By contrast, only 36 varieties (13 percent) were planted in half or more of the gardens.

Of the 67 plant families represented—which is nearly 50 percent of all families recorded to date in the *municipio*—3 families were disproportionately prominent. The Asteraceae, that is, the sunflower family, came first, with 45 cultivars; the rose family, next, with 23; and the Solanaceae—family of the tomato, potato, and tobacco plants—third, with 21. These three families together accounted for 99 (32 percent) of garden cultivars. Five additional families—the Fabaceae, Poaceae, Geraniaceae, Iridaceae, and Lamiaceae—each contributed 10 to 13 varieties to the total. Thus, eight prominent families (12 percent of the 67 total families) accounted for 155 (55 percent) of the 283 total varieties. On the other hand, half, or thirty-three families, were represented by just a single cultivar.

Though most garden cultivars were herbaceous plants (183, or 65 percent), trees (47, or 17 percent), shrubs (39, or 14 percent), vines (11, or 4 percent), and the odd agave or cactus suggest the structural complexity of San Juan gardens. They are similar in this respect to swidden plots and contrast notably with the structural simplicity of "modern" monocrop fields. San Juan gardeners are hardly unique with regard to their gardening strategies, as comparable data are reported for Mexican Indian household gardens elsewhere in Oaxaca and in other regions of the country, such as the Yucatán (Casas, Viveros, and Caballero 1994:100–102; Anderson et al. 2003:27–30).

Complementing the taxonomic and structural complexity of San Juan gardens is the functional diversity of the cultivars planted. Plant varieties may be classified broadly as useful for their ornamental, food, medicinal, and/or technological values, as well as for animal fodder. In our cases there were 126 ornamentals (45 percent), 97 food plants (34 percent), 56 medicinal plants (20 percent), 8 with technological applications (3 percent), and 6 reported as used as animal fodder (2 percent). The percentages total more than 100; the excess is due to cultivars with multiple use values.

San Juan is truly a garden village, a botanical garden with houses.

CHAPTER 8

Xpèëd / The Children

The Future of San Juan

I WAS VISITING with my friend Eucario Hernández one afternoon at his patio, to chat about plants and other topics. His wife, sister, sister-in-law, and daughter-in-law were meanwhile shelling corn, with one eye on five-year-old Jacobo, a grandson who was playing in a corner. I confessed to Eucario that I remained confused as to the distinction between two similar and similarly named plants, **blàg-wì** and **blàg-wì-làs**, whether they were the same or different, and if different how so, as I had been given apparently contradictory accounts of their use in treating the odd affliction called **chànêcw** < Sp. *chaneque*. Eucario's sister overhead my question and quietly sent the five-year-old out to bring in an appropriate sample. He popped back through the gate five minutes later with a branch in each hand, one **blàg-wì**, the other **blàg-wì-làs**. These clearly represented two species of the genus *Buddleia*, differing most obviously in the width of the leaves.

This feat of "precocious" learning proved not at all exceptional, though in the case of most five-year-olds it was difficult to measure. Jacobo's seven-year-old sister, Fabiola, however, was not the least shy. On the contrary, she eagerly displayed her mastery of the plants on a plant trail I had laid out in town, naming correctly 75 percent of the 55 species I had marked on the trail. It occurred to me that this phenomenon, which I call "precocious acquisition" (2002), may prove a point of some general significance with respect to our understanding of what is "normal" in human cognitive development and what is most fundamental with respect to the relationship between humans and their biotic environment. San Juan children seem quite unlike the children of urban societies in their easy familiarity with the rich diversity of plants and animals around them (table 8.1). Perhaps it is not the children of San Juan whose precocious acquisition needs to be explained, but the persistent ignorance of our own children, who very often, college degree in hand, are at a loss to see the difference between an oak and a maple, a thrush and a wren, or a bee and a wasp (cf. Dougherty 1979), the intellectual complement to Richard Louv's provocatively named "nature-deficit disorder" (2005).

The Theoretical Significance of Precocious Acquisition

The question of the production and reproduction of traditional environmental knowledge is also of interest to cognitive psychologists and linguists. The modularity of mind is the subject of much current research and theoretical speculation in these fields (Fodor 1983; Gardner 1983; Hirschfeld and Gelman 1994; Atran 1998). This research is motivated in large part by compelling evidence for specialization in the acquisition of language (Pinker 1994:297ff), that is, by the simple fact that children learn the fundamentals of the sound systems, morphology, and grammar of their mother tongue by age three, commonly without systematic instruction.

Children also master the process of *naming*, a process of abstraction of surpassing subtlety, in their first few years of life, seeming to know as if by instinct, for example, what an animal is and to appreciate the need to name each distinct animal kind. The neurological locus of such mental modules, specific in form and content, is as yet poorly known, but studies of selective aphasias due to localized brain damage indicate some tendency for modular localization of certain language functions. Of particular interest is evidence for semantic localization by domain. For example, there are documented cases of the highly selective loss of (or retention of) memory for plant and/or animal names. Pinker describes the effects of specific brain damage on the ability to retrieve vocabulary:

> different patients have problems with different kinds of nouns. . . . Some can use concrete nouns but not abstract nouns. . . . Some can use nouns for nonliving things but have trouble with nouns for living things; . . . some can name animals and vegetables but not foods, body parts, clothing, vehicles, or furniture. . . . One patient could not name fruits or vegetables: he could name an abacus and a sphinx but not an apple or a peach. (1994:314)

Pinker cautions that there is no simple correspondence of brain anatomy to semantic inventory. Rhetorically he asks, "Does this mean that the brain has a produce section?" If so, he notes, no one has yet found it. However, the fact that humans store critical information about plants or animals in some sort of *connected* cerebral space suggests that learning about plants or animals may be facilitated by some sort of innate memory formatting, with complementary learning protocols, finely attuned to the *natural kinds* of living things in the environment.

Striking cross-cultural parallels in the formal scope of ethnobiological nomenclature and classification support this view, unless we are to believe that these "universals" are adequately explained by the operation of more general learning strategies applied to the highly structured objective reality of species diversity. The "Magic Number/Nature's Fortune 500" (Berlin 1992) as a central tendency for the number of basic plant and animal taxa (and of place names [Hunn 1994]) is also suggestive of content-specific innate "formatting" of memory.

I believe that the evidence for the precocious acquisition of vocabulary for and knowledge of "natural kinds" (Gelman and Markman 1986; Keil 1986; Gelman and Coley 1991) may provide additional support for the view that there must be innate predispositions to acquire such knowledge. Furthermore, if learning about nature is "natural," we should consider the pedagogical implications. I would like to suggest that currently fashionable curricular strategies for early science education emphasizing experimentation and theoretical discovery may be quite "unnatural" and thus less likely to succeed than alternatives designed to build upon a child's innate natural-history learning module.

The Evidence from San Juan

I will present evidence that many children in San Juan Gbëë achieve near-adult mastery of local botanical knowledge between seven and twelve years of age. They acquire this knowledge without systematic instruction, while helping older relatives weed and harvest subsistence crops, tending household gardens, and gathering wild plants. By age twelve this knowledge includes several hundred plant names, the ability to apply those names with a high degree of accuracy, and the ability to extend nomenclatural patterns productively, plus knowledge of the characteristic features of each plant named and of the seasonal development, local habitat and community associations, and uses of a large majority of named plants. Data on individual ethnobotanical inventories were collected in several contexts, particularly in "rapid appraisal" plant-naming exercises, described below.

I assessed children's naming abilities by employing children to bring plant samples to my house, where they were to name and briefly describe each plant. Data were also collected by conversing with children about plants while on family collecting trips. The most complete data are for one twelve-year-old girl and for her seven-year-old niece (ages as of 1998).

If this were simply a matter of children learning what they are taught, it would be of limited significance. However, if acquisition of environmental knowledge is like first-language learning, "acquisition deprivation" at a critical age may be lasting. Traditional environmental knowledge systems provide detailed, empirically robust images of local natural environments (Berlin 1992; Williams and Baines 1993; Berkes 1999). Such knowledge may be a necessary, though obviously not a sufficient, basis for sustainable resource management by local communities. The production and reproduction of traditional environmental knowledge needs to be understood if TEK itself is to be conserved as a critical cultural resource for the future (Hunn 1999b).

Procedures

During July 1998 and September 2000, I commissioned local children to bring me plants and to teach me their names, uses, and habitats in exchange for a token payment. My two primary examples of "precocious" learning are Marielena and her niece, Lilia. The bulk of the data for Marielena was collected in the summer of 1998, when she was twelve; for Lilia in July 1998, when she was seven, and in September 2000, when she was nine. I hit on the idea of offering Marielena ten pesos (about $1 U.S.) for each bag of plants she could bring, with the understanding that she would tell me the names and uses of each. I made it clear that I did not want to pay for duplicates, but that she should bring me different plants each visit.

It was late July, school vacation, and time for the first weeding. The next evening I heard a soft knock on the door to our compound. It was Marielena, with a plastic bag of leaves, flowers, and other botanical odds and ends. An hour later I had listed 32 plants, with uses and commentary on when and where they could be found in flower. I made an initial assessment of the accuracy of the child's determination based on my sense of the range of admissible adult naming responses to the species in question. Very little of her information appeared to be in error. The next day she brought another bag. We spread the plants out on the floor and tallied another 16, none duplicating her previous haul. Three days later she brought 19 more, and Lilia presented her own bag of 17. Marielena stood by as Lilia proudly named her leaves. Marielena once or twice quietly corrected her. The next day Marielena brought 26 more. The score: Marielena 93, Lilia 17, for a total of 110, with still no duplication.

I returned in August 1998 for an additional extended visit. Marielena and I picked up where we had left off: 100 plants on the 18th, 96 more on the 19th, 25 on the 22nd, and 62 on the 23rd—for a running total of 376 different-named plants—at which time I had to return to Seattle. During this visit the word got out that a kid could earn easy money this way. Marielena's cousin Miguel came around with his younger sister on the 18th with 52 plants (including many of the same plants that Marielena had already brought). He brought another 77 on the 19th, and 60 more on the 22nd. Lilia came by herself on the 18th with 60 more of her own. Finally, Cesareo, Marielena's grandfather, 84 years old, needing some ready cash, dropped in with an additional 27 plants. Grand total for two short weeks' work: 669 identifications. In naming 376 plants, Marielena used 206 distinct folk generic names, names for 258 terminal taxa, and for 321 taxa at all ranks (table 8.2).

These dry statistics cannot convey the depth of the children's knowledge. To suggest this richness I will review in somewhat more detail one ninety-minute session with Lilia (then aged nine) in September 2000, in which she named and described eighty-two plants she had collected after school the afternoon before on a short walk in and near town. Her responses were necessarily brief, given the number of plants to be discussed and the limits of a nine-year-old's attention span. In table 8.3 I summarize her responses to three primary questions:

>*¿Zhá lḗ guìzh rí?* What is the name of this plant?
>*¿Pâr-né rquiă rí?* What is it used for?
>*¿Pá ló nŏ?* Where is it found? (not asked for all)

If the life-form assignment was not implicit in the name (as it most often is), I might have asked also, for example, *¿Pé yâg-á?* Is it a tree/shrub? or *¿Pé lbȅ-w?* Is it a vine? Finally, I noted my tentative Latin determinations. Lilia's mother, Inez, aunt Marielena, grandmother Roselía, and great-grandmother were nearby but offered to help only when specifically requested to do so. I have bracketed their contributions. Lilia's "errors" or "inadequate" responses are marked by asterisks.

Of eighty-two distinct identifications, she was unable to name the plant (*nàn-d náa* "I don't know") or named it "incorrectly" in seven cases (91 percent correct). Three correct responses were duplications. Thus, in one short walk on one afternoon Lilia collected and named correctly seventy-two distinct plant species. Furthermore, she noted whether or not the plant was used and if used, for what purpose. In several cases toward the end of our session she seemed to have tired, using the 'no use' *rguin-d-á* response rather freely. She noted nine plants used as medicines (*rmêd-á*; and her elders contributed another three species to that list), in most cases specifying for what illness the plant was used (e.g., *pâr-né yòob ní* 'for foot pain'; *pâr rò* 'for coughs'), even at times describing how the medicines are applied (e.g., *gâz né* 'we may bathe [with it]').

She also noted whether the plant was edible (e.g., *rôw né* 'we eat it'), used as fodder or forage by animals (e.g., *rôw chǐv* 'goats eat it'; *gôw nguǐd* 'chickens may eat it'), or was of ritual significance (e.g., *pâr ló mdiò* 'for [placing] on altars') or ornamental value (*pâr-né rgál-guièe* 'for decorating').

Lilia also characterized where most of the plants occurred in terms of habitat (e.g., *ló nȅz* 'on the trail'; *lén còrrâl* 'inside the fence' [i.e., 'in the garden']; *ró yù* 'in town'; *ló gòdz* 'in marshy places'; *chó quiè* 'on rocks') or specific locations (e.g., *ló x-còrrâl nánít* 'in grandmother's garden'; *guiět Ró-ctà* 'below Flat Rock), or simply by pointing (e.g., *nèc* 'here'; *cǎaní* 'over there').

Lilia used plant names just as San Juan adults do. The great majority of her naming responses are folk generic names, which in Gbëë Zapotec routinely incorporate the life-form or complex name as a prefixed element. She freely combines certain "nested" life-forms, as is common in adult speech (e.g., *guìzh-guièe-tǐ* 'Bidens spp.'). She adapts Spanish loanwords to the canonical syllabic forms and tonal conventions of Gbëë Zapotec (e.g., *guièe-jèrân* 'geranio flower' [*Pelargonium* spp.]) but uses

Spanish borrowings no more frequently than is general among San Juan adults. She employs the hedge, *xín-* 'relative of, similar to', as do adults (e.g., ***xín-gòrdòlôb*** 'relative of *gordolobo*' [*Gnaphalium* spp.]), and for many of the same species. Lilia also appropriately employs trinomial nomenclature for folk specific taxa (e.g., ***guìzh-guièe-tǐ-nquǐts*** '*Bidens* spp.'; ***yàg-yàaz-ngǎs*** '*Baccharis heterophylla*').

Her sample of plants is biased toward herbaceous species, but this may reflect their relative ease of collection in comparison with trees and shrubs, rather than any notable gaps in her repertoire. Finally, the plants collected represent a wide range of species, native and introduced as well as wild and cultivated. The eighty-two plants represent seventy-nine species of seventy genera in thirty-three families.

Analysis

Several questions come to mind in considering this evidence. First, are Marielena and Lilia unusual among San Juan children their age? I have no reason to think so, though I do not have a sufficient comparative sample to assess how typical their ethnobotanical mastery might be. Lilia's younger sister Griselda (age eight years in 2000) seems far less knowledgeable, but then she was raised in Pochutla, a coastal city, and is Spanish-dominant. The limited data I have for Miguel (age twelve in 2000), suggests that there is no dramatic gender difference in the acquisition of this knowledge.

Next we might inquire how Marielena and Lilia learned so much at such an early age. You can be sure they didn't learn it in school. The public school curriculum here is nationally standardized, not designed to be appropriate to local environmental conditions. The teachers are almost always temporary residents raised elsewhere in the state. Formal schooling may be authoritatively promoted as a means to escape the "ignorance and poverty" of village life, as was the essential message of the local priest's valedictory sermon to the inaugural secondary school graduating class of 1997. The notion that local primary-school children might be deeply knowledgeable with respect to local ecology is nowhere recognized by the public school system.

Rather, ethnobotanical knowledge is everyday knowledge acquired without apparent effort at an early age by virtually everyone in town. It is only from our "civilized" perspective that it seems remarkable, since we expect such elaborate knowledge of the natural world only of professional specialists or fanatic hobbyists.

They also learn a great deal at play. Children as young as five years old play at cultivating milpa and decorating altars (figs. 8.1, 8.2). For the Fiesta de la Santa Cruz, San Juan families climb to the summit of nearby Cerro San Isidro to leave offerings of flowers and votive candles, at an altar (fig. 8.3). Meanwhile, the children play in a protected grove of oaks at the western end of the summit, building miniature stone houses, plowing and planting miniature cornfields (fig. 8.4), and tending pinecone cattle, goats, and turkeys, in a celebratory enactment of the traditional *campesino* "good life" (fig. 8.5).

I believe this evidence, preliminary as it is, demonstrates how natural it is for children of primary-school age to absorb in great detail a body of local knowledge of natural history, particularly when that knowledge is constantly reinforced in the daily life of the family and community. For an urban child it is, I suppose, "natural" rather to master at a young age a vocabulary of machines, sports, entertainments, and social distinctions. The children of San Juan master *biodiversity*, while urban children master *commodity diversity*. It may be that as a consequence urban children lose the chance to develop a keen awareness of the diversity of life around them and thus, perhaps, grow up ill prepared to appreciate it and conserve it. Though we may learn as adults to appreciate the natural diversity of our surroundings, I believe that as adults such learning is neither so readily nor so deeply acquired. This was brought home to me when I met Valentín Martínez Miguel, a seventy-year-old blind man, in San Juan. He lost his sight at age eighteen, but since learned to write both Spanish and Zapotec in braille. I hired him to write accounts of local plants and animals. He was able to describe the appearance of many plants and animals despite being blind the last fifty-eight years of his life. What he had learned as a child was burned into his memory.

The Plant Trail (*Nèz-Guìzh*)

A small grant from the Jacobs Research Fund in 2001 financed a project designed to more systematically measure "precocious acquisition" of plant names and associated knowledge, to see if it was a general capability of San Juan children or an unusual talent unequally distributed among San Juan families.

In August 2001 I arrived in San Juan with a plan that I presented to the authorities. With their permission, I would lay out a loop trail along which I would mark a series of plants representative of the floral diversity in and about town, that is, some trees and shrubs, some herbs, some flowers, some vines; some of these large and conspicuous, others small and obscure; some native, others of exotic origin; some cultivated, others wild; some primarily useful for food, others for medicine, manufactures, or ornament (table 8.4). I would then accompany children on a tour of the trail, having them name the marked plants (fig 8.6). The goal was to document the extraordinary sophistication of San Juan children by charting their progress in mastering the local San Juan ethnobotanical vocabulary.

The authorities approved the plan and recommended that I seek the advice of Hermilo Silva, the immediate past municipal president, in the design of the trail. Hermilo agreed and accompanied me on a trial run along the half-kilometer route I had proposed, starting and finishing at the town marketplace, with fifty-five plants to be marked along the way (figs. 8.7, 8.8, 8.9). He provided authoritative "adult" identifications for fifty-two of the fifty-five plants (95 percent), indicating that three lacked names. He also noted local Spanish names for thirty-eight of the plants. Thus, fourteen were named in Zapotec only.

I set out small, plastic, numbered tags and drew a rough map of the route, but by the next day I noticed that several tags were missing, while a few had been cleverly transposed. A neighbor confided that some kids from neighboring San Pedro—said to be mischievous by nature—were responsible for the joke. Be that as it may, I could do without the tags, as I had each plant clearly located on my map. I was ready to begin lining up children willing to spend the forty-five minutes required to tour the route with me while naming as many plants as they could, in response to queries such as, *¿Zhá lḗ guìzh rí?* What is the name of this plant?

Ideally, I should have drawn a random sample of San Juan children, ages 6 to 14, stratified by sex and age (table 8.5), but such statistical niceties are not practical in most ethnographic circumstances, as one must first of all establish a personal relationship of trust with the family in question. I began with my expert ethnobotanical instructor, (now) ten-year-old Lilia, who had come forward as Marielena's teenage self-consciousness began to inhibit her readiness to instruct the *gringo* in Zapotec plant lore. Lilia, though eager to demonstrate her knowledge, preferred that her friend and cousin, Leticia, also ten years old and also in the fifth primary grade, accompany her to provide moral support. It became clear that girls would be reluctant to do the trail task with me alone, so I did my best to have them stand well apart when answering my queries so that each could offer her names and commentaries independently, the younger or less knowledgeable going first to minimize the likelihood of biased responses due to prompting.

Though less than ideal as a research protocol, I am confident that the results provide a reasonably accurate picture of San Juan children's plant knowledge (table 8.6). This procedure has the great advantage of relying on natural stimuli in natural contexts. The children often would pick a leaf, break the stem, smell it, or feel the texture and inspect the color of the sap, features not readily discerned in photos or dried and mounted specimens. On the other hand, the trail was very public, which was good from the standpoint of reducing suspicion among villagers as to my activities, but on the other hand not infrequently encouraged interruptions, as adults watching from their yards or passing in the street would "help us out" by providing the "correct" name or would engage me in conversation. Also, I would occasionally discover that one of my target plants had gone missing overnight, eaten by donkeys or harvested for soup or salad by a neighbor. I was then forced to find a functional equivalent plant as a replacement.

I had expected the statistical tabulation to show a dramatic correlation between age and recognition scores, but this proved not to be the case. The correlation of age with recognition score for the 36 children interviewed was just $r = 0.29$, which indicates that just 8.4 percent of the variation (r^2) in scores is attributable to differences in the children's ages (chart 8.1). A close examination of the data suggests why the expected correlation proved so weak. A few individual cases that strayed far from the trendline ("outliers") helped obscure the correlation of age with expertise. For example, the lowest (0.10) and one of the highest (0.85) individual scores were by seven-year-olds, the youngest age represented. Meanwhile, an eleven-year-old scored second-lowest at 0.26, and a ten-year-old scored third-lowest, while a fourteen-year-old scored 0.51, well below the overall average of 0.71. However, the two lowest scores of all were by children raised in Spanish-dominant households, the first the child of an in-marrying wife who does not speak Zapotec, the second raised in Miahuatlán in an emigrant family. By contrast, the seven-year-old who scored near the top is the daughter of our primary consultant and plant expert. The third-lowest score was by a painfully shy ten-year-old girl whose score certainly seriously underestimates her knowledge. Finally, the low-scoring fourteen-year-old may simply be not the brightest. It is noteworthy that there is a slightly stronger correlation of performance on the plant trail with school grade. This is contrary to the findings of a similar study in an indigenous forest community in Venezuela (Zent 1999) in which a strong negative correlation was found to hold between plant trail performance and formal schooling (chart 8.2). However, in that case formal schooling was associated with a radical dislocation from the forest environment in which older, unschooled adults had grown up. In San Juan formal schooling interferes only minimally with the traditional subsistence activities in which children learn about their local flora. While statistical summaries may expose interesting patterns in the data, I find it more instructive to consider the children's performances individually.

There is a second likely explanation for the rather weak correlation of scores with age. It would seem that children of seven years of age—the youngest in our sample—may already have learned to recognize the great majority of plants common in and about town. Thus, the differences within our sample are due more to other factors, such as family environment or individual intelligence and motivation. Unfortunately, it proved impractical to test children younger than seven with this plant trail, though if the interviews were to be conducted by a local young person fluent in Zapotec, it might be possible to get reliable data for children as young as four. Stross's (1973) and Zarger and Stepp's (2004) Tzeltal Maya data indicate that much relevant botanical learning takes place in those earlier years.

A Few Outstanding Performances

Lilia, whom you have met above, performed impressively on our first run over the original trail, scoring 84 percent of generic names and 75 percent of specific names, which may be compared to the adult standard for generic-name recognition set by Hermilo Silva and Floriana Cruz of 95 percent and 93 percent respectively. In fact, in a few instances Lilia's responses were more detailed than those of Hermilo, as she named #12, *Plumbago pulchella*, which Hermilo considered to lack a name, **guìzh-nàad** 'sticky plant'. We might presume that Lilia "invented" the name, except for the fact that many children subsequently and independently offered the same name, explaining how the plant was used as a "toy" by sticking it on one another's clothing. Lilia also provided a specific identification for an obscure solanaceous weed, naming it **yàg-pchùux-mèel** 'snake's tomato', while Hermilo considered it an unspecified type of *pchùux* 'tomato'. Her knowledge of Spanish plant names was also impressive, as she named thirty-three, in comparison with the thirty-eight named by Hermilo in Spanish. Her knowledge of uses was competent; she recognized a food (*dôw nè-w*), a medicine (*rmêd*), and an ornamental flower (*rgál-guièe*) among the five species targeted for this query.

A second Lilia, our eleven-year-old neighbor, proved more surprising still. She elaborated spontaneously on the ritual required when harvesting leaves of *Datura stramonium*, **blàg-rzûdz** 'leaf of drunkenness', to treat sore feet. She noted how one must leave seven pebbles beneath the plant as "payment" to "La Señorita" for the cure. I surmise that "La Señorita" is a title for a "virgin" or spiritual power that dwells in or cares for the plant, as *Datura* species are notorious throughout Mexico for their dangerous hallucinogenic properties. As noted earlier, *Datura stramonium* is used as medicine in San Juan, but only topically.

Nor is it the case that our top performers were all girls. Though the average score for boys was 63 percent, for girls 71 percent, three boys scored at 75 percent and above, while the correlation coefficient of score by sex was $r = 0.21$, indicating that sex can account for no more than 4 percent of the variance (chart 8.3). Though the difference is slight, it is nevertheless sensible in light of the fact that girls are likely to have more extensive opportunities to learn local plant names than are boys, as they spend more time working closely with their female seniors, who appear to more actively engage their daughters with respect to plants than is true of men and boys.

While children very quickly learn the basic vocabulary and some of the ethnoecological detail associated with each natural kind named, mature adults clearly have a far more refined and elaborated understanding of local flora and fauna, able to discourse on variation within and between categories of plants and animals, to analyze in great detail how plants and animals are put to use, and to reflect more self-consciously on the underlying nature of life in all its variety. Yet the framework for constructing adult understanding is set in place early in a child's life. It is worth considering how full adult understanding of the human role in the natural scheme of things may be undermined by depriving the child of the opportunity to construct that initial framework.

The Future of San Juan Gbëë

The modern world seems set on course toward an ever-tightening global web woven of instantaneous digital communications at the service of international megacorporations ever driven to maximize profits and aggrandize market share through economies of scale. Hundreds of millions of people all over the world have abandoned their rural village homes in pursuit of cash incomes and a piece of the global action, crumbs from the great commodity cornucopia that is the modern world.

In Mexico this process has sucked some 20 million ex-*campesinos* into Mexico City and enticed perhaps as many as 10 million more to the United States as undocumented workers. Some Oaxacan villages, notably Zapotec and Mixtec, have been reduced to a shell by the loss of the majority of their able-bodied male population to the osmotic pressure of the global market's demand for cheap labor. Some would say "good riddance" to the narrow confines of the hardscrabble subsistence lives of Mexico's rural villages. Yet one needn't be a romantic blinded by nostalgia to recognize what may be lost in this great historic transformation. My hope in compiling this indigenous natural history is that the reader might more fully appreciate the cultural legacy of San Juan Gbëë as one of the thousands of other indigenous communities that survive today at the global margins.

I have studied the environmental knowledge of North American native peoples for more than thirty years. My ethnobiological research in the Pacific Northwest is guided by the same vision that drew me to San Juan, the search for our common humanity in a shared fascination with the biodiversity that surrounds and nurtures us all. However, ethnobiological research with North American tribes is an intensely political exercise in salvage ethnography. The traditional environmental knowledge of these tribes is guarded in the memories of the few elders still living who by whatever fortuitous circumstance learned the native names for and cultural significance of the flora and fauna of the tribal homeland before the people were uprooted and their languages displaced.

My mentor and teacher for my Sahaptin ethnobiological research was James Selam, eighty-seven years old when he died in 2007, but with a vigorous intellect and penetrating sense of humor to the end. His family refused to abandon their traditional John Day River homes for reservation life after the treaties were ratified in 1859. James was born there and raised in a tule-mate longhouse. When the truant officer came by to round up children to take them off to the reservation boarding school, James's grandmother hid him in a trunk, because she "needed him" to help at home. As a result, James was one of very few fluent native speakers of the Sahaptin language still living and a highly regarded elder in all matters relating to Indian religious and ceremonial practice (Hunn 1990).

James Selam represents an endangered cultural resource for the Sahaptin tribes. Sahaptin traditional environmental knowledge—to the extent it depends upon a living indigenous language for its effective transmission down the generations—will soon survive only in the archives. Traditional harvests of fish, berries, roots, and game remain deeply meaningful for Sahaptin tribal members today, yet primarily as symbols of their Indian identities. Children on the reservation are raised speaking English, watching TV, and learning history in public schools devoted to the memory of the noble pioneers.

San Juan children, in sharp contrast, absorb a rich cultural heritage of environmental knowledge in the daily routines of play and work in the company of their siblings, parents, and grandparents, tending their home gardens, weeding their milpas, and foraging for herbal remedies in their forests. A San Juan child encounters plants and animals at every turn, learning their names, habits and habitats, and uses, as an apprenticeship for full citizenship in San Juan Gbëë. San Juan children are eager to show off their knowledge of plants and animals and take pride in their growing mastery of this cultural heritage. It seems to me a great waste if this vibrant connection of a people with their local habitat that endures from childhood to old age should be lost, severing the ancient umbilical cord that ties us to Mother Earth. Apologists for modernity in all its rich perversity see this cutting of the umbilicus as a birth process liberating humanity from the immediate dependence on the living earth. Yet, however "liberating" modern economic enterprise may be—liberating us from all ties to a home and a homeland—it is by the same token profoundly alienating.

San Juan is poised on the brink of this difficult birth. I ask whether it might not be possible for the people of San Juan to have their cake and eat it too, to hold fast to traditional lands and livelihoods and knowledge while carefully embracing the wider world. Why should it be necessary for the children of San Juan to choose between staying home and leaving it all behind? Consider the bilingual. A child of San Juan need not abandon all knowledge of his or her ancestral Zapotec language in favor of learning Spanish, as he or she is perfectly capable of mastering both: Zapotec for speaking of the land and the hometown, Spanish for the nation and the world.

During the twelve years of my Oaxaca research, I have seen the digital revolution take firm root. The first local Internet node was inaugurated in Oaxaca City the year my research began. Now there are Internet cafés on virtually every downtown street, and several are operational in the district center of Miahuatlán. A few more years, and I suspect there will be satellite links to *centros de computación* in every Mexican village. San Juan children will be able to e-mail their relatives working in California in Zapotec, Spanish, or English. San Juan weavers will be able to sell their hand-woven *rebozos* through the community Web site and download the images of *A Zapotec Natural History* to offer commentary and corrections to my text.

In the final analysis, traditional environmental knowledge will live on only if it is a meaningful part of the daily life of the people who own it. Use it or lose it. The people of San Juan will decide whether they wish to guard their sovereignty over the land that has sustained them for the past millennium, and if they so choose, their deep knowledge and appreciation of the living world around them will sustain them.

Literature Cited

Acosta, Salvador, Alejandro Flores, Alfredo Saynes, Remedios Aguilar, and Gladys Manzanero. 2003. Vegetación y flora de una zona semiárida de la cuenca alta del río Tehuántepec, Oaxaca, México. *Polibotánica* 16:125–52.

Agrawal, Arun. 1995. Dismantling the divide between indigenous and scientific knowledge. *Development and Change* 26:413–39.

Aguilar Castro, Salvador. 1992. Nosología tradicional entre los Zapotecos del distrito de Tlacolula. In *Medicina tradicional, herbolaria y salud comunitaria en Oaxaca*, Paola Sesia, editor, pp. 77–97. CIESAS, Gobierno del Estado de Oaxaca.

Anderson, Edgar, and Hugh C. Cutler. 1942. Races of *Zea mays*, I. Their recognition and classification. *Annals of the Missouri Botanical Garden* 29:69–89.

Anderson, Eugene N. 1984. "Heating and cooling" foods re-examined. *Social Science Information* 23:755–73.

Anderson, Eugene N. 1996. *Ecologies of the Heart: Emotion, Belief, and the Environment*. New York: Oxford University Press.

Anderson, Eugene N., with José Cauich Canul, Aurora Dzib, Salvador Flores Guido, Gerald Islebe, Felix Medina Tzuc, Odilón Sánchez Sánchez, and Pastor Valdez Chale. 2003. *Those Who Bring the Flowers: Maya Ethnobotany in Quintana Roo, Mexico*. San Cristóbal de las Casas, Chiapas, Mexico: El Colegio de la Frontera Sur (ECOSUR).

Annis, Sheldon. 1987. *God and Production in a Guatemalan Town*. Austin: University of Texas Press.

Artschwager Kay, Margarita. 1996. *Healing with Plants in the American and Mexican West*. Tucson: University of Arizona Press.

Atran, Scott. 1998. Folk biology and the anthropology of science: Cognitive universals and cultural particulars. In *Behavioral and Brain Sciences* 21:547–609.

Atran, Scott. 1999. Itzaj Maya folkbiological taxonomy: Cognitive universals and cultural particulars. In *Folkbiology*, Douglas L. Medin and Scott Atran, editors, pp. 119–203. Cambridge: Harvard University Press.

Aubague, Laurent. 1986. Desplazamiento o afianzamiento de las lenguas indígenas de Oaxaca. In *Etnicidad y pluralismo cultural: La dinámica étnica en Oaxaca*, Alicia Barabas and Miguel Bartolomé, editors, pp. 371–99. Mexico, DF: Instituto Nacional de Antropología e Historia.

Benítez Badillo, Griselda. 1986. *Arboles y flores del Ajusco*. Mexico, DF: Instituto de Ecología, Museo de Historia Natural de la Ciudad de México.

Berkes, Fikret. 1999. *Sacred Ecology: Traditional Ecological Knowledge and Resource Management*. Philadelphia: Taylor and Francis.

Berlin, Brent. 1970. A universalist-evolutionary approach in ethnographic semantics. In Current Directions in Anthropology, Ann Fischer, editor. Special issue of *Bulletin of the American Anthropological Association* 3 (3), pt. 2:3–18.

Berlin, Brent. 1972. Speculations on the growth of ethnobotanical nomenclature. *Language and Society* 1:51–86.

Berlin, Brent. 1973. The relation of folk systematics to biological classification and nomenclature. *Annual Review of Ecology and Systematics* 4:259–71.

Berlin, Brent. 1992. *Ethnobiological Classification: Principles of Categorization of Plants and Animals in Traditional Societies*. Princeton: Princeton University Press.

Berlin, Brent, Dennis E. Breedlove, and Peter H. Raven. 1973. General principles of classification and nomenclature in folk biology. *American Anthropologist* 75:214–42.

Berlin, Brent, Dennis E. Breedlove, and Peter H. Raven. 1974. *Principles of Tzeltal Plant Classification*. New York: Academic Press.

Berlin, Brent, and Paul Kay. 1969. *Basic Color Terms: Their Universality and Evolution*. Berkeley: University of California Press.

Berlin, Brent, and John O'Neill. 1981. The pervasiveness of onomatopoeia in the Jivaroan language family. *Journal of Ethnobiology* 1:95–108.

Berlin, Elois Ann, and Brent Berlin. 1996. *Medical Ethnobiology of the Highland Maya of Chiapas, Mexico: The Gastrointestinal Diseases*. Princeton: Princeton University Press.

Binford, Laurence C. 1989. *A Distributional Survey of the Birds of the Mexican State of Oaxaca*. Ornithological Monographs No. 43. Washington, DC: American Ornithologists' Union.

Blanton, Richard E., Gary Feinman, Stephen A. Kowalewski, and Linda M. Nicholas. 1999. *Ancient Oaxaca. The Monte Alban State*. Cambridge: Cambridge University Press.

Blurton-Jones, Nicolas, and Melvin J. Konner. 1976. !Kung knowledge of animal behavior (or: The proper study of mankind is animals). In *Kalahari Hunter-Gatherers*, R. B. Lee and I. DeVore, editors, pp. 325–48. Cambridge: Harvard University Press.

Borror, Donald J., and Richard E. White. 1970. *A Field Guide to the Insects of America North of Mexico*. Boston: Houghton Mifflin.

Breedlove, Dennis E., and Robert M. Laughlin. 2000. *The Flowering of Man: A Tzotzil Botany of Zinacantán*. Abridged ed. Washington, DC: Smithsonian Institution Press.

Brown, Cecil H. 1977. Folk botanical life-forms: Their universality and growth. *American Anthropologist* 79:317–42.

Brown, Cecil H. 1979. Folk zoological life-forms: Their universality and growth. *American Anthropologist* 81:791–817.

Brown, Cecil H. 1984. *Language and Living Things: Uniformities in Folk Classification and Naming*. New Brunswick, NJ: Rutgers University Press.

Browner, Carole H. 1985a. Criteria for selecting herbal remedies. *Ethnology* 24:13–32.

Browner, Carole H. 1985b. Plants used for reproductive health in Oaxaca, Mexico. *Economic Botany* 39:482–504.

Browner, Carole H. 1986. The politics of reproduction in a Mexican village. *Signs* 11:710–24.

Browner, Carole H., Bernard Ortiz de Montellano, and Arthur J. Rubel. 1992. El análisis comparativo de sistemas médicos. In *Medicina tradicional, herbolaria y salud comunitaria en Oaxaca*, Paola Sesia, editor, pp. 223–53. Mexico, DF: Centro de Investigaciones y Estudios Superiores en Antropología Social (CIESAS) y el Gobierno del Estado de Oaxaca.

Bulmer, Ralph N. H. 1974. Folk biology in the New Guinea highlands. *Social Science Information* 13:9–28.

Bye, Robert. 1993. The role of humans in the diversification of plants in Mexico. In *Biological Diversity of Mexico: Origins and Distribution*, T. P. Ramamoorthy, Robert Bye, Antonio Lot, and John Fa, editors, pp. 707–31. New York: Oxford University Press.

Caballero, Fray Juan. 1998. *Dendrología natural y botaneología Americana, o Tractado de los árboles y hiebas de América*. Oaxaca, Mex.: Exconvento de Santo Domingo.

Campbell, Howard. 1994. *Zapotec Renaissance: Ethnic Politics and Cultural Revivalism in Southern Mexico*. Albuquerque: University of New Mexico Press.

Campbell, Jonathan A., and William W. Lamar. 1989. *The Venomous Reptiles of Latin America*. Ithaca, NY: Cornell University Press.

Cancian, Frank. 1965. *Economics and Prestige in a Maya Community: The Religious Cargo System in Zinacantan*. Stanford, CA: Stanford University Press.

Caro, Tim, editor. 1998. *Behavioral Ecology and Conservation Biology*. New York: Oxford University Press.

Carroll, John B., editor. 1956. *Language, Thought, and Reality: Selected Writings of Benjamin Lee Whorf*. Cambridge: MIT Press.

Casas, Alejandro, Juan Luis Viveros, and Javier Caballero. 1994. *Etnobotánica Mixteca: Sociedad, Cultura y Recursos Naturales en la Montaña de Guerrero*. Mexico, D.F.: Instituto Nacional Indigenista—Consejo Nacional para la Cultura y las Artes.

Casas-Andreu, Gustavo, Fausto R. Méndez-de-la-Cruz, and Xóchitl Aguilar-Miguel. 2004. Anfibios y reptiles. In *Biodiversidad de Oaxaca*, edited by Abisaí J. García Mendoza, María de Jesús Ordóñez, and Miguel Briones-Salas, pp. 375–90. Mexico City: Instituto de Biología, Universidad Nacional Autónoma de México; Fondo Oaxaqueño para la Conservación de la Naturaleza; World Wildlife Fund.

Castañeda, Martha, Cristina Galante, Paola Sesia, and Ruth Piedrasanta. 1992. Metodología de los talleres de aprendizaje materno-infantil para regiones indígenas. In *Medicina tradicional, herbolaria y salud comunitaria en Oaxaca*, Paola Sesia, editor, pp. 265–91. CIESAS, Gobierno del Estado de Oaxaca.

Chiñas, Beverly N. 1991. *The Isthmus Zapotecs: A Matrifocal Culture of Mexico*, 2nd ed. Case Studies in Cultural Anthropology. Fort Worth, TX: Harcourt Brace Jovanovich.

Chiñas, Beverly N. 1993. *La Zandunga: Of Fieldwork and Friendship in Southern Mexico*. Prospect Heights, IL: Waveland Press.

Clément, Daniel. 1995. Why is taxonomy utilitarian? *Journal of Ethnobiology* 15:1–44.

Collier, George A, and Elizabeth Lowery Quaratiello. 1994. *Basta! Land and the Zapatista Rebellion in Chiapas*. New York: Food First.

Conklin, Harold C. 1954. The relation of Hanunóo culture to the plant world. PhD diss. New Haven: Yale University.

Conklin, Harold C. 1962. The lexicographic treatment of folk taxonomies. *International Journal of American Linguistics* 28:119–41.

Constitution of Mexico. 1917. Text translated from *Constitución política de los Estados Unidos mexicanos*, trigésima quinta edición, 1967. Editorial Porrua, S.A., Mexico, D.F. Originally published by the Pan American Union, General Secretariat, Organization of American States, Washington, DC, 1968.

Córdova, Fray Juan de. 1987 [1578]. *Vocabulario en lengua çapoteca*. Mexico, DF: Ediciones Toledo, INAH.

Croom, Edward M. Jr. 1983. Documenting and evaluating herbal remedies. *Economic Botany* 37:13–27.

Dahlgren, Barbro. 1990. *La grana cochinilla*. Mexico, DF: Instituto de Investigaciones Antropológicas, Universidad Nacional Autónoma de México.

de Ávila Blomberg, Alejandro. 2004. La clasificación de la vida en las lenguas de Oaxaca. In *Biodiversidad de Oaxaca*, edited by Abisaí J. García Mendoza, María de Jesús Ordóñez, and Miguel Briones-Salas, pp. 481–539. Mexico City: Instituto de Biología, Universidad Nacional Autónoma de México; Fondo Oaxaqueño para la Conservación de la Naturaleza; World Wildlife Fund.

Diamond, Jared. 1966. Zoological classification system of a primitive people. *Science* 151:1102–4.

Diamond, Jared. 1988. The golden age that never was. *Discover* 9:70–79.

Díaz Barriga, Horalia. 1992. *Hongos comestibles y venenosos de la Cuenca del Lago de Pátzcuaro, Michoacán*. Morelia, Mexico: Universidad de Michoacán de San Nícolas de Hidalgo.

Doebley, John F., Major M. Goodman, and Charles W. Stuber. 1985. Isozyme variation in races of maize from Mexico. *American Journal of Botany* 72:629–39.

Dougherty, Janet. 1979. Learning names for plants and plants for names. *Anthropological Linguistics* 21:298–315.

Ellen, Roy F. 1986. Ethnobiology, cognition, and the structure of prehension: Some general theoretical notes. *Journal of Ethnobiology* 6:83–98.

Esparza, Manuel. 1994. *Relaciones geográficas de Oaxaca, 1777–1778*. Oaxaca, Mexico: CIESAS.

Estabrook, George F. 1998. Maintenance of fertility of shale soils in a traditional agricultural system in central interior Portugal. *Journal of Ethnobiology* 18:15–33.

Fabrega, Horacio Jr., and Daniel B. Silver. 1973. *Illness and Shamanistic Curing in Zinacantan*. Stanford, CA: Stanford University Press.

Farjon, Aljos, and Brian T. Styles. 1997. *Pinus (Pinaceae). Flora Neotropica* Monograph 75. Bronx, NY: New York Botanical Garden.

Felger, Richard S., and Mary B. Moser. 1985. *People of the Desert and the Sea*. Tucson: University of Arizona Press.

Fodor, Jerry. 1983. *The Modularity of Mind*. Cambridge: MIT Press.

Foster, George M. 1953. Relationships between Spanish and Spanish-American folk medicine. *Journal of American Folklore* 66:201–17.

Foster, George M. 1987. On the origin of humoral medicine in Latin America. *Medical Anthropology Quarterly* 1:355–93.

Frati-Munari, Alberto C., Blanca E. Gordillo, Perla Altamirano, and C. Raúl Ariza. 1988. Hypoglycemic effect of *Opuntia* streptacantha Lemaire in NIDDM. *Diabetes Care* 11:63–66.

Fromkin, Victoria, and Robert Rodman. 1988. *An Introduction to Language*. 4th ed. Fort Worth, TX: Holt, Rinehart and Winston.

Gardner, Howard. 1983. *Frames of Mind: The Theory of Multiple Intelligences*. New York: Basic Books.

Gardner, Howard. 1985. *The Mind's New Science: A History of the Cognitive Revolution*. New York: Basic Books.

Gelman, Susan A., and Ellen Markman. 1986. Categories and induction in young children. *Cognition* 23:183–209.

Gelman, Susan A., and John D. Coley. 1991. The acquisition of natural kind terms. In *Perspectives on Language and Thought*, Susan A. Gelman and James P. Byrnes, editors. New York: Cambridge University Press.

Goodwin, George C. 1969. *Mammals from the State of Oaxaca, Mexico, in the American Museum of Natural History*. Bulletin of the American Museum of National History 141(1): 1–269.

González, Roberto J. 2001. *Zapotec Science: Farming and Food in the Northern Sierra of Oaxaca*. Austin: University of Texas Press.

Greenberg, James B. 1981. *Santiago's Sword: Chatino Peasant Religion and Economics*. Berkeley: University of California Press.

Greenberg, James B. 1989. *Blood Ties: Life and Violence in Rural Mexico*. Tucson: University of Arizona Press.

Guzmán, Ulises, Salvador Arias, and Patricia Dávila. 2003. *Catálogo de cactáceas mexicanas*. Mexico, DF: Universidad Nacional Autónoma de México (UNAM) and Comisión Nacional para el Conocimiento y Uso de la Biodiversidad (CONABIO).

Haraway, Donna. 1994. A game of cat's cradle: Science studies, feminist theory, cultural studies. *Configurations* 1:59–71.

Hardin, Garrett. 1968. The tragedy of the commons. *Science* 162:1243–48.

Hays, Terrence E. 1974. Mauna: Explorations in Ndumba ethnobotany. Unpublished Ph.D. dissertation. Seattle: University of Washington.

Hays, Terrence E. 1982. Utilitarian/adaptationist explanations in folk biological classification: Some cautionary notes. *Journal of Ethnobiology* 2:89–94.

Hernández, Francisco. 1959. *Historia natural de la Nueva España*. 2 vols. Mexico: UNAM (original 1577).

Hernández Díaz, Jorge. 1987. *El café amargo: Los procesos de diferenciación y cambio social entre los Chatinos*. Oaxaca, Mexico: CIESAS.

Hernández Pérez, Meinardo. 2002. Zha rnee zhow ¿Cómo se dice? Zapoteco de Mixtepec. Versión preliminar, November 2002. Published by the author.

Hill, Jane H., and Kenneth C. Hill. 1986. *Speaking Mexicano: The Dynamics of Syncretic Language in Central Mexico*. Tucson: University of Arizona Press.

Hirschfeld, Lawrence A., and Susan Gelman. 1994. *Mapping the Mind: Domain Specificity in Cognition and Culture*. New York: Cambridge University Press.

Hughes, Colin E. 1998. Monograph of *Leucaena* (Leguminosae-Mimosoideae). *Systematic Botany Monographs* 55:1–245.

Hunn, Eugene S. 1975a. Cognitive processes in folk-ornithology: The identification of gulls. Language Behavior Research Laboratory, University of California at Berkeley.

Hunn, Eugene S. 1975b. A measure of the degree of correspondence of folk to scientific biological classification. *American Ethnologist* 2:309–27.

Hunn, Eugene S. 1976. Toward a perceptual model of folk biological classification. *American Ethnologist* 3:508–24.

Hunn, Eugene S. 1977. *Tzeltal Folk Zoology: The Classification of Discontinuities in Nature*. New York: Academic Press.

Hunn, Eugene S. 1982. The utilitarian factor in folk biological classification. *American Anthropologist* 84:830–47.

Hunn, Eugene S. 1987. Science and common sense: A reply to Atran. *American Anthropologist* 89:114–49, with a reply by Atran.

Hunn, Eugene S. 1990. *Nch'i-Wána, "The Big River": Mid-Columbia Indians and Their Land*. Seattle: University of Washington Press.

Hunn, Eugene S. 1993. What is TEK? and The ethnobiological foundations for TEK. In *Ecologies for the 21st Century: Traditional Ecological Knowledge: Wisdom for Sustainable Development*, edited by Nancy M. Williams and Graham Baines,, pp. 11–29. Report of the Traditional Ecological Knowledge Workshop, Centre for Resource and Environmental Studies, Australian National University, Canberra, Australia.

Hunn, Eugene S. 1994. Place-names, population density, and the magic number 500. *Current Anthropology* 35(1): 81–85.

Hunn, Eugene S. 1996. Columbia Plateau Indian place names: What can they teach us? *Journal of Linguistic Anthropology* 6(1): 3–26.

Hunn, Eugene S. 1998. Mixtepec Zapotec ethnobiological classification: A preliminary sketch and theoretical commentary. *Anthropologica* 40:35–48.

Hunn, Eugene S. 1999a. Size as limiting the recognition of biodiversity in folk biological classifications; One of four factors governing the cultural recognition of biological taxa. In *Folkbiology*, Douglas L. Medin and Scott Atran, editors, pp. 47–69. Cambridge: Harvard University Press.

Hunn, Eugene S. 1999b. The value of subsistence for the future of the world. In *Ethnoecology*, Virginia Nazarea, editor, pp. 23–36. Tucson: University of Arizona Press.

Hunn, Eugene S. 2002. Evidence for the precocious acquisition of plant knowledge by Zapotec children. In *Ethnobiology and Biocultural Diversity*. John R. Stepp, Felice S. Wyndham, and Rebecca K. Zarger, editors, pp. 604–13. Athens, GA: International Society of Ethnobiology.

Hunn, Eugene. 2006. Meeting of minds: How do we share our appreciation of traditional environmental knowledge? *Journal of the Royal Anthropological Institute* (n.s.), 143–60.

Hunn, Eugene S., and Donato Acuca Vásquez. 2001. La etnobiología en el *Vocabvlario en lengva Çapoteca* de Fray Juan de Córdova. *Cuadernos del Sur: Ciencias Sociales* 16:21–32.

Hunn, Eugene S., Donato Acuca Vásquez, and Patricia Escalante. 2001. Birds of San Juan Mixtepec, district of Miahuatlán, Oaxaca, Mexico. *Cotinga* 16:14–26.

Hunn, Eugene S., and David French. 1984. Alternatives to taxonomic hierarchy: The Sahaptin case. *Journal of Ethnobiology* 3:73–92.

Hunn, Eugene S., Darryll Johnson, Priscilla Russell, and Thomas F. Thornton. 2003. Huna Tlingit traditional environmental knowledge and the management of a "wilderness" park. *Current Anthropology* 44(S5): 79–104.

Hutchins, Edwin. 1980. *Culture and Inference: A Trobriand Case Study*. Cambridge: Harvard University Press.

Hyam, Roger, and Richard Pankhurst. 1995. *Plants and Their Names: A Concise Dictionary*. Oxford: Oxford University Press.

Instituto Nacional de Estadística, Geografía e Informática (INEGI). 1990. *XI Censo General de Población y Vivienda, 1990: Oaxaca. Resultados Definitivos. Datos por Localidad (Integración Territorial)*. Aguascalientes: INEGI.

Jerez Salas, Martha Patricia, José Herrera Haro, and Marco Antonio Vásquez Dávila. 1994. *La gallina criolla en los Valles Centrales de Oaxaca. Reportes de investigación 1*. CIGA: Instituto Tecnológico Agropecuario de Oaxaca No. 23, Nazareño Xoxocotlán, Oaxaca, México.

Johns, Timothy. 1996. *The Origins of Human Diet and Medicine: Chemical Ecology*. Tucson: University of Arizona Press.

Katz, Esther. 1992. Del frío al exceso de calor: Dieta alimenticia y salud en la Mixteca. In *Medicina tradicional, herbolaria y salud comunitaria en Oaxaca*, Paola Sesia, editor, pp. 99–115. CIESAS, Gobierno del Estado de Oaxaca.

Katz, Solomon H., Mary L. Hediger, and Linda A. Valleroy. 1974. Traditional Maize Processing Techniques in the New World. *Science* 184:172–85.

Kay, Charles E. 1994. Aboriginal overkill: The role of Native Americans in structuring Western ecosystems. *Human Nature* 5:359–398.

Kay, Paul. 1971. Taxonomy and semantic contrast. *Language* 68:866–87.

Kay, Paul. 1975. A model-theoretic approach to folk taxonomy. *Social Science Information* 14:151–66.

Keil, Frank C. 1986. The acquisition of natural kind and artifact terms. In *Language Learning and Concept Acquisition*, edited by Ausonio Marras and William Demopoulos. Norwood, NJ: Ablex.

Kesby, John. 1986. *Rangi Natural History: The Taxonomic Procedures of an African People*. New Haven, CT: Human Relations Area Files.

King, Judy. 2004. Los Diás de los Muertos (Days of the Dead). http://www.mexconnect.com/mex—/travel/jking/jkdayofthedead.html

King, Steven R., and Helio H. C. Bastien. 1990. *Oxalis tuberosa* Mol. (Oxalidaceae)

in Mexico: An Andean tuber crop in Meso-America. *Advances in Economic Botany* 8:77–91.
Klein, Janice. 1978. "Susto": The anthropological study of the diseases of adaptation. *Social Science & Medicine* 12:23–28.
Kleinman, Arthur M. 1973. Toward a comparative study of medical systems: An integrated approach to the study of the relationship of medicine and culture. *Science, Medicine and Man* 1:55–65.
Lampman, Aaron M. 2007. General principles of ethnomycological classification among the Tzeltal Maya of Chiapas, Mexico. *Journal of Ethnobiology* 27:11–27.
León-Portilla, Miguel. 1963. *Aztec Thought and Culture: A Study of the Ancient Nahuatl Mind*. Translated by Jack Emory Davis. Norman: University of Oklahoma Press.
Lévi-Strauss, Claude. 1966. *The Savage Mind*. London: Weidenfeld and Nicolson.
Levine, Seymour D., Richard E. Adams, Robert Chen, Mary Lou Cotter, Allen F. Hirsch, Vinayak V. Kane, Ramesh M. Kanojia, Charles Shaw, and Michael P. Wachter. 1979. Zoapatanol and montanol, novel oxepane diterpenoids from the Mexican plant zoapatle (*Montanoa tomentosa*). *Journal of the American Chemical Society* 101:3404–5.
Linares, Edelmira, Robert Bye, and Beatriz Flores. 1999. *Plantas medicinales de México: Usos y remedios tradicionales*. Mexico, DF: Instituto de Biología, Universidad Nacional Autónoma de México.
Logan, Michael H., Kimberly D. Gwinn, Tina Richey, Beth Maney, and Charles T. Faulkner. 2004. An empirical assessment of epazote (*Chenopodium ambrosioides* L.) as a flavoring agent in cooked beans. *Journal of Ethnobiology* 24:1–12.
López Austin, Alfredo. 1980. *Cuerpo humano e ideología*. 2 vols. Mexico: Universidad Nacional Autónoma de México.
Louv, Richard. 2005. *Last Child in the Woods*. Chapel Hill: Algonquin Books.
Mabberley, D. J. 1997. *The Plant-Book: A Portable Dictionary of the Vascular Plants*. 2nd ed. Cambridge: Cambridge University Press.
Maffi, Luisa. 1994. A Linguistic Analysis of Tzeltal Maya Ethnosymptomatology. PhD diss., University of California, Berkeley.
Maffi, Luisa, editor. 2001. *On Biocultural Diversity: Linking Language, Knowledge, and the Environment*. Washington, DC: Smithsonian Institution Press.
Malinowski, Bronislaw. 1974 [1925]. *Magic, Science, and Religion, and Other Essays*. Garden City, NJ: Doubleday Anchor Books.
Marcus, George E., and Michael M. J. Fisher. 1986. *Anthropology as Cultural Critique: An Experimental Moment in the Human Sciences*. Chicago: University of Chicago Press.
Marcus, Joyce. 1976. The origins of Mesoamerican writing. *Annual Review of Anthropology* 5:35–67.
Marcus, Joyce. 2003. Escritura y representación en el viejo y el nuevo mundo. In *Escritura zapoteca: 2,500 años de historia*, María de los Ángeles Romero Frizzi, coordinadora, pp. 73–94. Mexico, DF: Conaculta; INAH.
Marcus, Joyce, and Kent Flannery. 1996. *Zapotec Civilization: How Urban Society Evolved in Mexico's Oaxaca Valley*. London: Thames and Hudson.

Martin, Gary J. 1995. *Ethnobotany: A "People and Plants" Conservation Manual*. London: Chapman and Hall.

Martin, Gary J. 1996. Comparative ethnobotany of the Chinantec and Mixe of the Sierra Norte, Oaxaca, Mexico. PhD diss. Berkeley: University of California.

Martínez, Maximino. 1967. *Las plantas medicinales de México*. 6th ed. Mexico, DF: Ediciones Botas.

Martínez, Maximino. 1979. *Catálogo de nombres vulgares y científicos de plantas mexicanas*. Mexico, DF: Fondo de Cultura Económica.

Mata Pinzón, Soledad, et al., editors. 1994. *Diccionario enciclopédico de la medicina tradicional mexicana*. Vol. 2. Tlacopac, Mexico, DF: Instituto Nacional Indigenista.

McClain, Carol Shepherd. 1975. Ethno-obstetrics in Ajijic. *Anthropological Quarterly* 40:38–56.

McVaugh, Rogers, editor. 1983–. *Flora Novo-Galiciano: A Descriptive Account of the Vascular Plants of Western Mexico*. Vols. 3, 5, 12–17. Ann Arbor: University of Michigan Press.

Messer, Ellen. 1978. *Zapotec Plant Knowledge: Classification, Uses, and Communication about Plants in Mitla, Oaxaca, Mexico*. Memoirs of the Museum of Anthropology, University of Michigan, No. 10.

Mickel, John T., and Joseph M. Beitel. 1988. *Pteridophyte Flora of Oaxaca, Mexico*. Memoirs of the New York Botanical Gardens. Bronx, NY: New York Botanical Garden.

Miranda, Faustino, and Efraím Hernández X. 1963. Los tipos de vegetación de México y su classificación. *Boletín de la Sociedad Botánica de México* 28:29–179.

Mishler, Elliot G. 1981. Viewpoint: Critical perpectives on the biomedical model. In *Social Contexts of Health, Illness, and Patient Care*, E. G. Mishler, Lorna R. Amarasingham, Samuel D. Osherson, and Stuart T. Hauser, editors. London and New York: Cambridge University Press.

Moerman, Daniel E., Robert W. Pemberton, David Kiefer, and Brent Berlin. 1999. A comparative analysis of five medicinal floras. *Journal of Ethnobiology* 19:49–67.

Munro, Pamela, and Felipe H. Lopez. 1999. *Di'csyonaary X:tèe'n Dìi'zh Sah Sann Lu'uc: San Lucas Quiaviní Zapotec Dictionary*. Vol. 1. Los Angeles: Chicano Studies Research Center.

Nadasdy, Paul. 1999. The politics of TEK: Power and the "Integration" of knowledge. *Arctic Anthropology* 36(1–2): 1–18.

O'Nell, Carl W. 1975. An investigation of reported "fright" as a factor in the etiology of susto, "magical fright." *Ethos* 3:41–63.

O'Nell, Carl W., and Henry Selby. 1968. Sex differences in the incidence of susto in two Zapotec pueblos: An analysis of the relationship between sex role expectations and a folk illness. *Ethnology* 7:95–105.

Ortiz de Montellano, Bernard R. 1975. Empirical Aztec medicine. *Science* 188:215–20.

Ortiz de Montellano, Bernard R. 1986. Aztec medicinal herbs: Evaluation of therapeutic effectiveness. In *Plants in Indigenous Medicine and Diet: Behavioral Approaches*, Nina L. Etkin, editor. Bedford Hills, NY: Redgrave.

Ortiz de Montellano, Bernard R. 1990. *Aztec Medicine, Health, and Nutrition*. New Brunswick, NJ: Rutgers University Press.

Perry, Jesse P. Jr. 1991. *The Pines of Mexico and Central America*. Portland, OR: Timber Press.

Peters, Charles M., Silvia E. Purata, Michael Chibnik, Berry J. Brosi, Ana M. López, and Myrna Ambrosio. 2004. The life and times of *Bursera glabrifolia* (H. B. K.) Engl. in Mexico: A parable for ethnobotany. *Economic Botany* 57:431–41.

Pinker, Steven. 1994. *The Language Instinct: How the Mind Creates Language*. New York: Harper Collins.

Plotkin, Mark. 1994. *Tales of a Shaman's Apprentice*: An Ethnobotanist Searches for New Medicines in the Rain Forest. New York: Penguin.

Randall, Robert A., and Eugene S. Hunn. 1984. Do life forms evolve or do uses for life? *American Ethnologist* 11:329–49.

Rao, Rajesh P. N., George J. Zelinsky, Mary M. Hayhoe, and Dana H. Ballard. 1997. Eye movements in visual cognition: A computational study. Technical Report 97.1, National Resource Laboratory for the Study of Brain and Behavior, Department of Computer Science, University of Rochester, Rochester, New York.

Redford, Kent H., and Allyn MacLean Stearman. 1993. Forest-dwelling native Amazonians and the conservation of biodiversity: Interests in common or in collision? *Conservation Biology* 7:248–55.

Reeck, Roger. 1991. A Trilingual Dictionary in Zapotec, English and Spanish. Master's thesis, Puebla, Mexico: University of the Americas.

Rodríguez-Trejo, Dante Arturo. 2003. Fire ecology of the mountain pine, *Pinus hartwegii*. Paper presented at the 2nd International Wildland Fire Ecology and Fire Management Conference in Orlando, Florida. http://www.imacmexico.org/ev.php?ID=9733 —201&102=DO—TOPIC.

Rojas, Basilio. 1992. *Miahuatlán, un Pueblo de México*. Oaxaca, Mexico: Secretaría de Desarrollo Económico y Social, Consejo Estatal para la Cultura y las Artes, Gobierno del Estado de Oaxaca.

Rosch, Eleanor. 1978. Principles of categorization. In *Cognition and Categorization*, Eleanor Rosch and Barbara Lloyd, editors. Hillsdale, NJ: Erlbaum.

Rowley, J. Stuart. 1966. Breeding records of birds of the Sierra Madre del Sur, Oaxaca, Mexico. *Proceedings of the Western Foundation of Vertebrate Zoology* 1:107–204.

Rubel, Arthur J. 1967. El susto en Hispanoamérica. *América Indígena* 26:69–90.

Rubel, Arthur J., Carl W. O'Nell, and Rolando Collado-Árdon. 1989. *Susto, una enfermedad popular*. Mexico, DF: Fondo de Cultura Económica.

Rus, Jan, and George Collier. 2003. A generation of crisis in the Central Highlands of Chiapas: The cases of Chamula and Zinacantán, 1974–2000. In *Mayan Lives, Mayan Utopias: The Indigenous Peoples of Chiapas and the Zapatista Rebellion*, Jan Rus, Rosalva Aída Hernández Castillo, and Shannan L. Mattiace, editors, pp. 33–61. Lanham, MD: Rowman and Littlefield.

Rus, Jan, Rosalva Aída Hernández Castillo, and Shannan L. Mattiace, editors. 2003. *Mayan Lives, Mayan Utopias: The Indigenous Peoples of Chiapas and the Zapatista Rebellion*. Lanham, MD: Rowman & Littlefield.

Rzedowski, Jerzy. 1978 [1994]. *La vegetación de México*. Mexico, DF: Limusa.
Rzedowski, Jerzy, and Graciela Calderón de Rzedowski. 2004. Copales y cuajiotes. In *Biodiversidad de Oaxaca*, Abisaí J. García-Mendoza, María de Jesús Ordóñez, and Miguel Briones-Salas, editors, pp. 193–98. Mexico City: Instituto de Biología, Universidad Nacional Autónoma de México; Fondo Oaxaqueño para la Conservación de la Naturaleza; World Wildlife Fund.
Sahagún, Fr. Bernardino de. 1950–69. 12 vols. *Florentine Codex. General History of the Things of New Spain*, edited and translated by Arthur J. O. Anderson and Charles E. Dibble. Salt Lake City: University of Utah Press (original 1560–65).
Salazar, Gerardo A., and Eugene S. Hunn. n.d. A new species of *Platanthera* (Orchidaceae) from Oaxaca, Mexico. In preparation.
Sánchez G., José J., Major M. Goodman, and Charles W. Stuber. 2000. Isozymatic and morphological diversity in the races of maize of Mexico. *Economic Botany* 54:43–59.
Sánchez López, Alberto. 1989. *Oaxaca: Tierra de Maguey y Mezcal*. Oaxaca, Mexico: Instituto Tecnológico de Oaxaca.
Sánchez Sánchez, Oscar. 1968. *La Flora del Valle de México*. Mexico, D.F.: published by the author.
Sapir, Edward. 1921. *Language: An Introduction to the Study of Speech*. New York: Harcourt Brace Jovanovich.
Sapir, Edward. 1956. *Selected Writings in Language, Culture, and Personality*, David Mandlebaum, editor. Berkeley: University of California Press.
Saussure, Ferdinand de. 1996 [1907]. *Saussure's First Course of Lectures on General Linguistics (1907)*. Edited and translated by George Wolf. Tarrytown, NY: Pergamon Press.
Schalkwijk-Barendsen, Helene M. E. 1991. *Mushrooms of Northwest North America*. Redmond, WA: Lone Pine Publishing.
Sesia, Paola, editor. 1992. *Medicina tradicional, herbolaria y salud comunitaria en Oaxaca*. Mexico, D.F.: Centro de Investigaciones y Estudios Superiores en Antropología Social (CIESAS) y el Gobierno del Estado de Oaxaca.
Sillitoe, Paul. 1983. *Roots of the Earth*. Manchester, UK: University of Manchester.
Smith, Eric A., and Mark Wishnie. 2000. Conservation and subsistence in small-scale societies. *Annual Reviews of Anthropology* 29:493–524.
Smith, J. Bryan, E. F. Smith, Alan M. Lefer, and K. C. Nicolau. 1981. Spasmogenic effects of the anti-fertility agent zoapatanol. *Life Sciences* 28:2743–46.
Smith Stark, Thomas C. 2001. Algunas isoglosas zapotecas. Presented at Las Actas del III Coloquio Internacional de Lingüística Mauricio Swadesh, UNAM, Mexico, DF, 29 August 2001.
Soto Arenas, Miguel Ángel, and Gerardo A. Salazar. 2004. Orquídeas. In *Biodiversidad de Oaxaca*, Abisaí J. García-Mendoza, María de Jesús Ordóñez, and Miguel Briones-Salas, editors, pp. 271–95. Mexico: Instituto de Biología, UNAM-Fondo Oaxaqueño para la Conservación de la Naturaleza–World Wildlife Fund.
Standley, Paul, editor. 1946. *The Flora of Guatemala*. Chicago: Chicago Natural History Museum.

Stoll, David. 1990. *Is Latin America Turning Protestant? The Politics of Evangelical Growth*. Berkeley: University of California Press.

Stross, Brian. 1973. Acquisition of botanical terminology by Tzeltal children. In *Meaning in Mayan Languages*, Munro S. Edmonson, editor, pp. 107–41. The Hague: Mouton.

Stubblefield, Morris, and Carol Miller de Stubblefield. 1991. *Diccionario zapoteco de Mitla, Oaxaca*. Mexico, DF: Instituto Linguistico del Verano.

Sturtevant, William C. 1964. Studies in ethnoscience. *American Anthropologist* 66:99–113.

Summer Institute of Linguistics (SIL). 2004. *Ethnologue: Languages of the World*. 14th ed. http://www.ethnologue.com/show—family.asp?subid=1907.

Tapia-Pérez, María Esther, Amparo Tapia-Contreras, Roberto Cedillo-Rivera, Lidia Osuna, and Mariana Meckes. 2003. Screening of Mexican medicinal plants for antiprotozoal activity—part II. *Pharmaceutical Biology* 41:180–83.

Taylor, Paul M. 1987. *The Ethnobiology of the Tobelorese People*. Smithsonian Contributions to Anthropology. Washington, DC: Smithsonian Institution Press.

Thompson, Max C. 1962. Noteworthy records of birds from the Republic of Mexico. *Wilson Bulletin* 74:173–76.

Turner, Billie L. 1995. A new species of *Lupinus* (Fabaceae) from Oaxaca, Mexico: A shrub or tree mostly three to eight meters high. *Phytologia* 79(2): 102–7.

Turner, Nancy J. 1974. Plant taxonomic systems and ethnobotany of three contemporary Indian groups of the Pacific Northwest (Haida, Bella Coola, and Lillooet). *Syesis* 7:1–107.

Turner, Nancy J. 1987. General plant categories in Thompson and Lillooet, two Interior Salish languages. *Journal of Ethnobiology* 7:55–82.

Tyler, Stephen A. 1991. A post-modern in-stance. In *Constructing Knowledge: Authority and Critique in Social Science*, Lorraine Nencel and Peter Pels, editors, pp. 78–94. London: Sage.

Vogt, Evon Z. 1970. *The Zinacanteco of Mexico: A Modern Maya Way of Life*. New York: Holt, Rinehart and Winston.

Wackernagel, Mathis, and William Rees. 1996. *Our Ecological Footprint: Reducing Human Impact on the Earth*. Gabriola Island, BC: New Society.

Waddy, Julie A. 1988. *Classification of Plants and Animals from a Groote Eylandt Aboriginal Point of View*. 2 vols. Darwin: Australian National University.

Wellhausen, Edwin J., L. M. Roberts, and Efrain Hernández X. 1951. *Razas de maíz en México*. Folleto Técnico No. 5. Oficina de Estudios Especiales, Secretaría de Agricultura y Ganadería. Mexico.

Whitecotton, Joseph W. 1977. *The Zapotecs: Princes, Priests, and Peasants*. Norman: University of Oklahoma Press.

Williams, Nancy M., and Gregory Baines, editors. 1993. *Traditional Ecological Knowledge: Wisdom for Sustainable Development*. Canberra: Centre for Resources and Environmental Studies, Australian National University.

Wilson, Edward O. 1986. *Biophilia*. Reprint edition. Cambridge: Harvard University Press.

Wilson, Edward O. 2002. *The Future of Life*. New York: Alfred A. Knopf.

Winter, Marcus. 1997. Inspección de sitios arqueológicos. Sección de Arqueología, Centro INAH Oaxaca, 7 July 1997.

Wittgenstein, Ludwig. 1999. *Philosophical Investigations*. 3rd ed. Englewood Cliffs, NJ: Prentice Hall.

Zarger, Rebecca K., and John R. Stepp. 2004. Persistence of botanical knowledge among Tzeltal Maya children. *Current Anthropology* 45:413–18.

Zent, Stanford. 1999. The quandary of conserving ethnoecological knowledge: A Piaroa example. In *Ethnoecology: Knowledge, Resources, and Rights*. Ted L. Gragson and Ben G. Blount, editors, pp. 90–152. Athens: University of Georgia Press.

Zolla, Carlos, Sofía del Bosque, Antonio Tascón, and Virginia Mellado. 1988. *Medicina tradicional y enfermedad*. Mexico: Centro Interamericano de Estudios de Seguridad Social.

Index

Explanatory note: Entries referring to part 2 of this publication (online at www.uapress.arizona.edu/Books/bid1957.htm) are specified as follows: for example, in "B.Tb5.10," "B" specifies the major sections of the table of contents listed on the left margin of your screen—in this case, "B. Illustrations and Tables. . . ." "Tb5.10" stands for "table 5.10," the tenth table cited in chapter 5 of part 2. Other symbols are "Ch" for *chart*, "Fg" for *figure*, "Mp" for *map*, and "Sc" for *sound clip*. Citations to section A, the Preface, are by paragraph number; to section C, Background, by section and subsection numbers. For example, "C1.2" indicates the "Cacti" subsection of the "Catalog of Woody Vegetation"; "C2.4" indicates the "Taxonomies" heading (4) within the "Ethnobotanical Principles" subsection (2) of the "Background" section on the website. Section C of part 2 also includes Latin, English, Spanish, and Zapotec name indexes, which should allow the interested reader to locate desired information.

acquisition of ethnobiological knowledge, 54
  gardens, role in learning about plants, C3.3, C3.4
  "Magic Number 500," 226
  modular learning, 225–226, 230–231
  plant trail, 224, 231–233. *See also* methods of research: plant trail
    correlation of scores by sex, B.Ch8.3
    list of participants, B.Tb8.5
    list of plant trail species, B.Tb8.4
    scatterplot of scores, B.Ch8.1, B.Ch8.2
    scores by sex, age, schooling, B.Tb8.6
    statistical analysis of results, 233–236
  precocious acquisition, 224–226
    evidence from San Juan, 226–230
    summary of individual inventories, B.Tb8.2
  rapid appraisal method, 227–228
  rates compared across cultures, B.Tb8.1

Acuca Vásquez, Donato, 33–34, 75–77
agaves, 55–57, 61–62, 67–68, 137, 144–145
  classification of, C2.2
  diversity of in San Juan, C1.1
  names for, C1.1
  not "trees," C1.1
  related species, 32, C1.1
  uses, C1.1
    for aguamiel and pulque, 68, 144–145, C1.1
    for fences, 146, C1.1
    for fiber, 67, 146, C1.1
    for food, 144–145, C1.1
    for medicine, 189, C1.1
    for mezcal, 68, C1.1
agriculture, 120. *See also* cultivated food plants; fruits; gardens
Almud as measure, 129
cultivars, 131–137. *See also* beans; chilis; maize; squash
fallow cycles, 122–123
fertilizer, 122, 139, 140, 143–144, 221, C3.3

irrigation, 71, 125
milpa, 72–73, 122, 125, 131, 138–139
orchards in riparian zone, 123, 138–139,
    B.Tb5.10
pests, 137–138, B.Tb5.8. See also
    insect pests
planting, 124–125, 127–129
plowing, 125, 144
    with donkeys, 141, 144
    with oxen, 126–127, 142, 144
rituals, 125. See also fiestas
slash-and-burn, 125
statistical summaries by function,
    B.Tb5.15
terraces, 124
tree species cultivated, B.Tb5.10
weeding, 131
amphibians. See reptiles, amphibians, fishes
animal husbandry, 120, 140–144
    census of animals, 143
        statistical summaries, B.Tb5.17
    chickens, 140–141
        eggs, 141
        named varieties, B.Tb5.16
    dogs, 105, 142, 195–196
    donkeys, 104, 141–142, 144
    goats, 104, 143–144
        ecological role of, 143–144
        for meat, 144
        sale value of, 141, 144
        as source of fertilizer, 140–144
        statistical summaries, 143, B.Tb5.18
    oxen, 142
    pigs, 104–105, 142
    rabbits, 103, 104, 105, 142
    sheep, 141
    turkeys, 140
animal names. See nomenclature in
    ethnobiology
Article 27, Mexican constitution, 21
Aztecs, 15–16, 158, 167, 187, 198, 204
    Aztec merchants in San Juan, 32, 120
    and medicine, 16, 158, 167, 174–175, 187

beans, 122
    classification and nomenclature, C2.7
    cultivars, 129, 134–135
    pests of, 138
    varieties named in San Juan Zapotec,
        B.Tb5.6
Berlin, Brent, 16
    principles of classification and nomen-
        clature, 16, 93–94, C2
    applicability to Zapotec, C2.8
    ranks, in folk taxonomies, C2.4
biocultural diversity, 6, 25
biophilia, 13
birds, 101, 109–113. See also ethnozoology
    dipper, 71
    hummingbirds, C2.2
    as life-form, 109–110, C2.5
    onomatopoetic names, 110–113
    plant associations, C1.10
    rare species, C1.8
    taxonomic correspondence, 110,
        B.Tb4.10, C2.2
Bulmer, Ralph N. H., 16, C2.1

cacti, 137, C1.2
    barrel, 66, C1.2
    columnar, 55, 66, 68–69, 124, C1.2
    nopal, C1.2
    prickly pear, 58, 66, 124, C1.2
Chatino, 48
children
    acquisition of ethnobiological knowl-
        edge, 54, 224, 226–230
    one child's inventory, B.Tb8.3
    interest in flowers, C3.3
    recognition of plants, 213–214, 224
    toys, 150, 214
    variation in ethnobiological knowl-
        edge, 233–234
chilis, 122, 167
cochineal, C1.2, C3.4
conflict, between Indian communities,
    75–76, B.Sc2.3

Conklin, Harold, 16, C2.1, C2.4
conservation
  biocultural diversity, 6, 25
  biodiversity, 6
copal trees (*Bursera* spp.), 70
cross shrines, 59
cultivars. *See* beans; chilis; maize; squash
cultivated food plants
  fruits, 122
  grown outside San Juan, B.Tb5.3
  guajes (*Leucaena* spp.), C1.3
  introduced, B.Tb5.2
  list of all species, B.Tb5.11
    introduced, 121–122, B.Tb5.2
    native, B.Tb5.1
  seasonings, 122, 139
  trees in orchards, B.Tb5.10
  tubers, 122, 135–136, B.Tb5.9

de Ávila, Alejandro, 30–33
Díaz, Porfirio, 21
diet
  adequacy of, 118–119, 129–131, 144
  contribution of gardens to, C3.3
  edible invertebrates, 146–147
  malnutrition, 118–119, 181
  vitamins, 122, 181
diseases
  aires malos, 174, 177, 183–184, 193–194. *See also* diseases: chaneque
    remedies for, B.Tb6.18
  of animals, remedies for, 166, B.Tb6.19
  "cancer," 158–159, 179–180
  chaneque, 9, 166, 173, 184, 193–194, 224
    "great fight," 191–192
    remedies for, B.Tb6.18
  childbirth, 166, 186–190
    remedies for, B.Tb6.15
  classification of, 163–166
  coughs, 175, 177–178
  dental problems, 179
  diet related, 119, 181
  emotional, 166, 190–192. *See also* diseases: fright
  epilepsy, 192
  rage, 192
    remedies for, B.Tb6.17
  separation anxiety, 192
  empacho, 9, 169, 176
  of eyes, ears, nose, throat, 165, 177–179
    remedies for, B.Tb6.11
  fever, 165–166, 184, 190
    remedies for, B.Tb6.13
  fright (espanto, susto), 9, 159–160, 164, 190–192, 195
    remedies for, B.Tb6.16
  gastrointestinal, 165, 175–177
    remedies for, B.Tb6.10
  hernias, 186
  injuries, 182
    remedies for, B.Tb6.12
  pain, 161, 165, 166, 177, 182–183, 194
    remedies for, B.Tb6.13
  parasites, 176, 182, 192
  pasmo, 166, 185
  skin problems, 165, 179–182
    burns, 180
    "cancer," 179–180
    contact dermatitis, 181
    manchas (paño, vitiligo), 166, 180–181
    remedies for, B.Tb6.12
    wounds, 180
  spiritual maladies, 166, 191–192, 193–195
  urogential, 166, 183–184, 185–186
    remedies for, B.Tb6.14
  Zapotec terminology for diseases, 161–163, 165–166
    terms with **–guîdz** suffix, 161, B.Tb6.5
dye plants, C3.4. *See also* cochineal

Ellen, Roy, C2.1
ethnobiology. *See also* nomenclature in ethnobiology

classification, C2. *See also* taxonomies
   natural kinds, 104
   psychological implications, C2.4
   correspondence to Linnaean taxonomy, 113, C2.2, C2.8
   ecological salience as factor, C2.2
   overdifferentiation, 113
   underdifferentiation, 112, C2.2
   field of, 13–14, 15–18
   historical phases, 15–18
   personal motivations, 13–15
   utilitarian factor, 11–12, 15–16, 116, 198–201, C2.2
ethnoscience, 10–11. *See also* ethnobiology; ethnozoology
ethnoecology, 17
ethnoethology of !Kung San, 12
ethnozoology, A.6. *See also* animal husbandry; birds; invertebrates; mammals; reptiles, amphibians, fishes
   animacy, 97–101, C2.6. *See also* worldview
   life-forms, 101–102, 115–116, B.Fg4.3b
   naming animals, 97–101

fences, living, 59, 67, 124, 146, C1.2, C1.5, C1.6, C1.11
   edible plants in, 123–124
ferns, C2.2, C2.5
   medicinal, 175
fertilizer, 122, 125, 140. *See also* agriculture
   in gardens, 221, C3.3
   role of goats, 143–144
fiestas
   Christmas, 49, 198, 206
   Fiesta de la Santa Cruz, 10, 46–48, 125, 215, 231
   graduation or clausura, 28–29, 50–51
   lenten, primer viernes, 50
   patron saint, 49–50
   Todos Santos, 10, 49, 198
firewood. *See* wood
fish. *See* reptiles, amphibians, fishes

flowers
   aesthetic value of in Mesoamerica, 198
   beggar-ticks (*Bidens* spp.), 202–203
   Castilleja spp., C2.2
   children gather, C3.3
   composites, 201, 210–211
   cultivars, 202, 204–205, 218–220
   dahlias (and *Cosmos* spp.), 204–205
   as decoration on altars, graves, 199–201, 215–217, C3.3
   frangipani (*Plumeria*), 213
   hummingbird flowers, 207–208
   as life-form, C2.5
   lilies, 207
   marigolds (*Tagetes* spp.), 176, 201–202
   mistletoes (*Loranthaceae* spp.), 209, C2.2
   morning-glories (*Ipomoea* spp.), 208–209
   naming, 210, 211, 218–220
   orchids, 206–207, C2.2
   poinsettias (*Euphorbia pulcherrima*), 206
   roses, 188, 212–213
fodder, 139–140, C1.5
   list of fodder plants, B.Tb5.13
foliage, as decoration, 215–217
   decorative sotol "stars," 216
   fern fronds, 215, 217
   pine needle garlands, 215
fruits, 83, 138–139, B.Tb5.10, C1.2
   of cacti, C1.2
   cultivated fruit trees, 71, 123, 138, B.Tb5.10, C1.11, C3.2
   trees, 83, 138–139
fuel. *See* wood
funerals, 216–217
fungi, 75, 94–97, 98, A.6, C2.6
   edible, 96, 147–148
   as life-form, C2.6
   list of species recorded in San Juan, B.Tb4.17
   medicinal, 96, 174

names for, C2.6
neither plant nor animal, C2.6
poisonous, 96
residual categories of, 96

gardens (huertos familiares), 123, 138. See also agriculture
  care of plants in gardens, C3.2, C3.3
  design of, C3.2
  edible plants in, 220–221, C3.3
  as experimental plots, 217–218, 221, C3.2, C3.3
  marketing of garden plants, 138, C3.2
  medicinal plants in, C3.3
  native versus introduced plants, 123, 218–220, C3.2, C3.3
  ornamental plants in, C3.3
  San Juan garden survey, C3
    methods, C3.2
    survey data, 217–223, C3
    statistical summaries, B.Tb7.1, C3.3
    value of, C3.4
  variability among San Juan gardens, C3.2, C3.3
  weeds in gardens, C3.2
  women as gardeners, C3.2, C3.3, C3.4
globalization, impact of, 5–6, 24, 27, 28–29, 119, 231, 236–238
grasses, C2.2, C2.5
guajes (*Leucaena* spp.), 146

habitats
  fallow fields (acahuales), 59, 124
  field and trail margins, 124, 139, 160, C1.11
  hot country, 66–67, C1.3, C1.5, C1.8, C1.11
  matorral, 59–60, 70–71, C1.8, C1.11
  of medicinal plants, 171, B.Tb6.8
  montane forests, C1.3, C1.8, C1.10, C1.11
  riparian woodland, 138, C1.4, C1.11
  selva baja caducifolia, 59, 67–68, C1.2, C1.6, C1.7, C1.11

herbaceous plant, as life-form, C2.5
hot versus cold, 9, 154, 160, 166–170, 175–179, 181, 183–185, C3.2. See also diseases; medicine
  balancing in compound cures, 172, 189
  in childbirth, 169–170, 188–189
  consistency of application, 167–168, 169, B.Tb6.6
  criteria for distinction, 143–144, 167–168, 169–170
  diarrheas, 161, 169, 175
  of dung, 143–144
  of foods, 168
  Mesoamerican origins, 166–168
  Mixtec concepts, 168–169
house construction, 22
hunting, 148–149
  list of potential prey species, B.Tb5.20

incense, 183, 216, C1.6. See also copal trees
indigenous ethnobiological collaboration, 17–18
indigenous life, 6, 8, 17, 20
insect pests
  of crops, 125, 137–138, B.Tb5.8
  of people, 195–196
invertebrates, 102, 114–117. See also ethnozoology
  butterflies and moths, 115, 137
  edible species, 50, 116, 146–147, B.Tb4.13, B.Tb5.19
  host plants, 114–115
  as life-form, 115
  Linnaean correspondence, 116–117
  medicinal species, 116, B.Tb4.14
  miscellaneous utility, B.Tb4.15
  pests, 116, B.Tb4.16
  summary of names, B.Tb4.12
  summary of taxa by order, 115, 117
  summary of taxa by type, B.Tb4.11
irrigation, 71, 125. See also agriculture

land tenure, 20–21, 124
language, xiii, 13–14, 19, 26–28. *See also* Zapotec
  language loss, 25–28
  Nahuatl, 85
    loan words, 85, 178, C1.2, C1.3, C2.5
  Spanish bilingualism, 26–27
  Spanish loans in plant names, 84–88, 103–104, 232, 234, 235
Latin names, 14, 79, 89
  translation of native names, 91–92
Lévi-Strauss, Claude, 199, C2.4
lizards. *See* reptiles, amphibians, fishes
logging, C1.8

maize, 122. *See also* agriculture: milpa
  cultivars, 125–126, 131–134
  planting strategies, 128–129
  varieties named in San Juan Zapotec, B.Tb5.4
    specialized maize terminology, B.Tb5.5
Malinowski, Bronislaw, 199
mammals, 102–105. *See also* ethnozoology
  domestic, 148–149. *See also* animal husbandry
  list of species reported from region, 105, B.Tb4.8
  pests of crops, 137
  predatory, 103
  as prey, 104–105
  summary of taxa by type, B.Tb4.7
market production, of flowers in gardens, C3.2, C3.4
medicinal plants, 138, 151, 154–155, 159, 160
  for childbirth, 169–170, 172, 187–190
  compound cures (compuestos), 170, 172
  in disturbed sites, B.Tb6.2
  habitats, 171, B.Tb6.8
  hallucinogenic, 193–194
  hypoglycemic, C1.2
  introduced plants, 154, 160
  mode of application, 170, 173–175

  bathing, 174–175, 183, 185, 189
  dressings, 174
  in eyes, 173–174, 179
  limpias, 174, 194–195, B.Tb6.9
  teas, 174–175
  topical, 173–174
  plant part used, 170–171, B.Tb6.7
  plant species by origin and management status, 160, 191, B.Tb6.1
  statistical summaries, 160, 196–197
    comparison of regional floras, B.Tb6.21
    distribution by plant family, 196–197, B.Tb6.20
  types of treatments, B.Tb6.3
medicine. *See also* diseases
  Aztec, 16, 158, 167, 174–175, 187
  for childbirth, 154–155, 166, 172, 174–175, 186–190, B.Tb6.15
  government clinics, 152–153, 186–187
  judging effectiveness, 156–158
  for mouth sores, C1.7
  for parasites, 195
  for poisoning, 196
  spiritualist, 156
  traditional, 151
    local specialists, 151–155
methods of research
  first contacts, 32–33
  flora and, 89–90
  insect collections, 59, 114
  Linnaean correspondence, 90, 91–92
  measuring children's acquisition
    plant trail, 224
    rapid appraisal, 227–228
  permissions, 36–37
  plant trail, 54, 231–233
  in San Juan, 53–54, 72–73
  statistical comparisons, 88–90, 105, 110, 113, 115, 117, C2.2
    Scientific Species Recognition Ratio (SSRR), 105, C2.2
  voucher specimens, 90, 95, 114, A.2, A.7

INDEX 259

mezcal, 68, 122, 145–146, 173. See also agaves
  medicinal use of, 176, 177, 183, 193–194
Miahuatlán, 30, 56, 72, 145, 156, 234
  flowers in market, C3.3
Mixtecs, 167
Monte Albán, 19–20

names
  definition of, 78, 92–93
  what names do, 78, 91–92
nomenclature in ethnobiology, 27, 78ff
  animal names, 94–95, 97–98
    agentive prefix, 98
    animate prefix, 97–98
  binomial nomenclature, 79, 94, 104, C2.3
  color terms as modifiers, 86–87
  descriptive force, 79, 82
  of diseases, 161–163, 165–166
  of flowers, 210, 211, 218–220
  generalized descriptive phrases, A.5
  lexemes, 91–93, 211
  lexeme types, 78–82, C2.8
    complex primary names, 80–82
    simple primary names, 80
  nonce forms, 114–115, A.5
  onomatopoeia, 113
  polysemy, 80
  primary versus secondary names, C2.3, C2.8
  Spanish loans, 85–88, 103–104

oaks (*Quercus*), 56, 58, 61, 71, 74–75, 89, C1.9
  for construction, C1.9
  San Juan classification of, B.Tb4.5, C1.9, C2.2
Oaxaca, 19–20, 153
  Dominican missions of, 21–22
  Zapotecs in, 19, 26–27
orchards. See agriculture

Oxalis, 68, 145
  for baking agaves, 145, C1.1
  edible tuber (oca), 76, 136

palms, 57
peasant versus campesino, 28–29
pines, 57–58, 74, 89, C1.8
  for construction, 149, C1.8
  for pitch, C1.8
  San Juan classification of, 89, 91, B.Tb4.4, C1.8
Plotkin, Mark, 16
plows, 149–150. See also agriculture
  terms for plowing and plow parts, B.Tb5.21
poisonous plants, 69, 95–96, 181, 195–196, C1.7
poverty as problematical, 6, 23–24, 28–29, 43, 119, 230
pulque, 23, 62, 68, 122, 145, 205, C1.1. See also agaves

quelites, 123, 134, 162, 199
  list of weedy greens, B.Tb5.12
  of Mitla, 162

religion. See also fiestas
  Catholic versus Protestant, 44–46
  missionaries, 21–22, 43–46
reptiles, amphibians, fishes, 101–102, 105–109, B.Tb4.9
  amphibians, 107, 108
  fish, 105–106
  lizards, 106–108
  snakes, 106–107
  turtles, 107
  worms, 106–107

Sahagún, Fray Bernardino de, 15–16
Sahaptin Indians, compared to San Juan Zapotecs, 237
San Juan Gbëë, 3–5, 23
  cargo service, 20, 48–49

census summaries, 37–40, B.Ch2.3
  economically active population, 38
  education, 28, 38, 41–42
  government, 20–21, 24, 51–53
    Comisariado de Bienes Comunales, 51
    presidentes municipales, 36–37, 51
    usos y costumbres, 20, 51–53
  history, 20, 22, 58, 63, 69, 71
  infrastructure, 42–44
  land tenure, 20–21
  linguistic conservatism, 26–27, 40
  medical resources, 151–155, 186
  migration, 24–25, 29, 39–40, 120, 236
  morning chorus, B.Sc2.1, B.Sc2.4, B.Sc2.5
  people, 3–4, 34–35
  population, 20, 39
  prehistory, 20, 64–65, 70, 120, 151
    ball court, 64, 70
    cave dwellings, 64–65
    terraces, 65
    tombs, 65
  rainfall, 23, B.Ch2.1
  religion, 21–22, 43–46
  road from Oaxaca City, 56–58
  seting, 30–33, 59–60, B.Mp2.1–Mp2.5
  in song, 52, B.Sc2.2, B.Sc2.3
  statistical summaries, 14, 20, 24–25, 37–44
  temperature, 23, B.Ch2.2
  tequio, 52
  territory, 75–76
  water system, 75
  women's political role, 53
San Pedro Gbëë, 30–33, 138
  medicine in, 153–154, 156
  Rancho Conejo, 76–77, 136, C1.3
  selling cut flowers in San Juan, C3.3
Sapir-Whorf hypothesis, 14–15, C2.1
Schneider, Lisa, and garden survey, C3
science. *See also* ethnobiology; ethnoscience
  applied versus theoretical, 12
  critical science studies, 8, 157
  Darwin's approach, 8
  folk versus modern, 3, 7–10, 157, 186–187
seasonings. *See* cultivated food plants
shrines, on mountain tops, 77. *See also* fiestas: Fiesta de la Santa Cruz
silk production, C3.4
snakes. *See* reptiles, amphibians, fishes
Sociedad para el Estudio de los Recursos Bióticos de Oaxaca, A.C. (SERBO), 30, 33
squash, 122, 135
  named in San Juan Zapotec, B.Tb5.7
subsistence strategies, 6, 24, 119–120
Summer Institute of Linguistics (SIL), 45

taxonomies, 91, C2.4
  Berlin's analytic framework, 93–94, C2, C2.8
  covert taxa, C2.4, C2.8
  extended ranges of taxa, 84, A.5
  folk generics, 80–82, 93, 102–103, 110–113, 114, C2.3, C2.7, C2.8
  folk specifics, 81–82, 93–94, 112–113, 116, C2.3, C2.7, C2.8
  fungi, where do they fit?, 94–97
  intermediate rank, 82–83, 93, 103, C1.5, C2.4, C2.8
  life-forms, 80, 83–84, 93–95, 115–116, C2.3, C2.5, C2.8
    animal, 101–102
    plant, 83, 101, B.Fg4.3
    overlapping, 211–213, B.Tb4.2, B.Tb4.3, C2.5
    tree, C2.5
  polythetic taxa, C2.7
  polytypic taxa, C2.4
  prototypes, 80, 84
  psychological reality, 92, C2.4, C2.7
  rank, in folk taxonomies, C2.4

San Juan plant taxa summarized,
    B.Tb4.6
San Juan taxonomic hierarchy, B.Tb4.1
special purpose categories, 91, C2.5
terminal taxa, C2.2
unaffiliated taxa, 94, C2.6
varietal taxa, 93–94, C2.7
tepache, 62, 122. *See also* pulque
thorn trees, 82, C1.5
tools. *See also* fences, living
    plows, 149–150. *See also* plows: terms
        for plowing and plow parts
toys, 150
traditional environmental knowledge
    (TEK), 6–7, 8–9, 11, 17, 121, 227
    critiques of, 7, 9
traditional resource management
    (TRM), 17
tree, as life-form, C2.5
turtles. *See* reptiles, amphibians, fishes
Tzeltal Mayan comparisons, 84, 88, 175,
    234, C2.6

virgins, appeals to, 193–195

wage labor, 120
weaving, dye plants in gardens, C3.4
weeds
    edible. *See* quelites
    in gardens, C3.2
wheat, for bread, 72, 122
wild edible plants, 121, 124, 207
    agaves, 144–145

guajes (*Leucaena* spp.), C1.3
    list of all edible species, B.Tb5.11
Winter, Marcus, 64
witchcraft, 156, 194–195
wood
    in construction, 120, 149–150, C1.8,
        C1.9, C1.10
    as fuel, 119, 138–140, C1.8, C1.10
        list of firewood plants, B.Tb5.14
    for plows, 149–150
    for toys, 150
worldview
    animacy, 94–95, 97–101, C2.6
    heart, 99–100
    intelligence of animals, 99–100
    life, 99
worms. *See* reptiles, amphibians, fishes

Zapata, Emiliano, 21
Zapotec. *See also* beans; diseases; language; maize; squash
    bilingualism, 26, 28, 42
    future prospects, 26–27
    Isthmus Zapotec, 22, 28
    loan words from Spanish, 80–81,
        84–88
    number of Zapotec languages, 19
    orthography, xiii–xiv, B.TbP1, B.TbP2
    phonemic inventory, xiii–xiv, B.TbP1,
        B.TbP2
    terms with **guiél-** prefix, B.Tb6.4
    vocabulary and traditional environmental knowledge, C3.4

About the Author

Eugene Hunn is Professor Emeritus, Department of Anthropology, University of Washington, Seattle. He received his Ph.D. in anthropology from the University of California, Berkeley, in 1973. His primary research interests are ethnobiology, ethnoecology, and cognitive anthropology. He has conducted field work in Mexico and with Native North American communities. His books include *Tzeltal Folk Zoology: The Classification of Discontinuities in Nature* (Academic Press, 1977), *Resource Managers: North American and Australian Hunter-Gatherers*, co-edited with Nancy M. Williams (Westview, 1981), and *Nch'i-Wána, "The Big River": Mid-Columbia Indians and Their Land* (University of Washington Press, 1990).